The Silver Coin

Art and lettering by
Michael Walsh

6 "High Score" written by
Joshua Williamson

7 "Tzompanco" written by
Ram V.

8 "Rising and Falling..." written by
Matthew Rosenberg

9 "The Dancer" written by
Vita Ayala

10 "Covenant: Abomination" written by
Michael Walsh

Colored by
Michael Walsh and Toni Marie Griffin

Edited by
Chris Hampton

"The Bronx is Burning" by
Vita Ayala and Salomée Luce-Antoinette

The Silver Coin is created by
Michael Walsh, Ed Brisson, Jeff Lemire, Kelly Thompson, and Chip Zdarsky

IMAGE COMICS, INC. • Robert Kirkman: Chief Operating Officer • Erik Larsen: Chief Financial Officer • Todd McFarlane: President • Marc Silvestri: Chief Executive Officer • Jim Valentino: Vice President • Eric Stephenson: Publisher / Chief Creative Officer • Nicole Lapalme: Controller • Leanna Caunter: Accounting Analyst • Sue Korpela: Accounting & HR Manager • Marla Eizik: Talent Liaison • Jeff Boison: Director of Sales & Publishing Planning • Lorelei Bunjes: Director of Digital Services • Dirk Wood: Director of International Sales & Licensing • Alex Cox: Director of Direct Market Sales • Chloe Ramos: Book Market & Library Sales Manager • Emilio Bautista: Digital Sales Coordinator • Jon Schlaffman: Specialty Sales Coordinator • Kat Salazar: Director of PR & Marketing • Monica Garcia: Marketing Design Manager • Drew Fitzgerald: Marketing Content Associate • Heather Doornink: Production Director • Drew Gill: Art Director • Hilary DiLoreto: Print Manager • Tricia Ramos: Traffic Manager • Melissa Gifford: Content Manager • Erika Schnatz: Senior Production Artist • Ryan Brewer: Production Artist • Deanna Phelps: Production Artist • IMAGECOMICS.COM

High Score

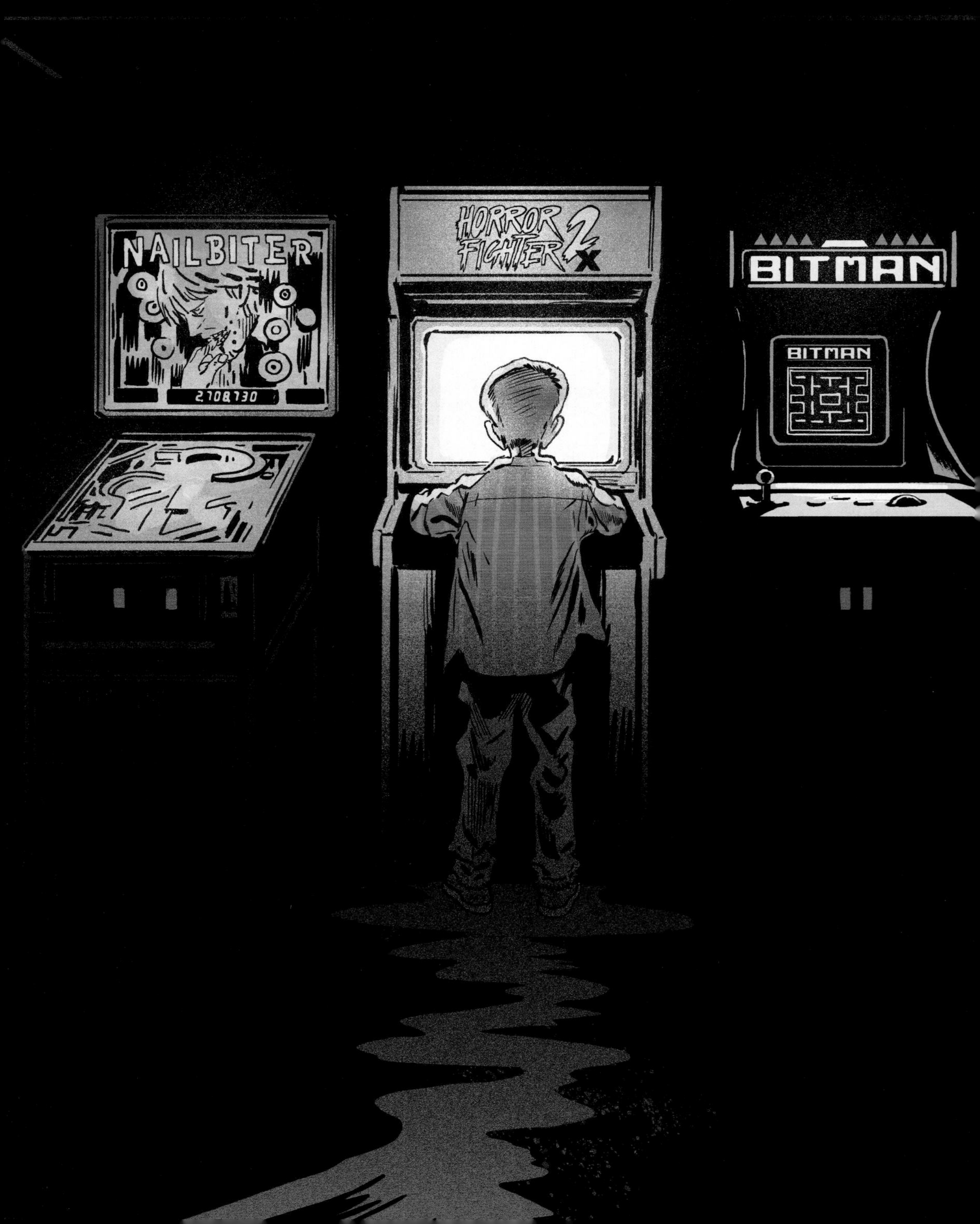
NAILBITER
2708730
HORROR FIGHTER 2X
BITMAN
BITMAN

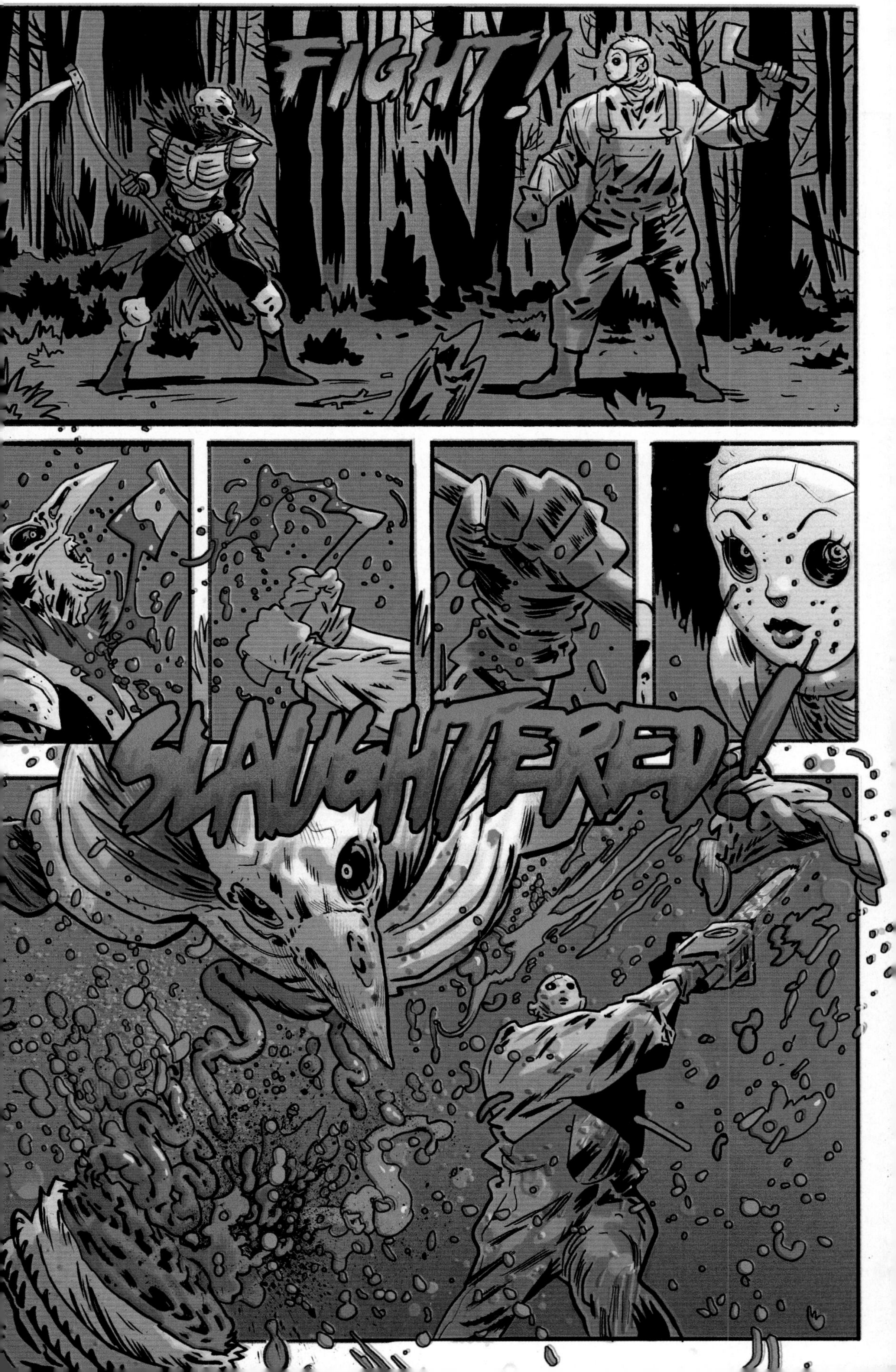
FIGHT!
SLAUGHTERED!

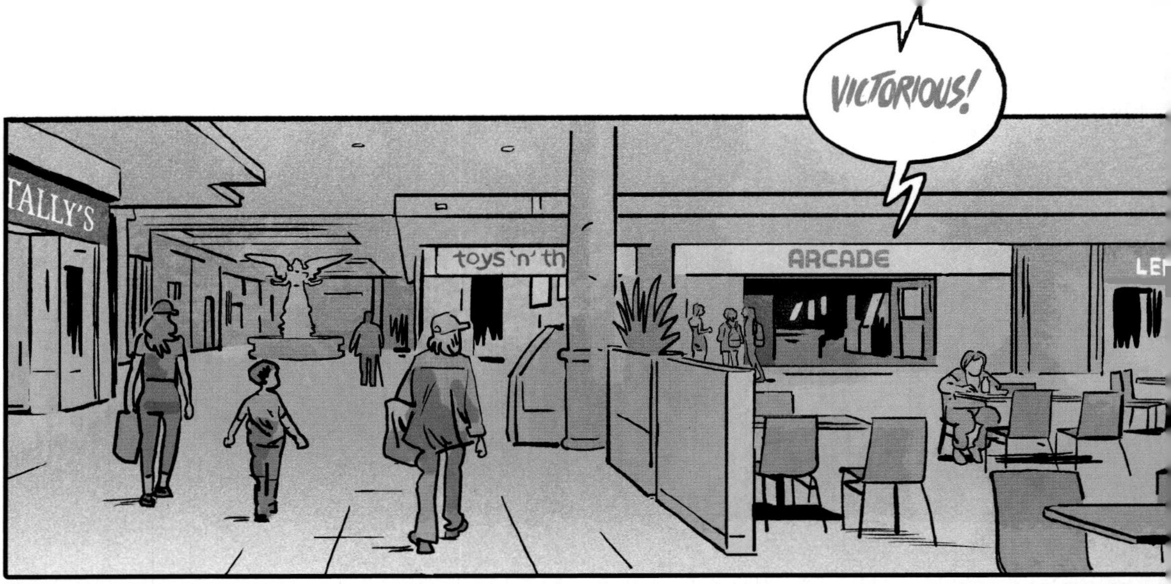
VICTORIOUS!
TALLY'S
toys 'n' th
ARCADE

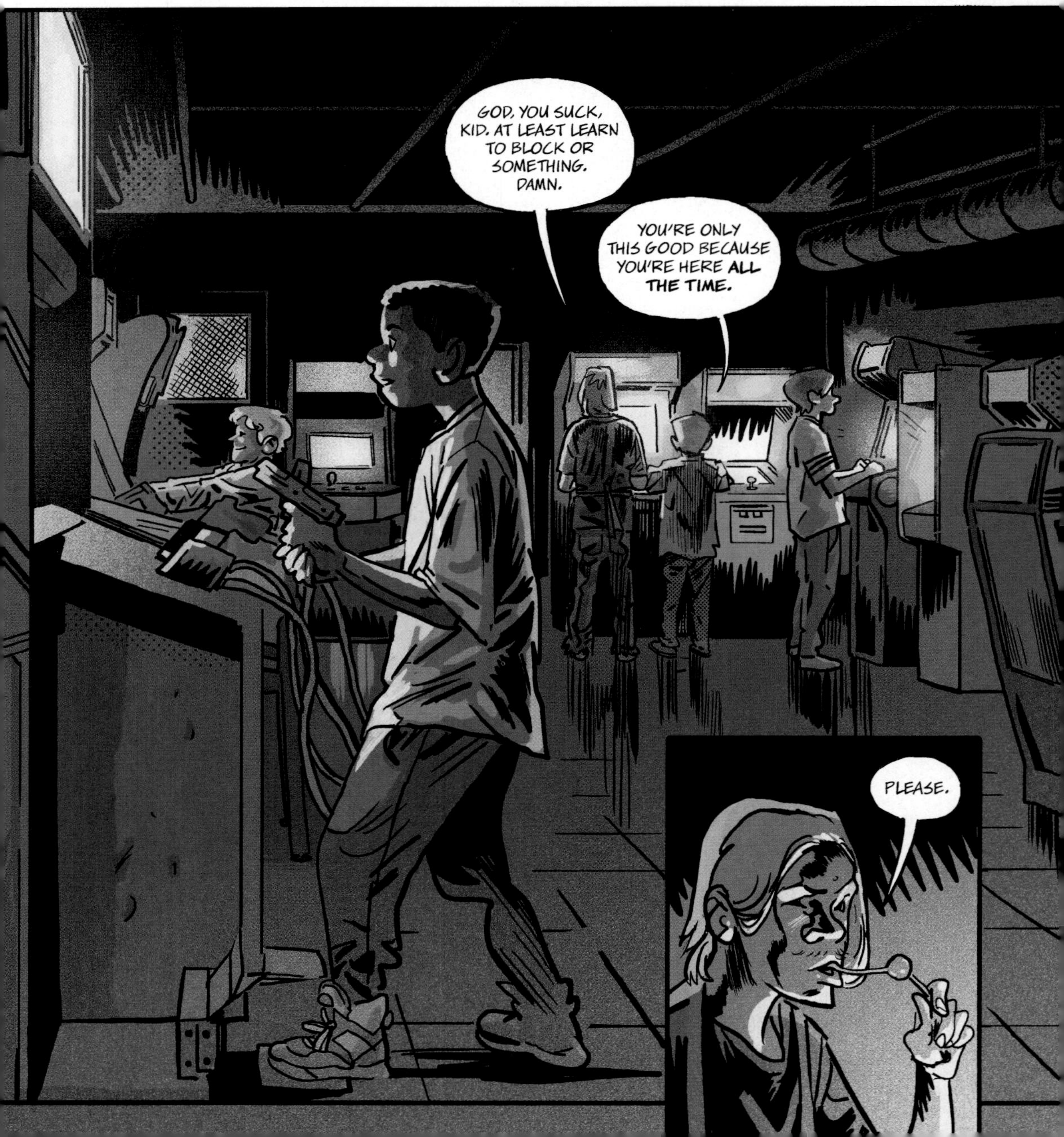
GOD, YOU SUCK, KID. AT LEAST LEARN TO BLOCK OR SOMETHING. DAMN.
YOU'RE ONLY THIS GOOD BECAUSE YOU'RE HERE **ALL THE TIME.**
PLEASE.

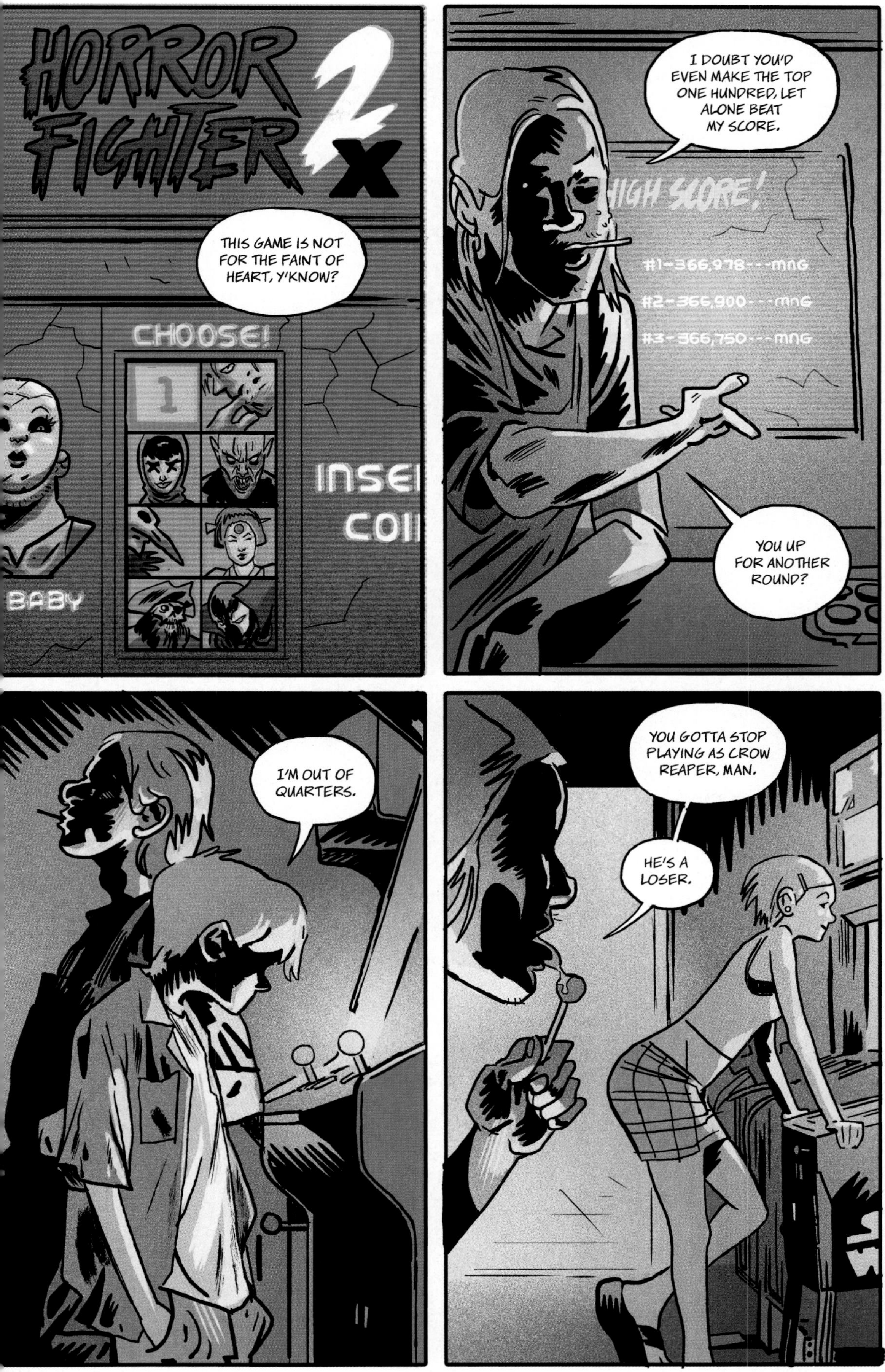
HORROR FIGHTER 2 X
THIS GAME IS NOT FOR THE FAINT OF HEART, Y'KNOW?
CHOOSE!
1
BABY
INSE
COI
I DOUBT YOU'D EVEN MAKE THE TOP ONE HUNDRED, LET ALONE BEAT MY SCORE.
HIGH SCORE!
#1-366,978---MNG
#2-366,900---MNG
#3-366,750---MNG
YOU UP FOR ANOTHER ROUND?
I'M OUT OF QUARTERS.
YOU GOTTA STOP PLAYING AS CROW REAPER, MAN.
HE'S A LOSER.

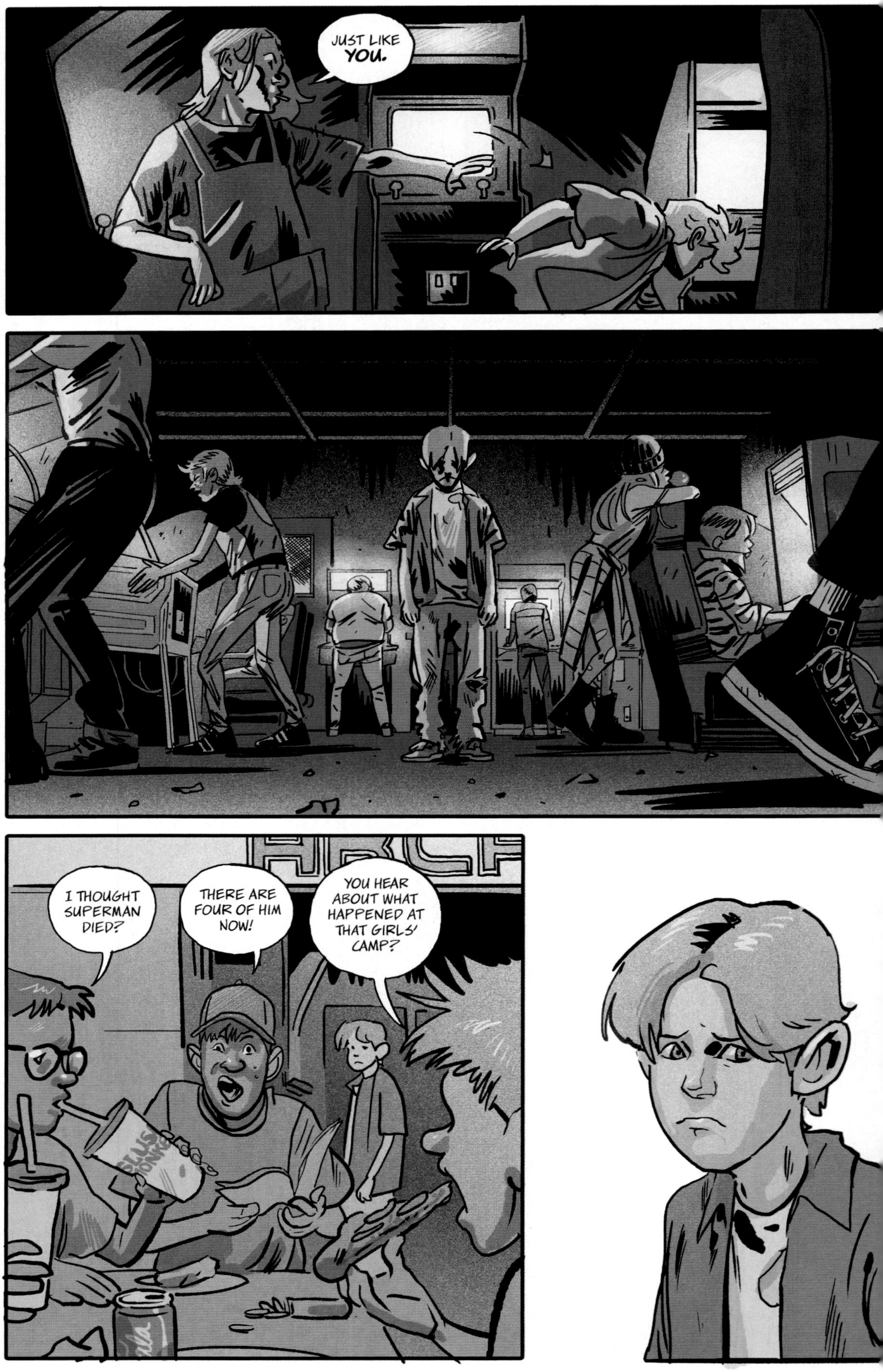
JUST LIKE YOU.
I THOUGHT SUPERMAN DIED?
THERE ARE FOUR OF HIM NOW!
YOU HEAR ABOUT WHAT HAPPENED AT THAT GIRLS' CAMP?

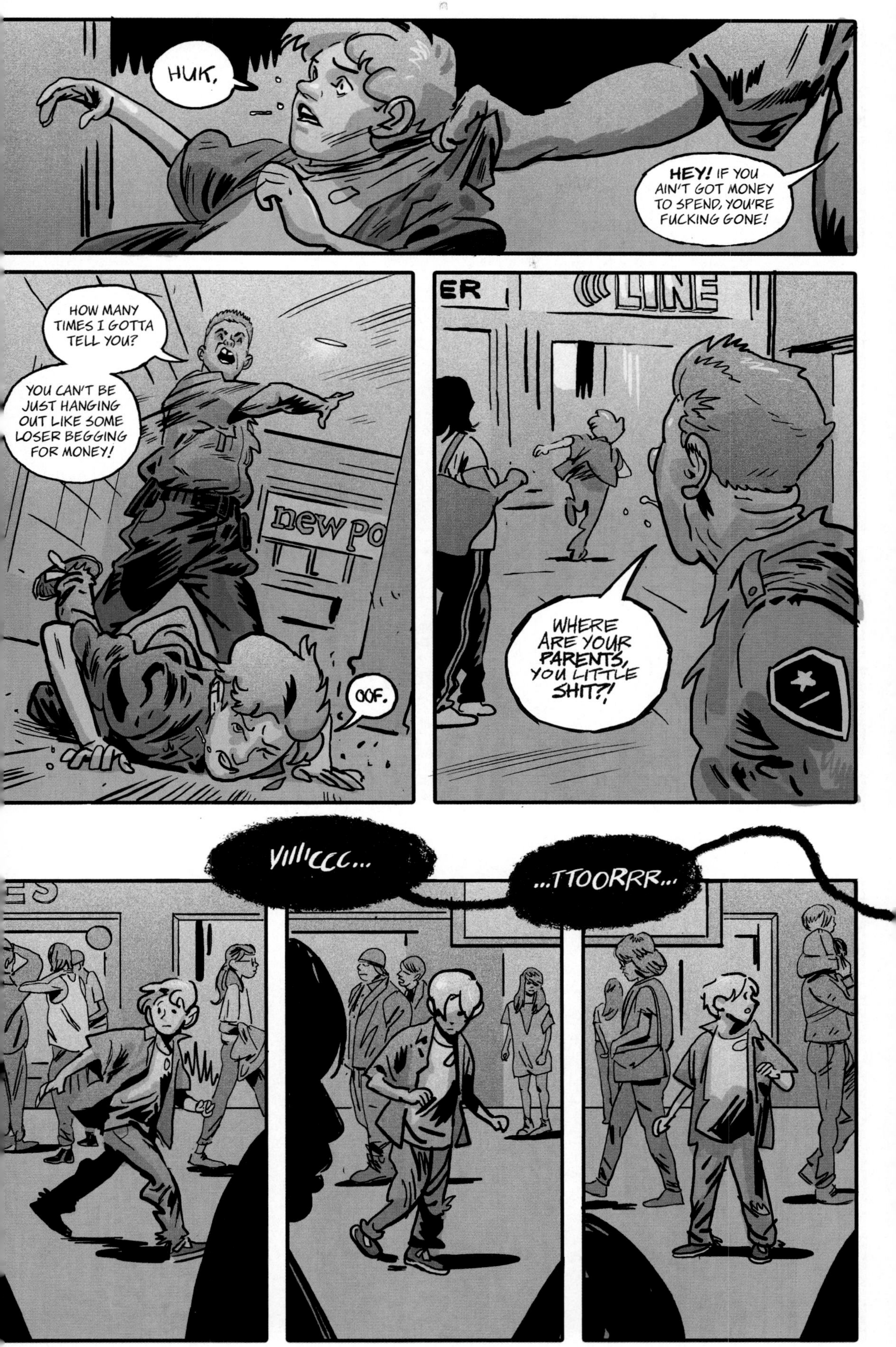
HUK,
HEY! IF YOU AIN'T GOT MONEY TO SPEND, YOU'RE FUCKING GONE!
HOW MANY TIMES I GOTTA TELL YOU?
YOU CAN'T BE JUST HANGING OUT LIKE SOME LOSER BEGGING FOR MONEY!
new po
OOF.
ER
LINE
WHERE ARE YOUR PARENTS, YOU LITTLE SHIT?!
VIIIICCC...
...TTOORRR...

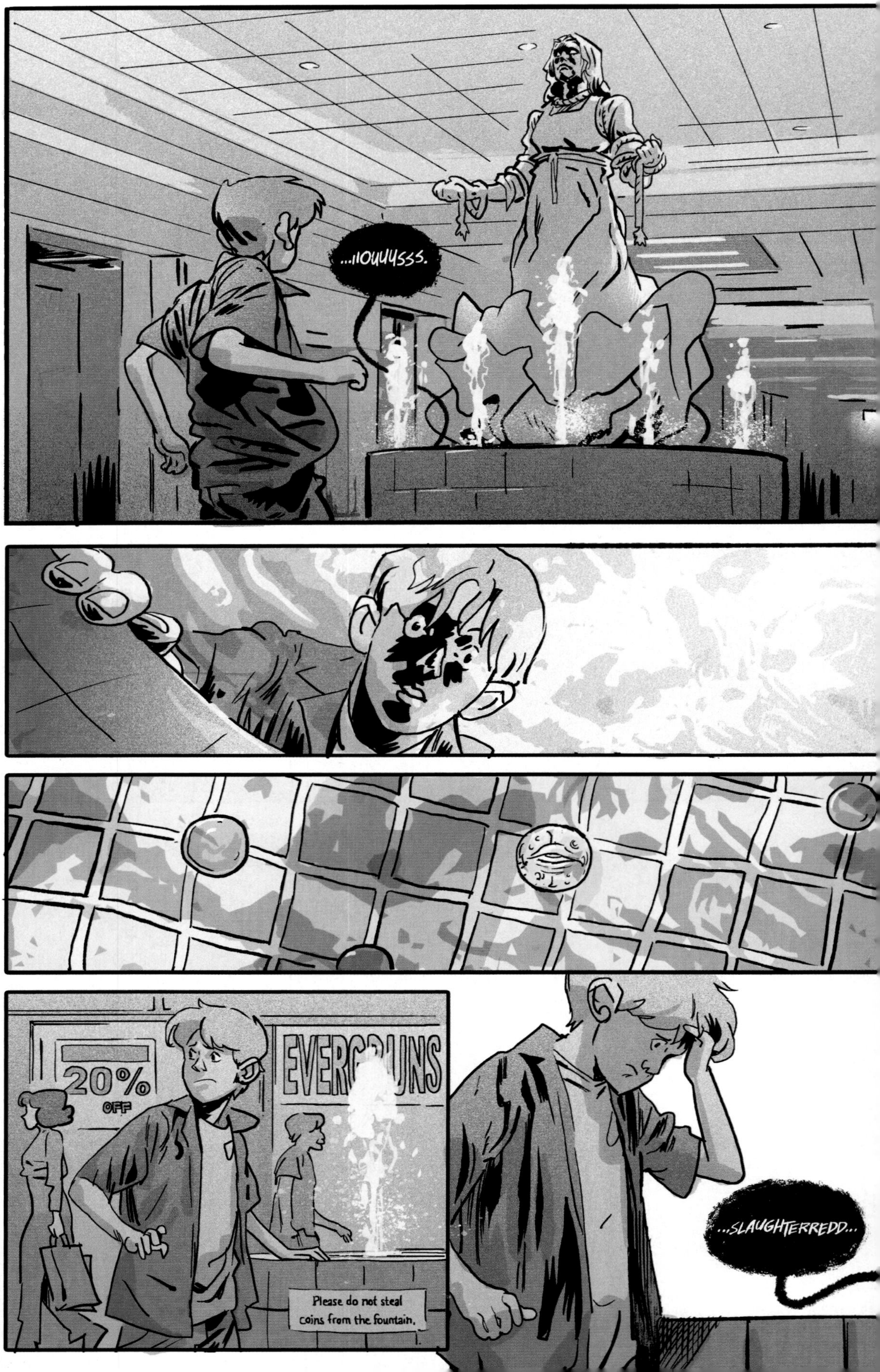
...llouuyss.
20% OFF
EVERGRUNS
Please do not steal coins from the fountain.
...SLAUGHTERREDD...

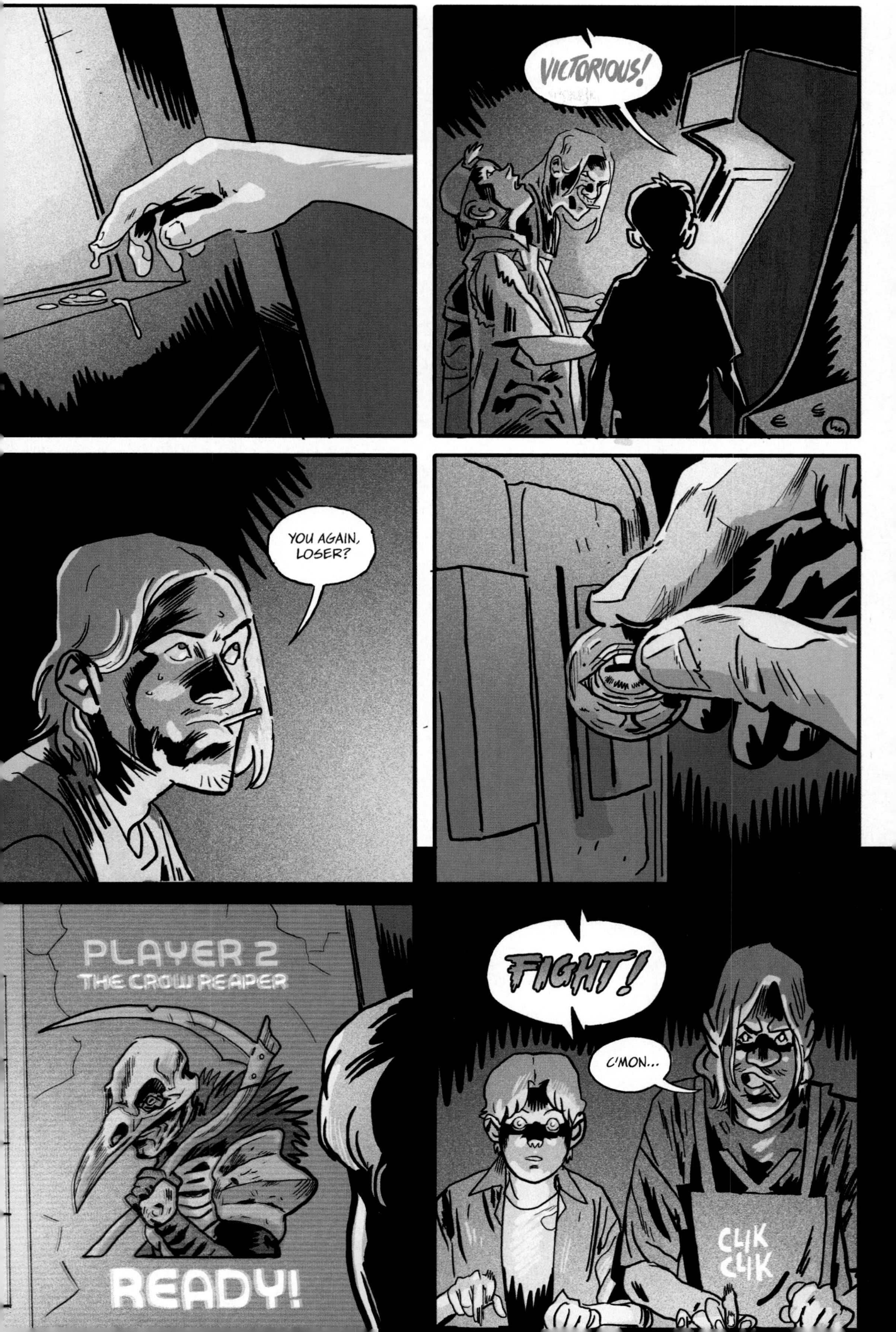
VICTORIOUS!
YOU AGAIN, LOSER?
PLAYER 2
THE CROW REAPER
READY!
FIGHT!
C'MON...
CLIK CLIK

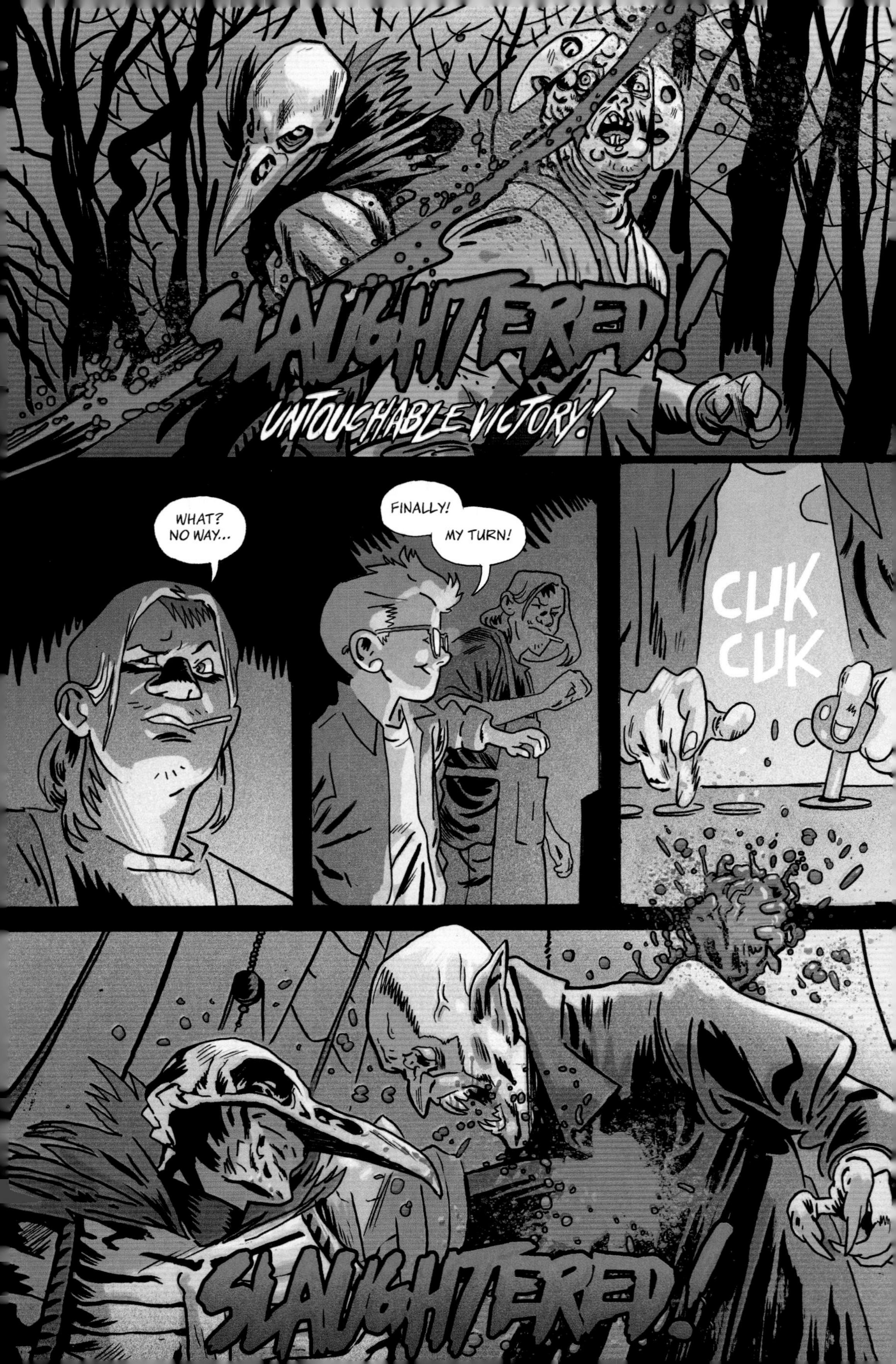
SLAUGHTERED!
UNTOUCHABLE VICTORY!
WHAT? NO WAY...
FINALLY!
MY TURN!
CUK CUK
SLAUGHTERED!

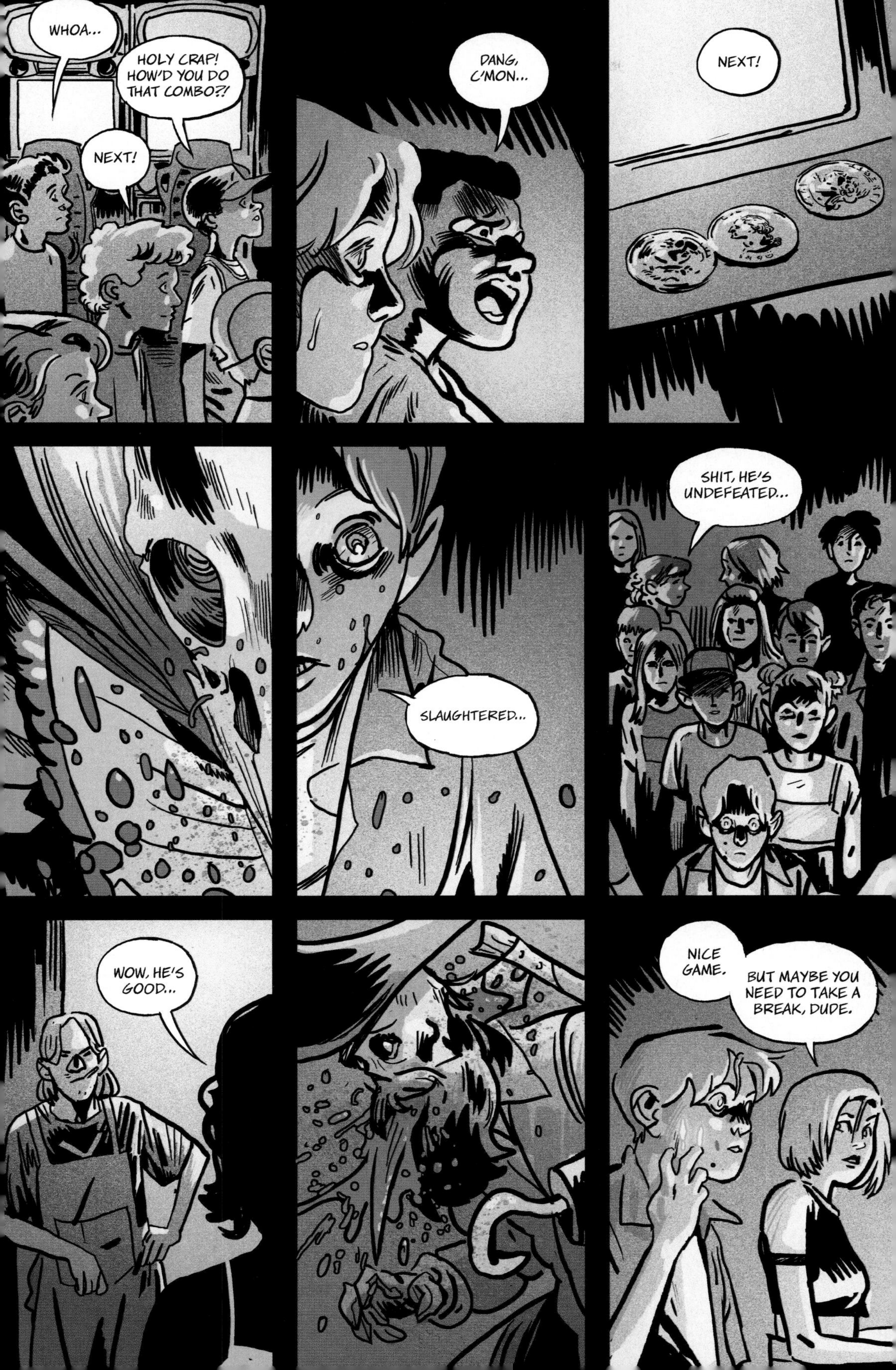
WHOA...
HOLY CRAP! HOW'D YOU DO THAT COMBO?!
NEXT!
DANG, C'MON...
NEXT!
SLAUGHTERED...
SHIT, HE'S UNDEFEATED...
WOW, HE'S GOOD...
NICE GAME.
BUT MAYBE YOU NEED TO TAKE A BREAK, DUDE.

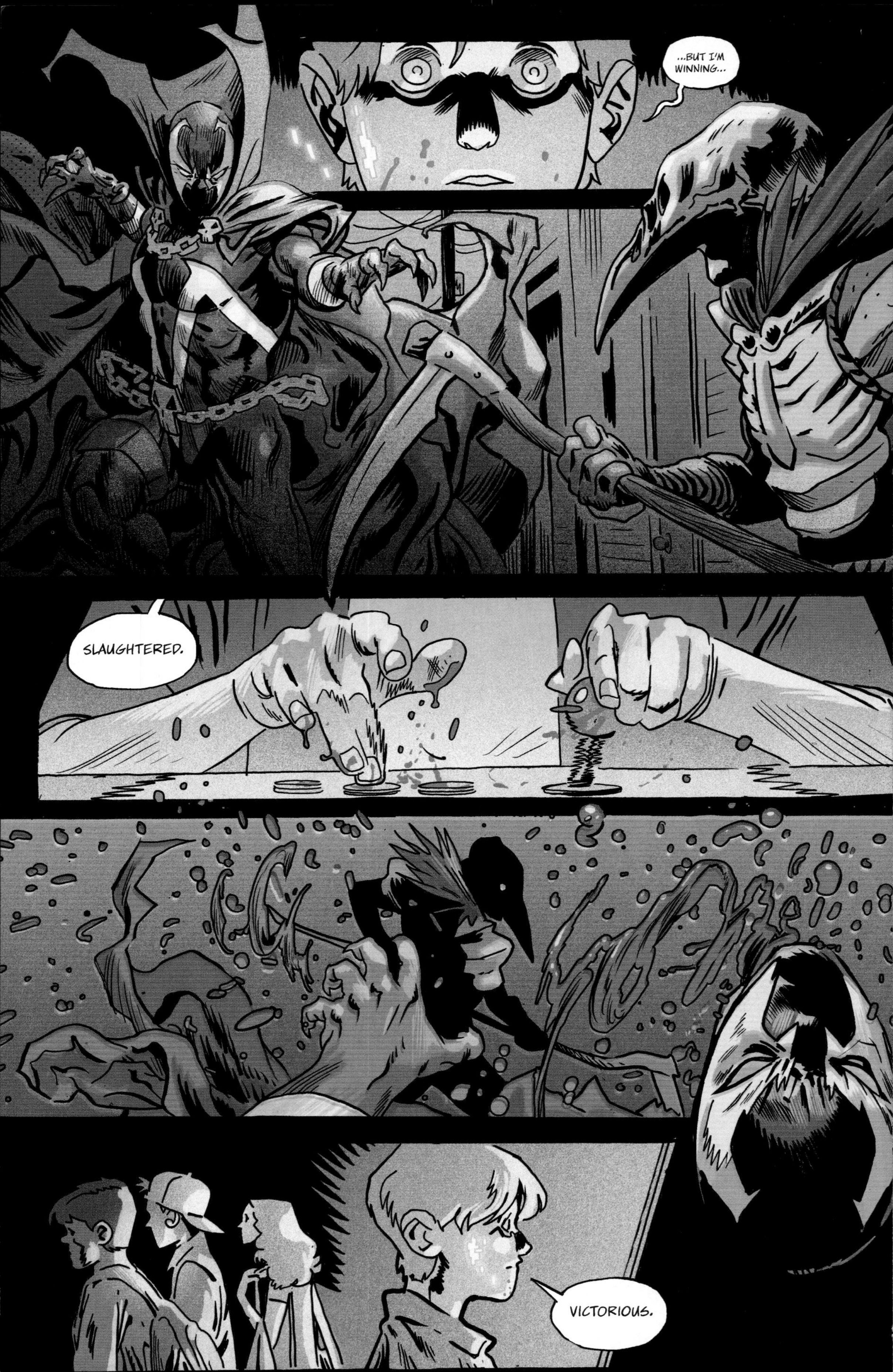
...BUT I'M WINNING...
SLAUGHTERED.
VICTORIOUS.

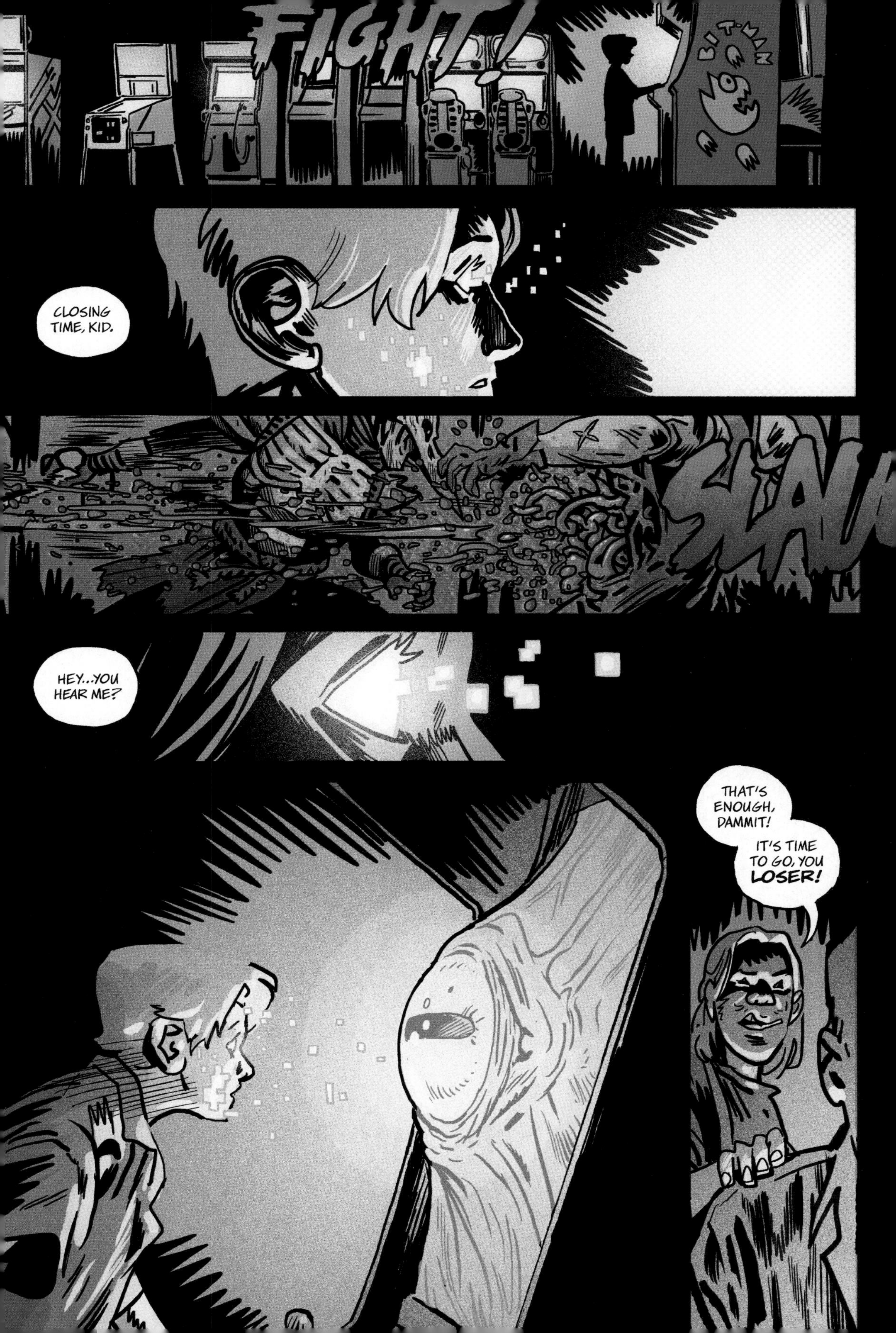
FIGHT!
BIT-MAN
CLOSING TIME, KID.
SLAU
HEY...YOU HEAR ME?
THAT'S ENOUGH, DAMMIT!
IT'S TIME TO GO, YOU **LOSER!**

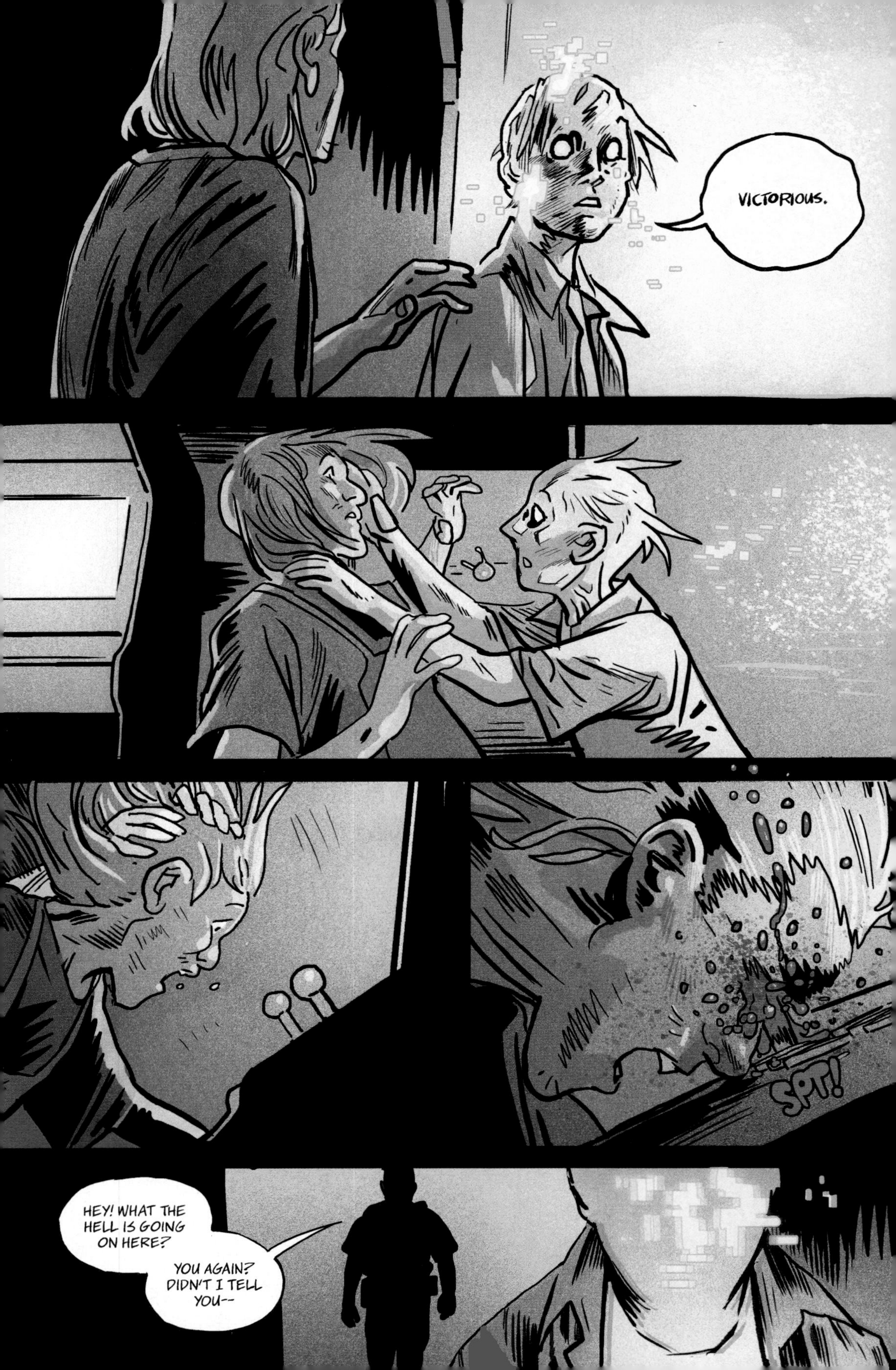
VICTORIOUS.
SPIT!
HEY! WHAT THE HELL IS GOING ON HERE?
YOU AGAIN? DIDN'T I TELL YOU--

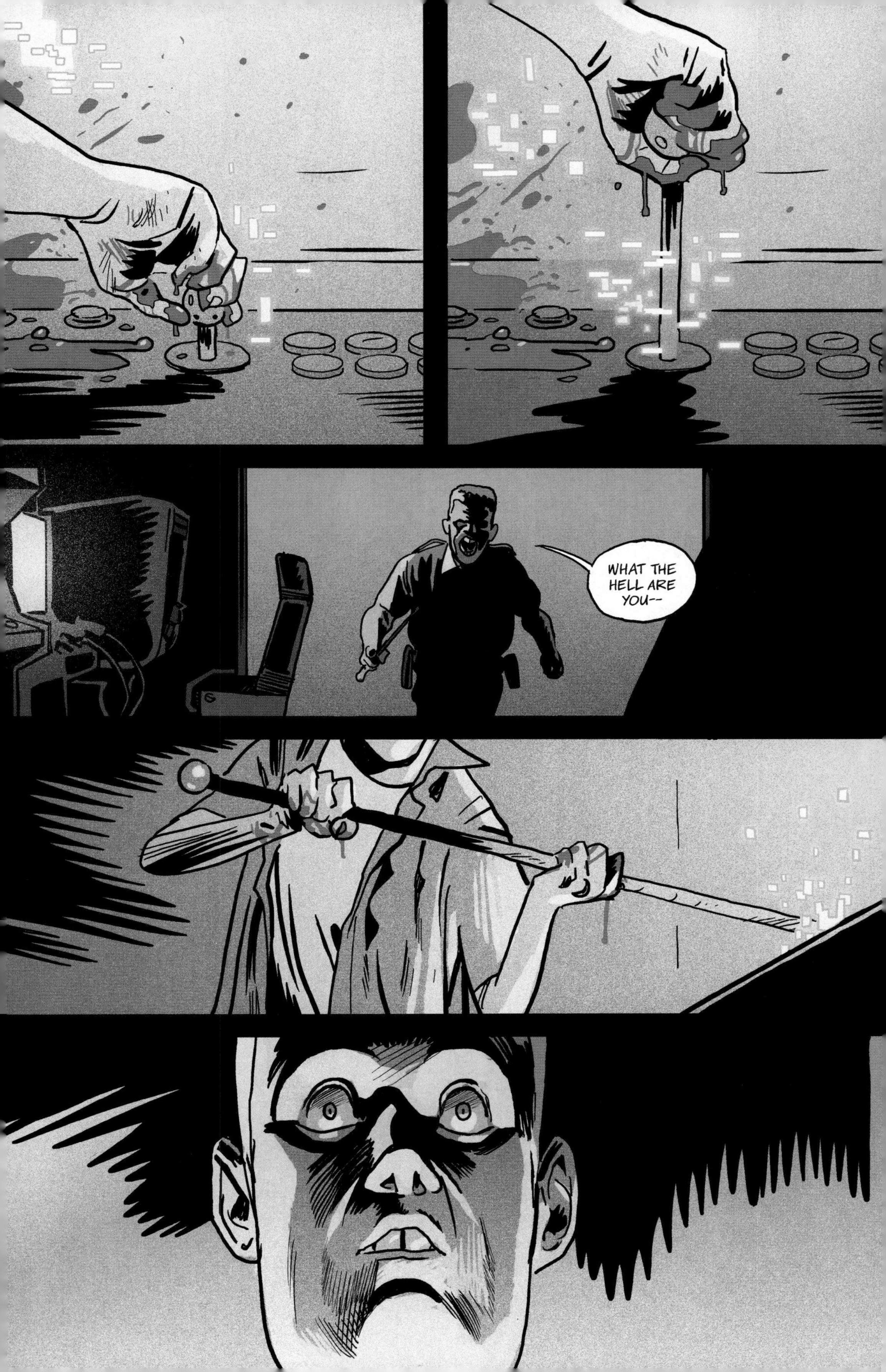
WHAT THE HELL ARE YOU--

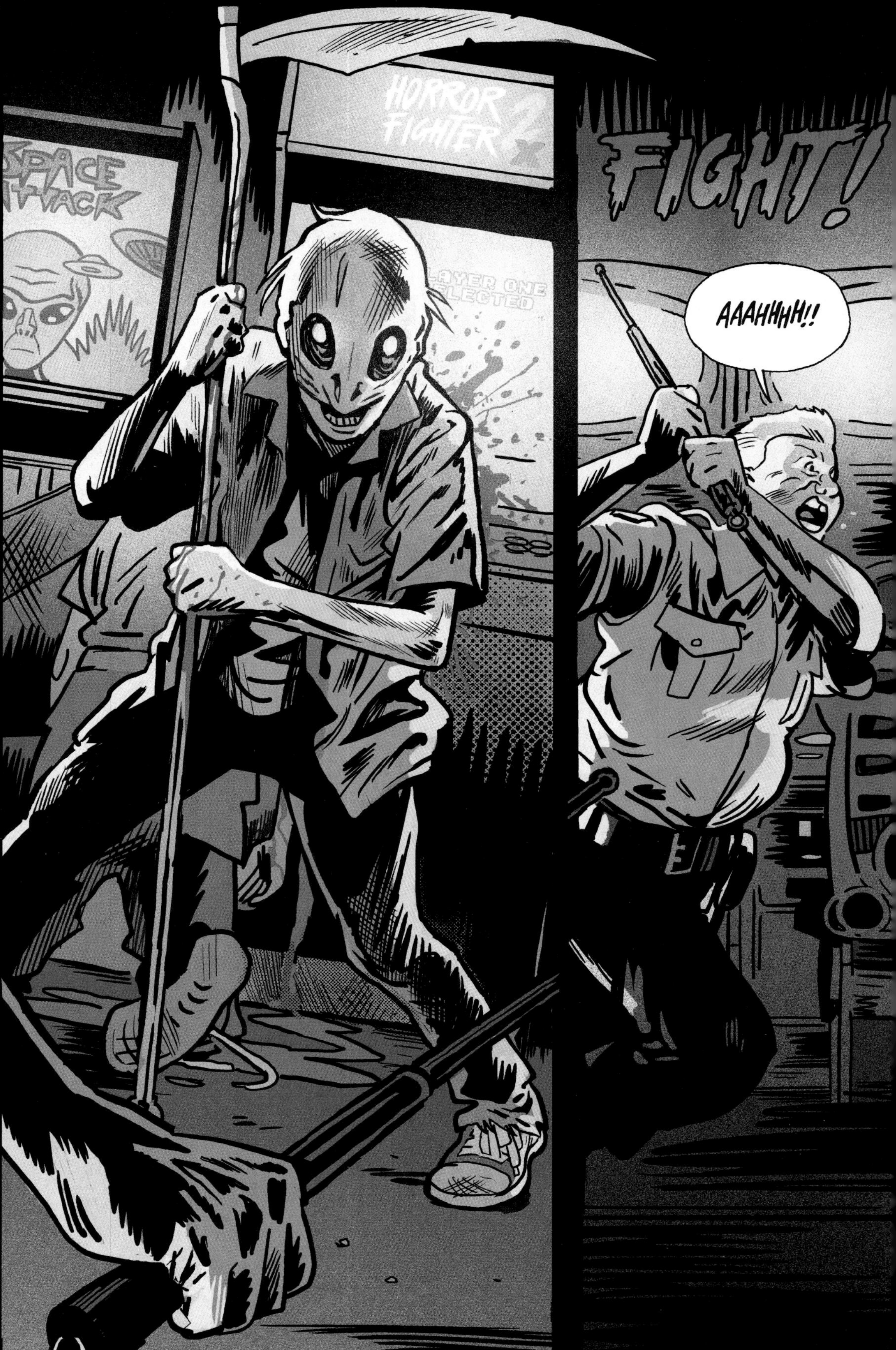
SPACE
HORROR FIGHTER
FIGHT!
AAAHHHH!!

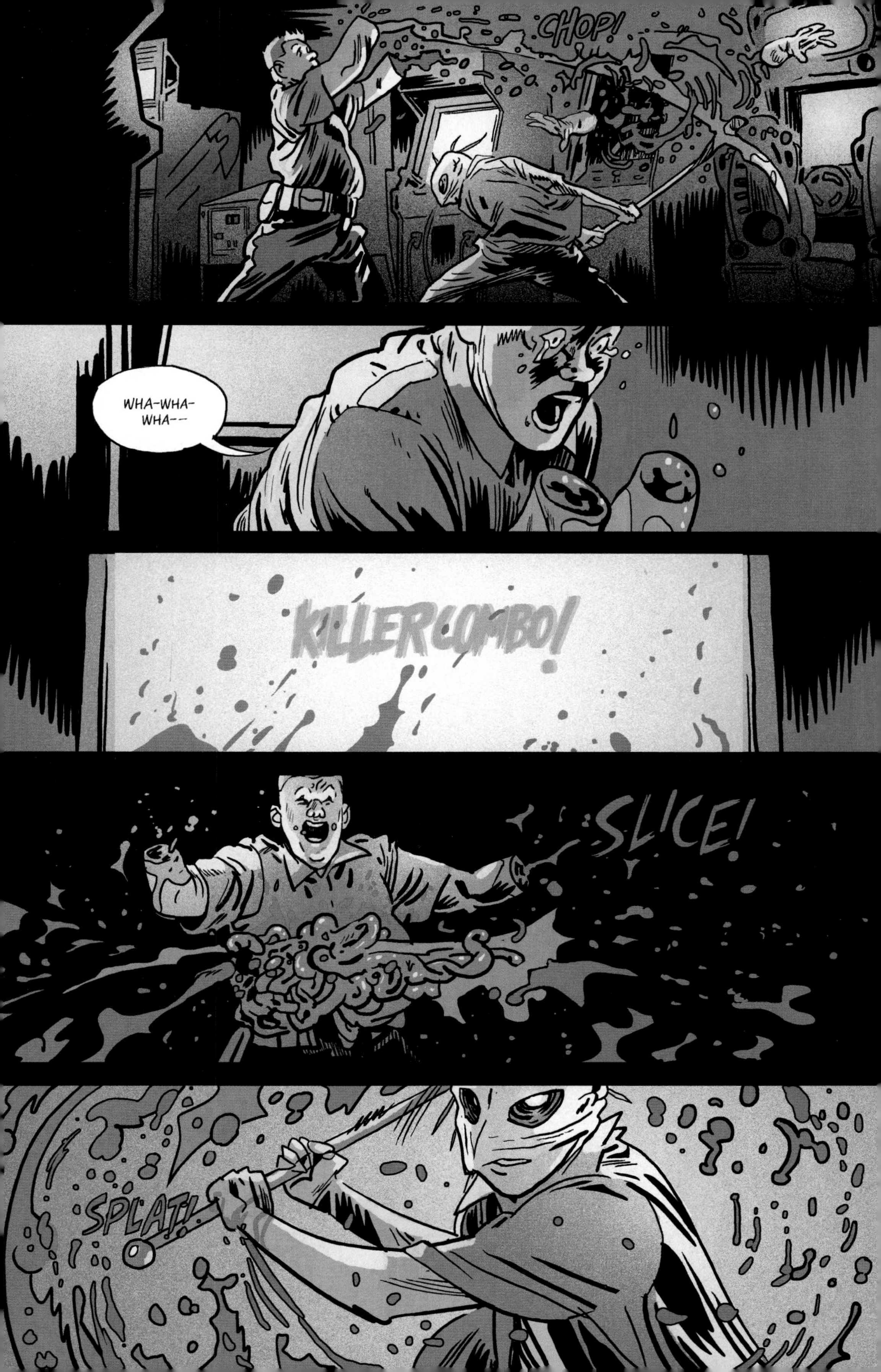
CHOP!
WHA-WHA-WHA--
KILLER COMBO!
SLICE!
SPLAT!

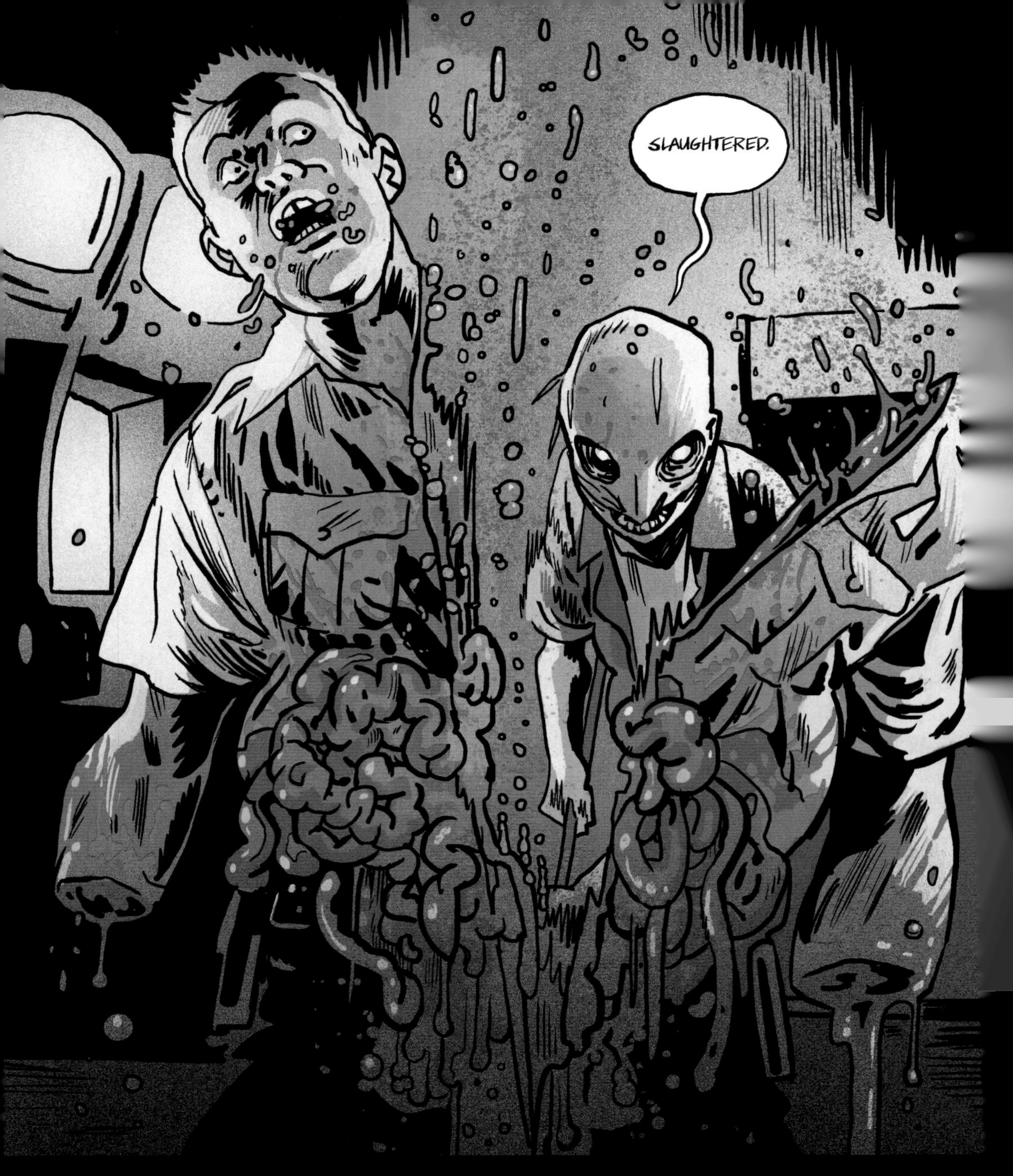
SLAUGHTERED.

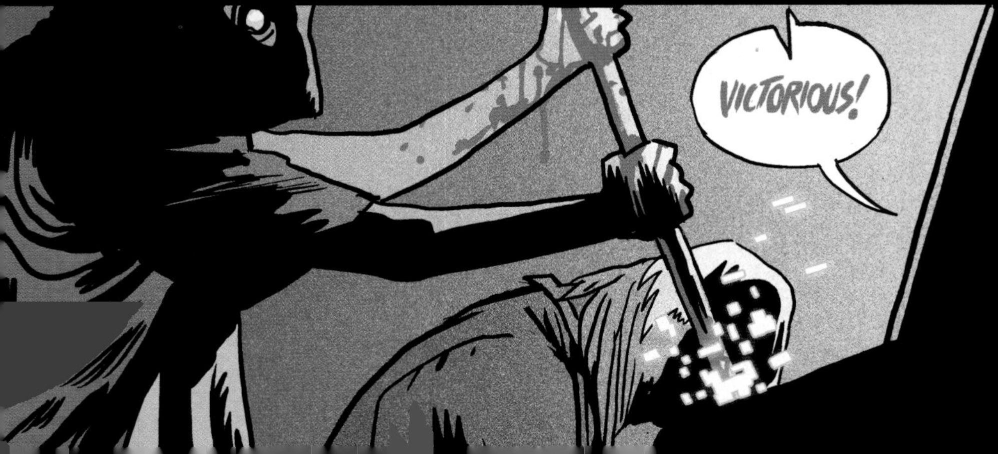
VICTORIOUS!

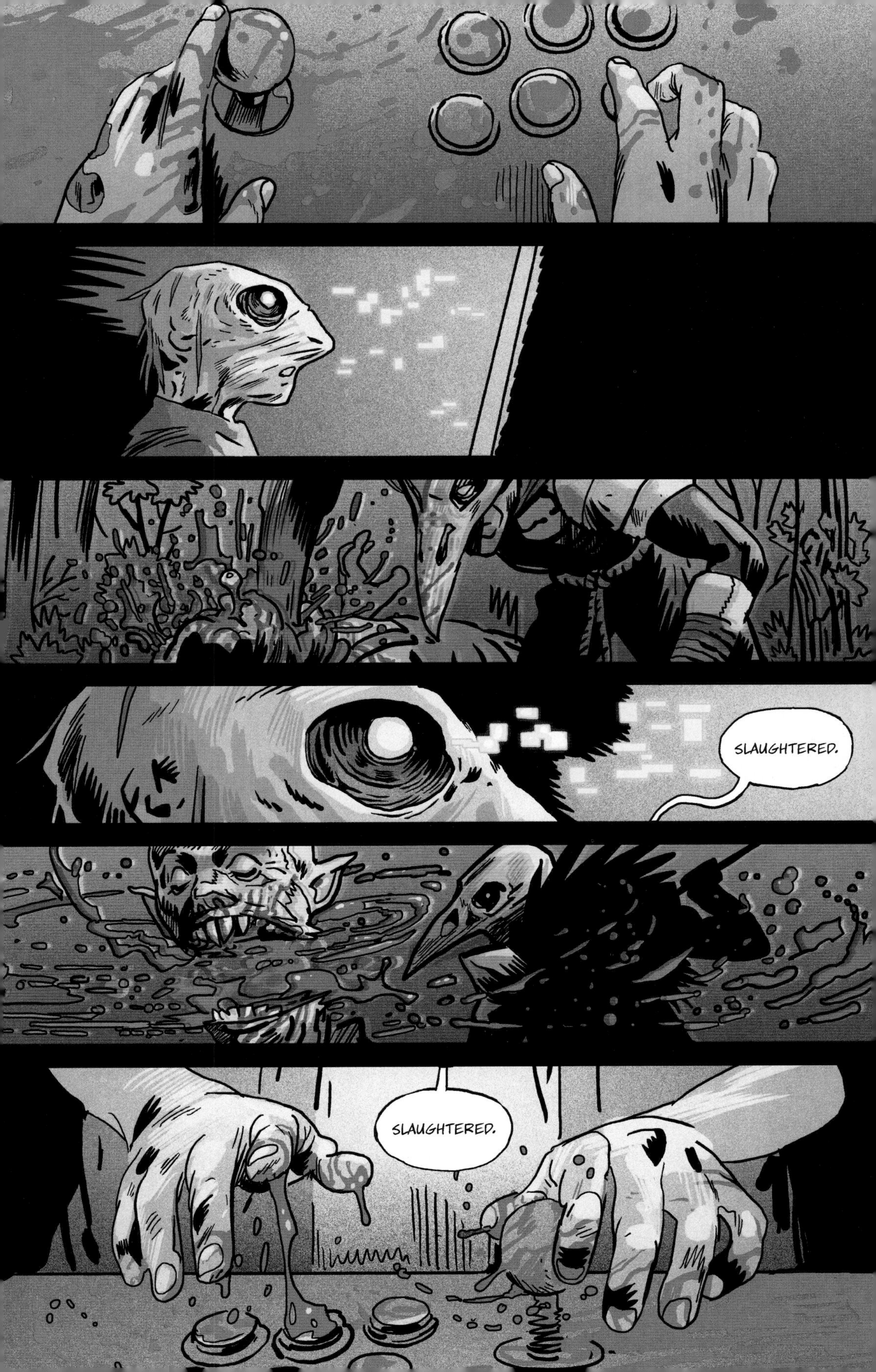
SLAUGHTERED.
SLAUGHTERED.

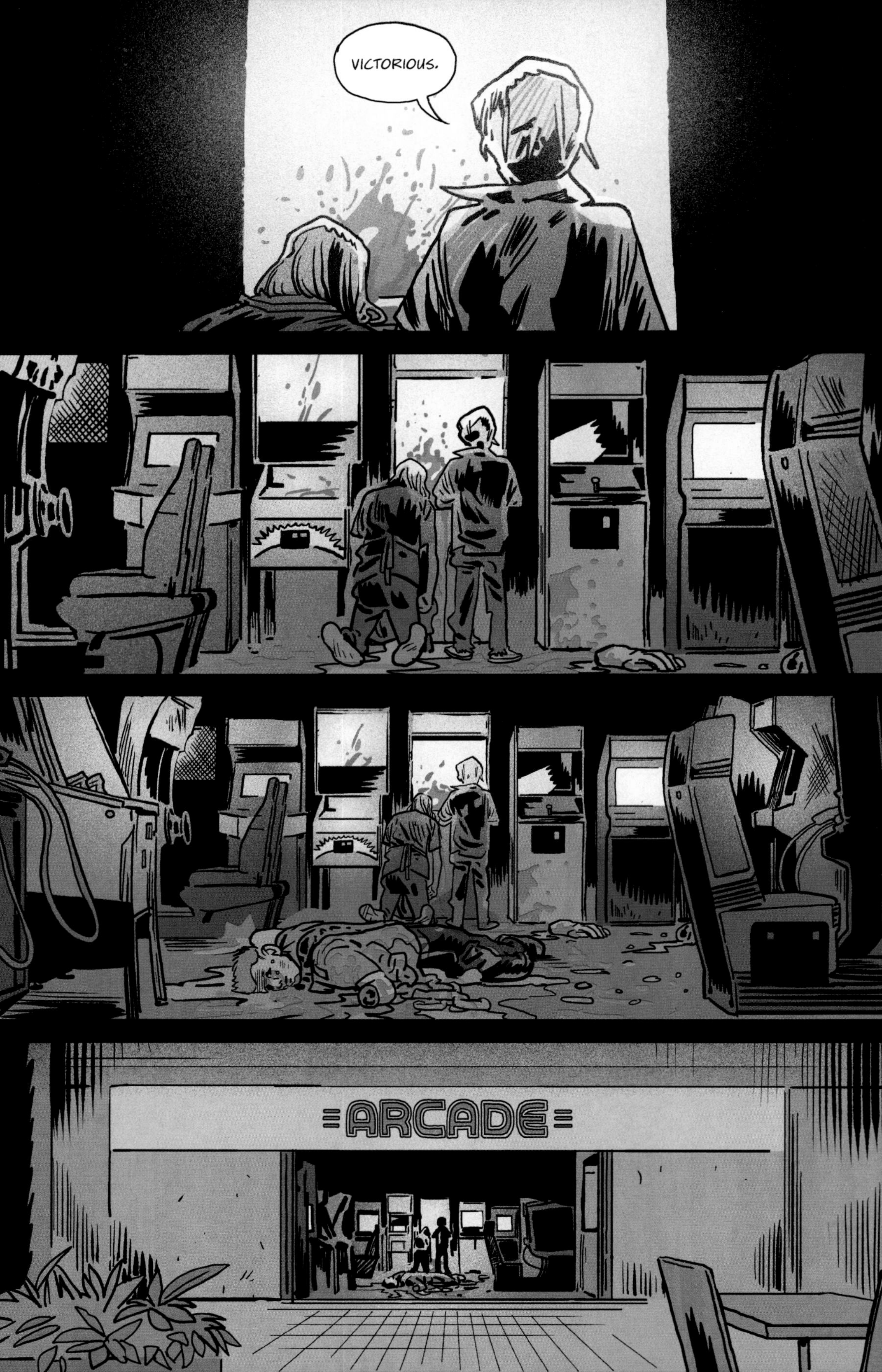
VICTORIOUS.
ARCADE

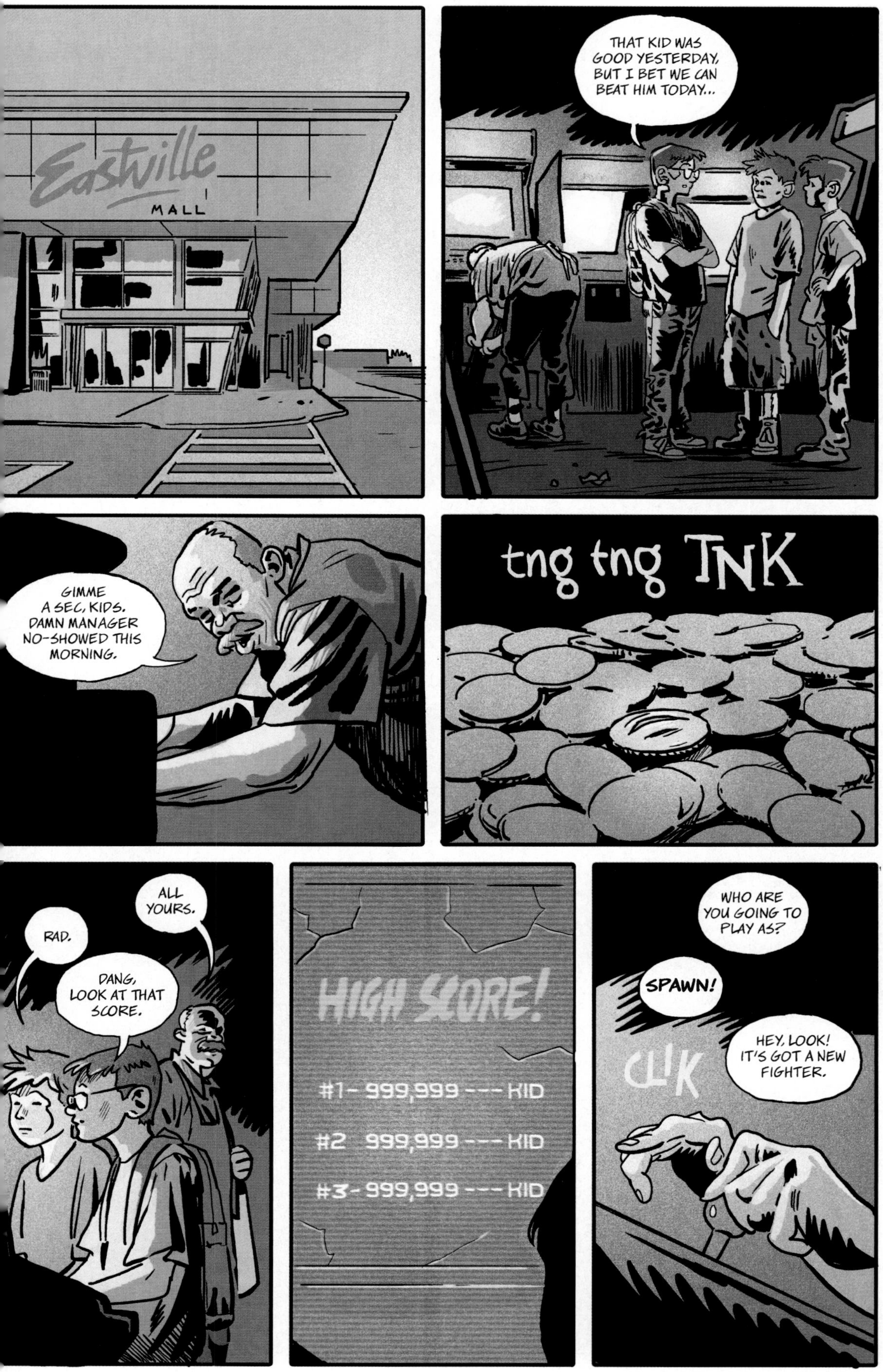
Eastville
MALL
THAT KID WAS GOOD YESTERDAY, BUT I BET WE CAN BEAT HIM TODAY...
GIMME A SEC, KIDS. DAMN MANAGER NO-SHOWED THIS MORNING.
tng tng TNK
ALL YOURS.
RAD.
DANG, LOOK AT THAT SCORE.
HIGH SCORE!
#1- 999,999 --- KID
#2 999,999 --- KID
#3- 999,999 --- KID
WHO ARE YOU GOING TO PLAY AS?
SPAWN!
HEY, LOOK! IT'S GOT A NEW FIGHTER.
CLIK

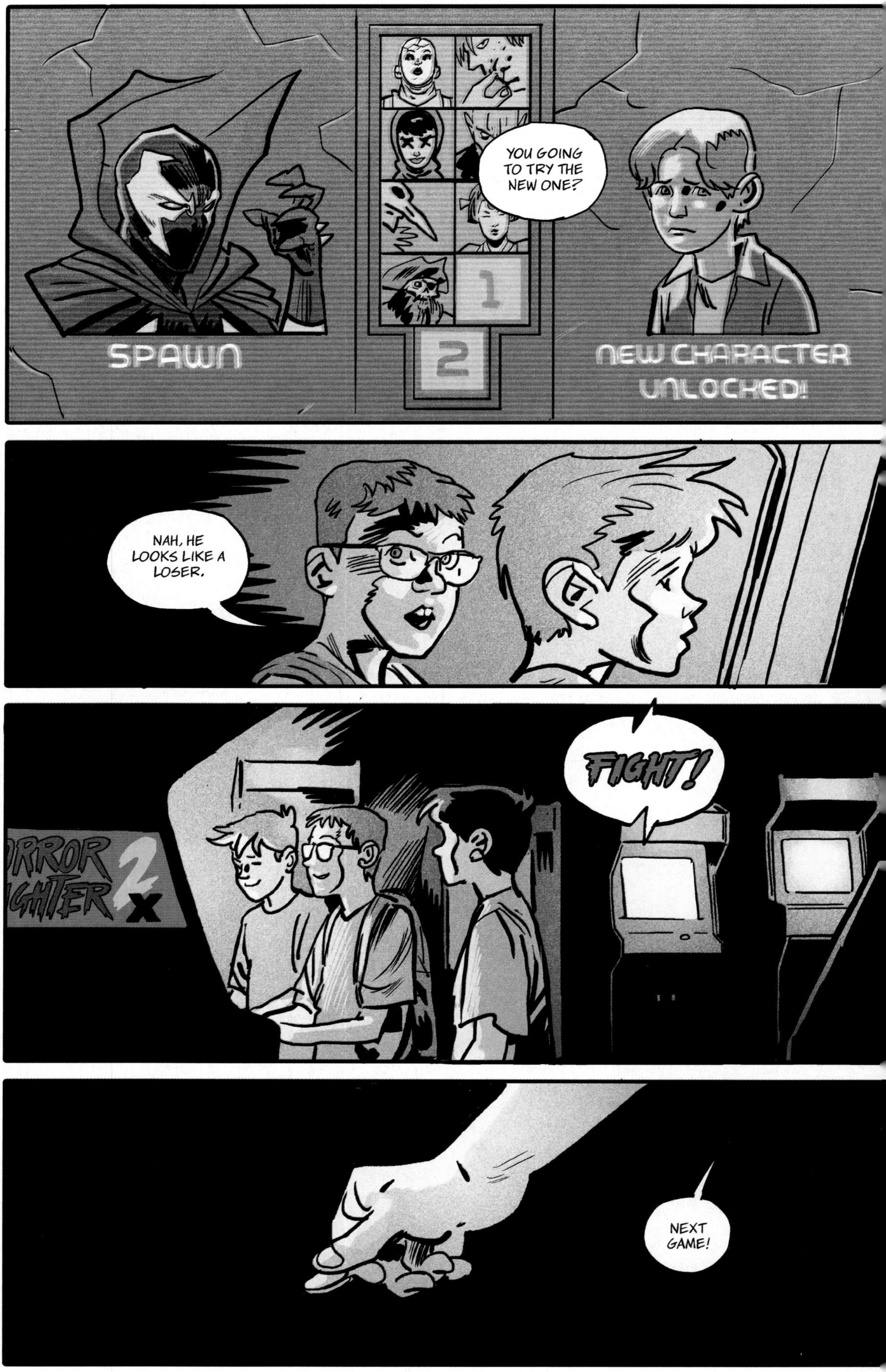
SPAWN
1
2
YOU GOING TO TRY THE NEW ONE?
NEW CHARACTER UNLOCKED!
NAH, HE LOOKS LIKE A LOSER.
RROR
GHTER 2 X
FIGHT!
NEXT GAME!

Tzompanco

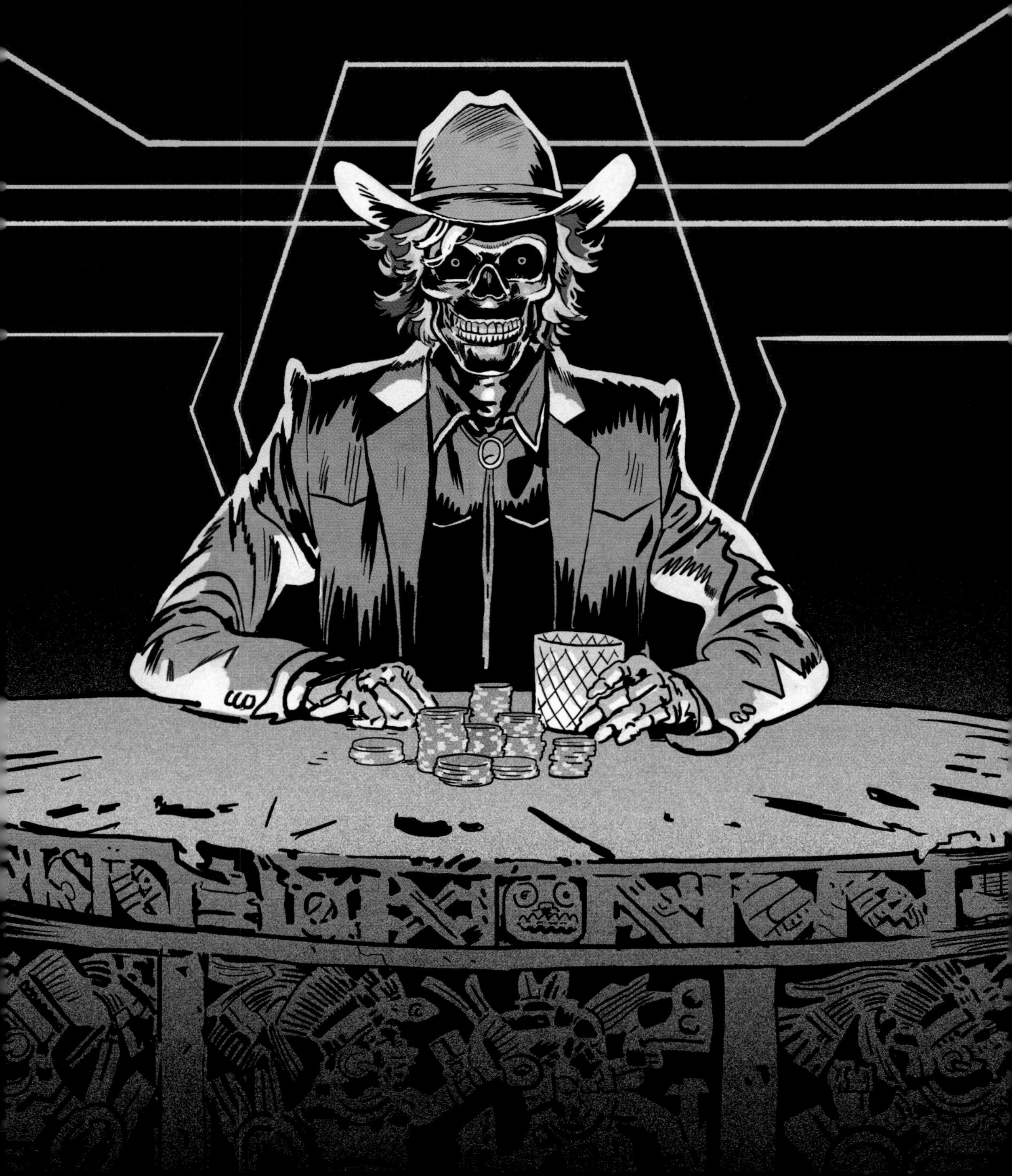

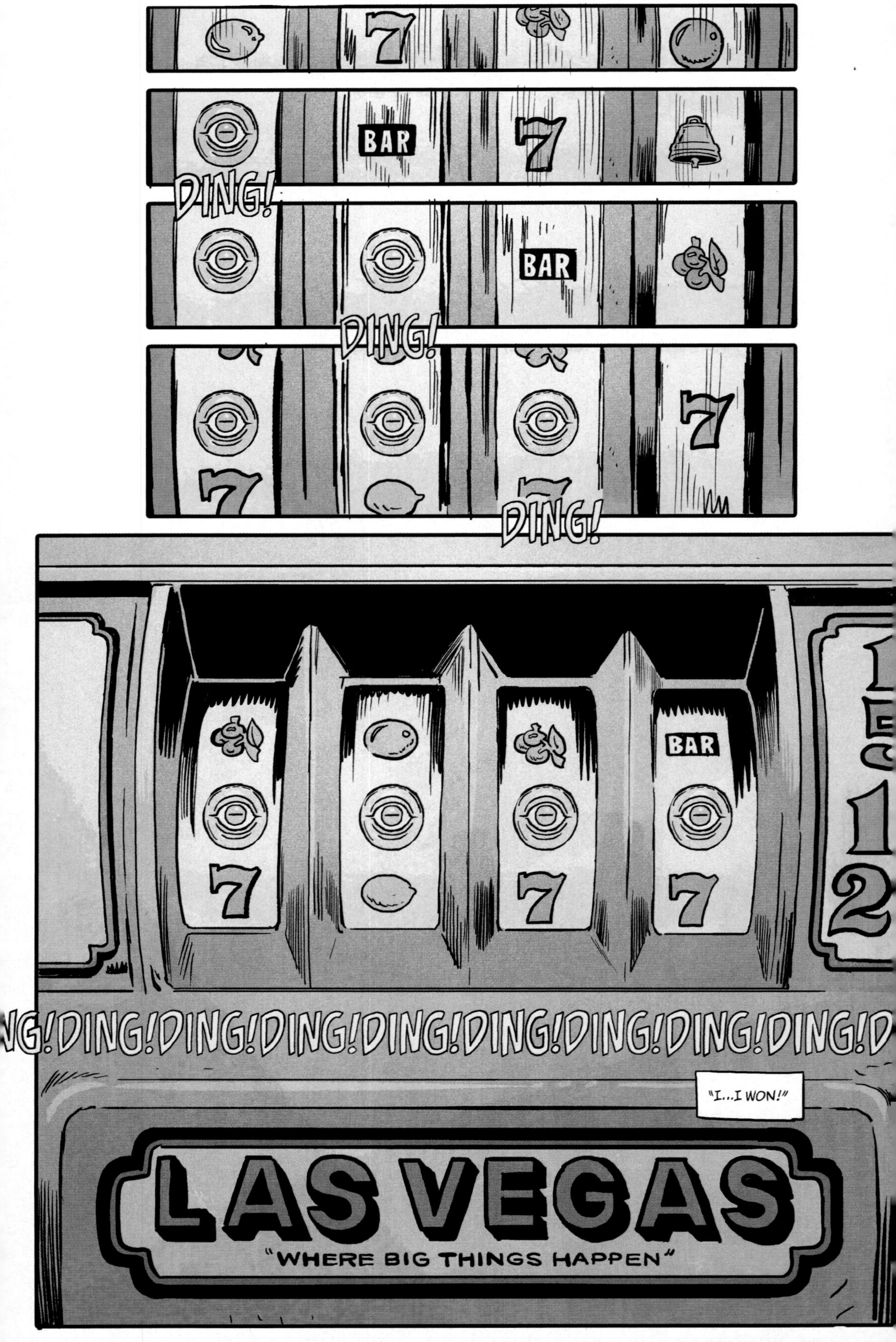
BAR
DING!
BAR
DING!
DING!
BAR
NG!DING!DING!DING!DING!DING!DING!DING!DING!D
"I...I WON!"
LAS VEGAS
"WHERE BIG THINGS HAPPEN"

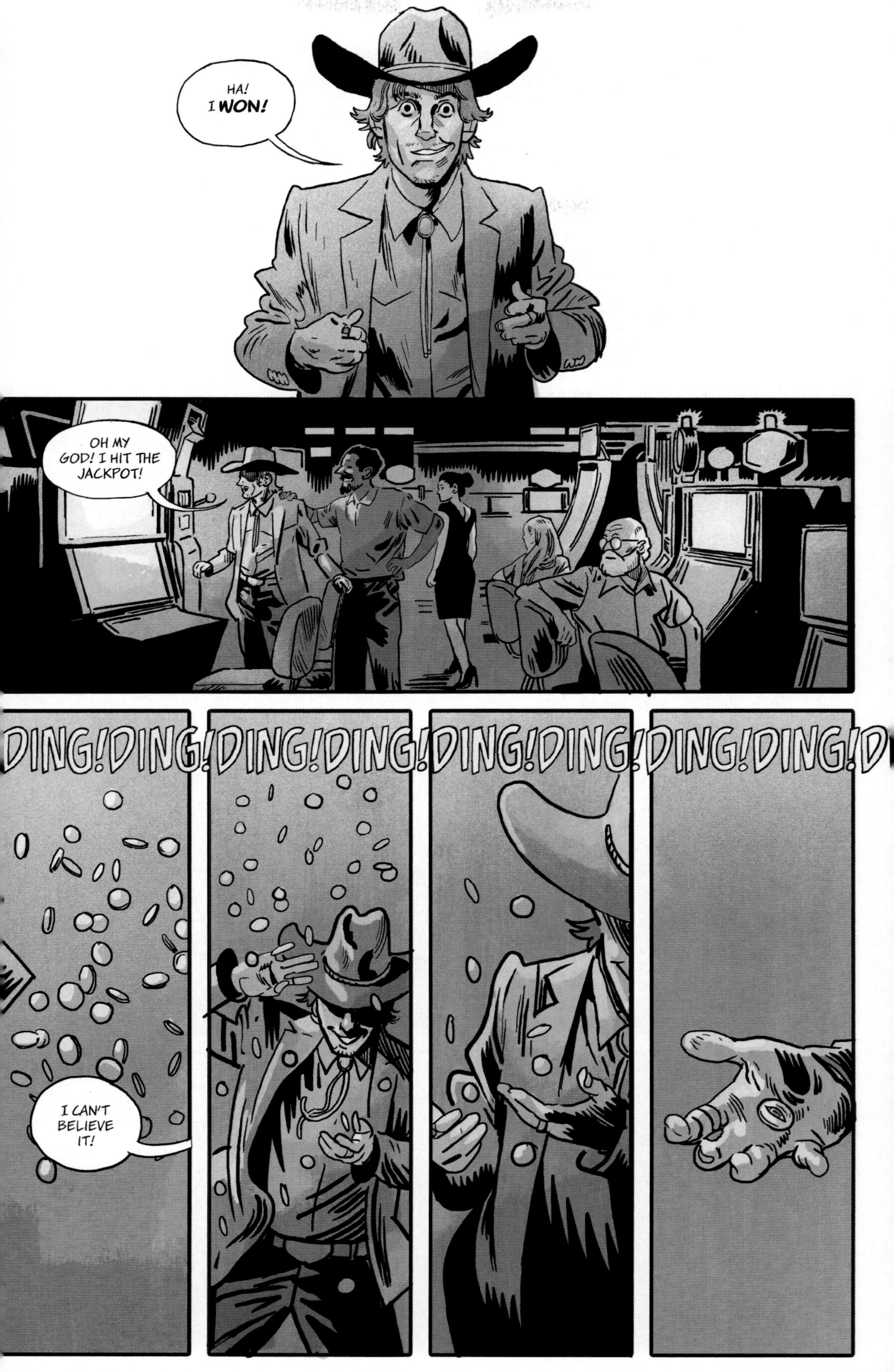
HA!
I WON!
OH MY GOD! I HIT THE JACKPOT!
DING!DING!DING!DING!DING!DING!DING!DING!D
I CAN'T BELIEVE IT!

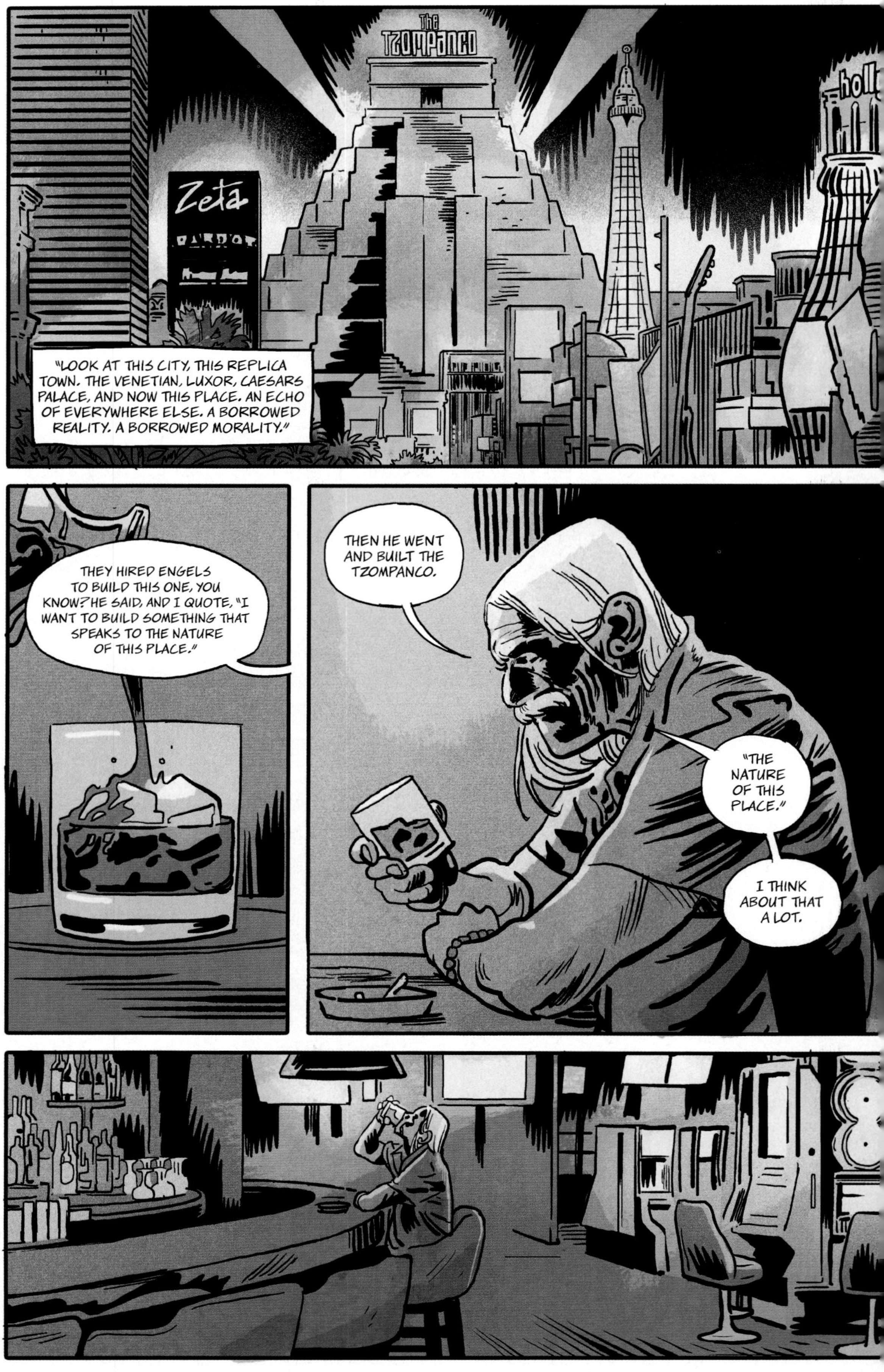
The TZOMPANCO
Zeta
"LOOK AT THIS CITY, THIS REPLICA TOWN. THE VENETIAN, LUXOR, CAESARS PALACE, AND NOW THIS PLACE. AN ECHO OF EVERYWHERE ELSE. A BORROWED REALITY. A BORROWED MORALITY."
THEY HIRED ENGELS TO BUILD THIS ONE, YOU KNOW? HE SAID, AND I QUOTE, "I WANT TO BUILD SOMETHING THAT SPEAKS TO THE NATURE OF THIS PLACE."
THEN HE WENT AND BUILT THE TZOMPANCO.
"THE NATURE OF THIS PLACE."
I THINK ABOUT THAT A LOT.

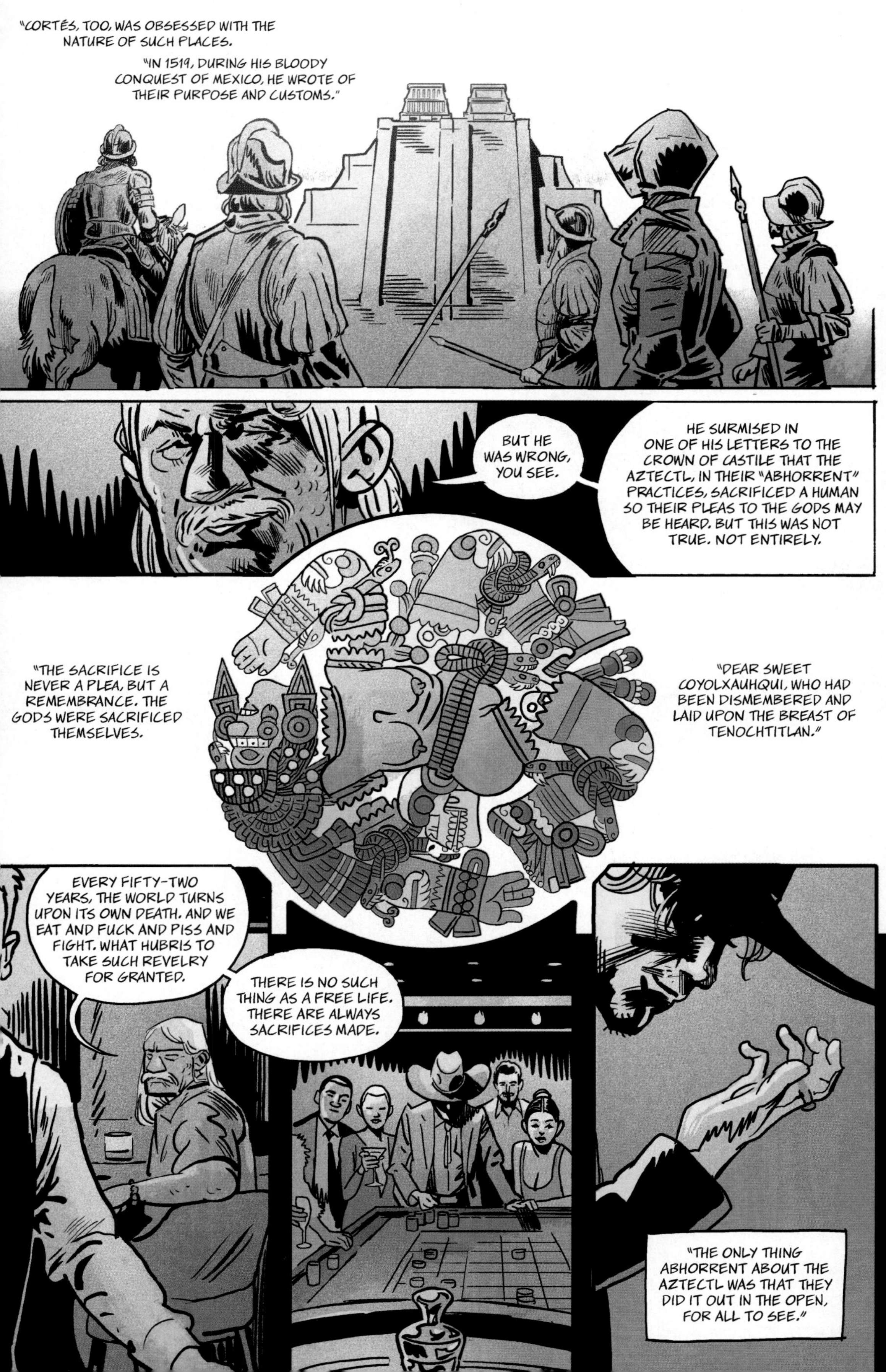

"CORTÉS, TOO, WAS OBSESSED WITH THE NATURE OF SUCH PLACES.
"IN 1519, DURING HIS BLOODY CONQUEST OF MEXICO, HE WROTE OF THEIR PURPOSE AND CUSTOMS."
BUT HE WAS WRONG, YOU SEE.
HE SURMISED IN ONE OF HIS LETTERS TO THE CROWN OF CASTILE THAT THE AZTECTL, IN THEIR "ABHORRENT" PRACTICES, SACRIFICED A HUMAN SO THEIR PLEAS TO THE GODS MAY BE HEARD. BUT THIS WAS NOT TRUE. NOT ENTIRELY.
"THE SACRIFICE IS NEVER A PLEA, BUT A REMEMBRANCE. THE GODS WERE SACRIFICED THEMSELVES.
"DEAR SWEET COYOLXAUHQUI, WHO HAD BEEN DISMEMBERED AND LAID UPON THE BREAST OF TENOCHTITLAN."
EVERY FIFTY-TWO YEARS, THE WORLD TURNS UPON ITS OWN DEATH. AND WE EAT AND FUCK AND PISS AND FIGHT. WHAT HUBRIS TO TAKE SUCH REVELRY FOR GRANTED.
THERE IS NO SUCH THING AS A FREE LIFE. THERE ARE ALWAYS SACRIFICES MADE.
"THE ONLY THING ABHORRENT ABOUT THE AZTECTL WAS THAT THEY DID IT OUT IN THE OPEN, FOR ALL TO SEE."

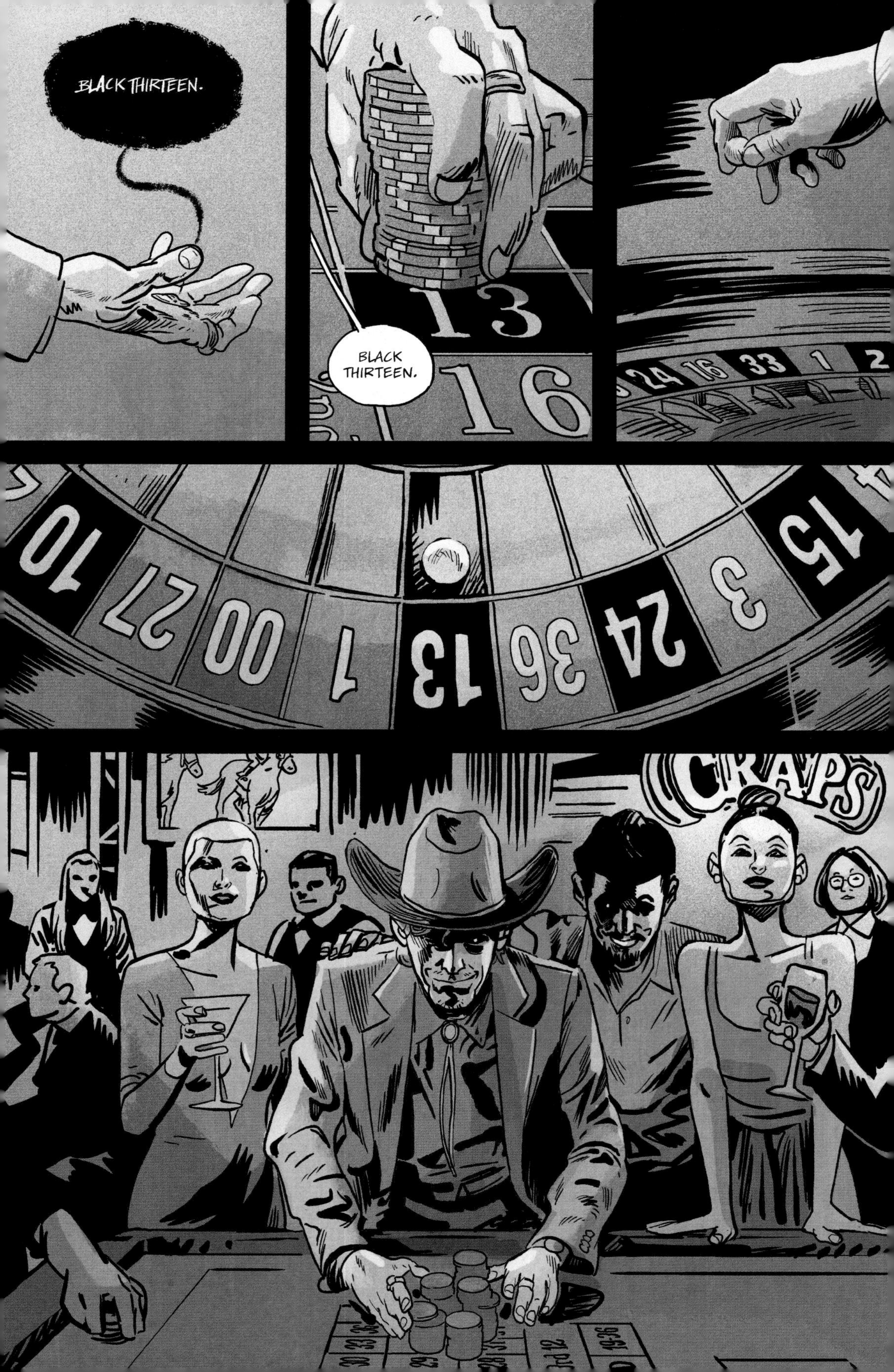
BLACK THIRTEEN.
BLACK THIRTEEN.
CRAPS

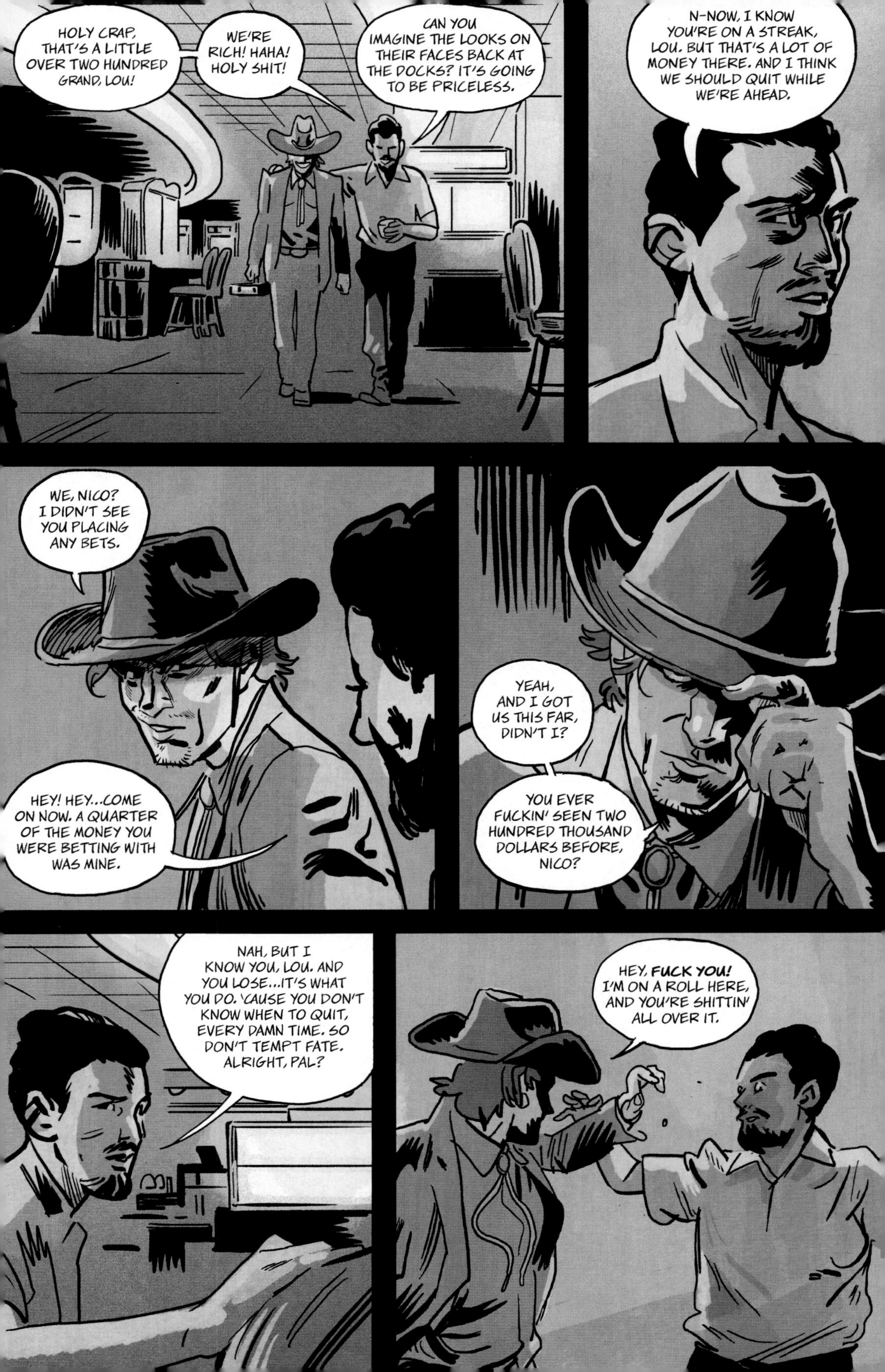
HOLY CRAP, THAT'S A LITTLE OVER TWO HUNDRED GRAND, LOU!
WE'RE RICH! HAHA! HOLY SHIT!
CAN YOU IMAGINE THE LOOKS ON THEIR FACES BACK AT THE DOCKS? IT'S GOING TO BE PRICELESS.
N-NOW, I KNOW YOU'RE ON A STREAK, LOU. BUT THAT'S A LOT OF MONEY THERE. AND I THINK WE SHOULD QUIT WHILE WE'RE AHEAD.
WE, NICO? I DIDN'T SEE YOU PLACING ANY BETS.
HEY! HEY...COME ON NOW. A QUARTER OF THE MONEY YOU WERE BETTING WITH WAS MINE.
YEAH, AND I GOT US THIS FAR, DIDN'T I?
YOU EVER FUCKIN' SEEN TWO HUNDRED THOUSAND DOLLARS BEFORE, NICO?
NAH, BUT I KNOW YOU, LOU. AND YOU LOSE...IT'S WHAT YOU DO. 'CAUSE YOU DON'T KNOW WHEN TO QUIT, EVERY DAMN TIME. SO DON'T TEMPT FATE. ALRIGHT, PAL?
HEY, **FUCK YOU!** I'M ON A ROLL HERE, AND YOU'RE SHITTIN' ALL OVER IT.

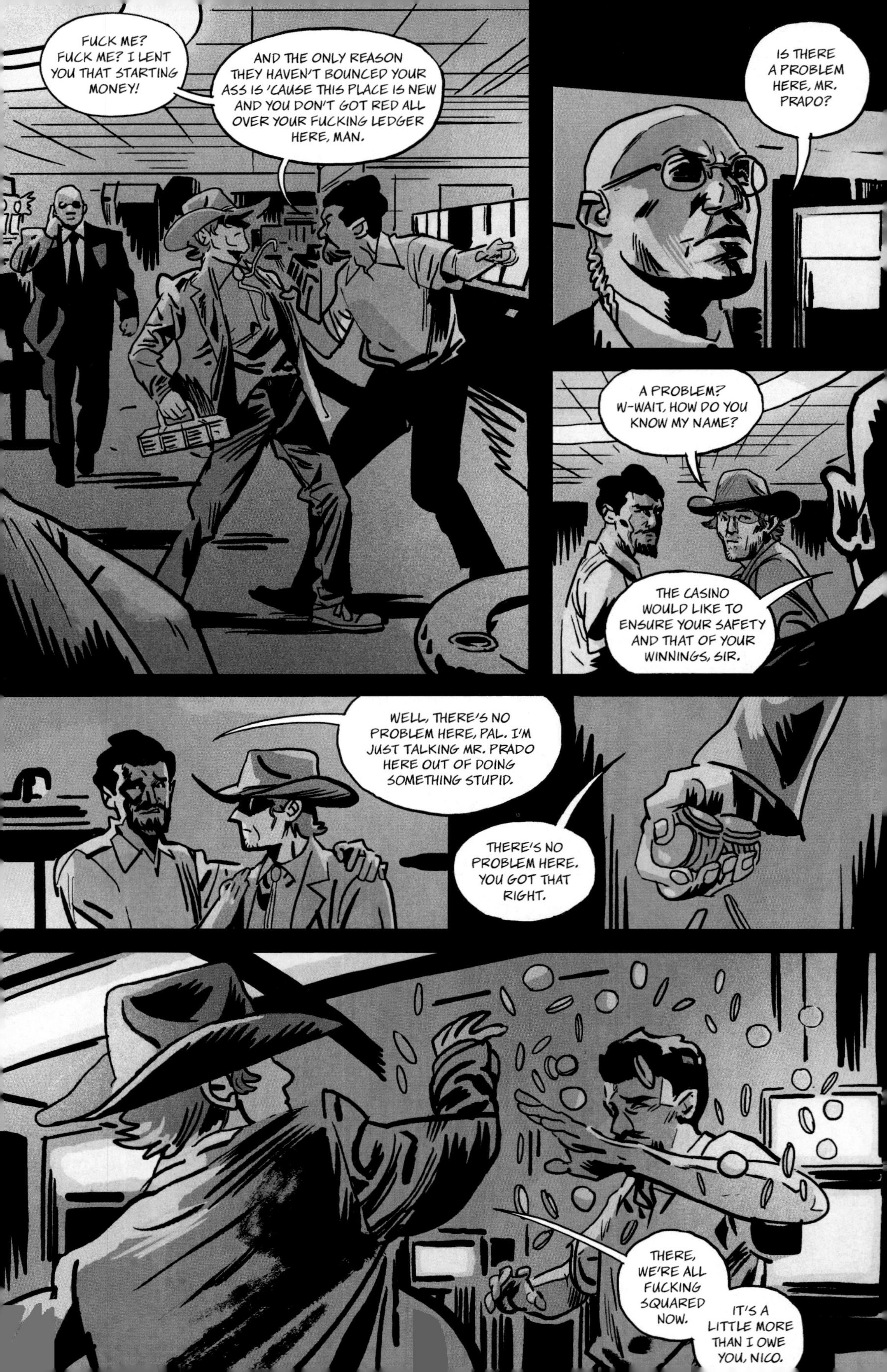
FUCK ME? FUCK ME? I LENT YOU THAT STARTING MONEY!
AND THE ONLY REASON THEY HAVEN'T BOUNCED YOUR ASS IS 'CAUSE THIS PLACE IS NEW AND YOU DON'T GOT RED ALL OVER YOUR FUCKING LEDGER HERE, MAN.
IS THERE A PROBLEM HERE, MR. PRADO?
A PROBLEM? W-WAIT, HOW DO YOU KNOW MY NAME?
THE CASINO WOULD LIKE TO ENSURE YOUR SAFETY AND THAT OF YOUR WINNINGS, SIR.
WELL, THERE'S NO PROBLEM HERE, PAL. I'M JUST TALKING MR. PRADO HERE OUT OF DOING SOMETHING STUPID.
THERE'S NO PROBLEM HERE. YOU GOT THAT RIGHT.
THERE, WE'RE ALL FUCKING SQUARED NOW.
IT'S A LITTLE MORE THAN I OWE YOU, NICO.

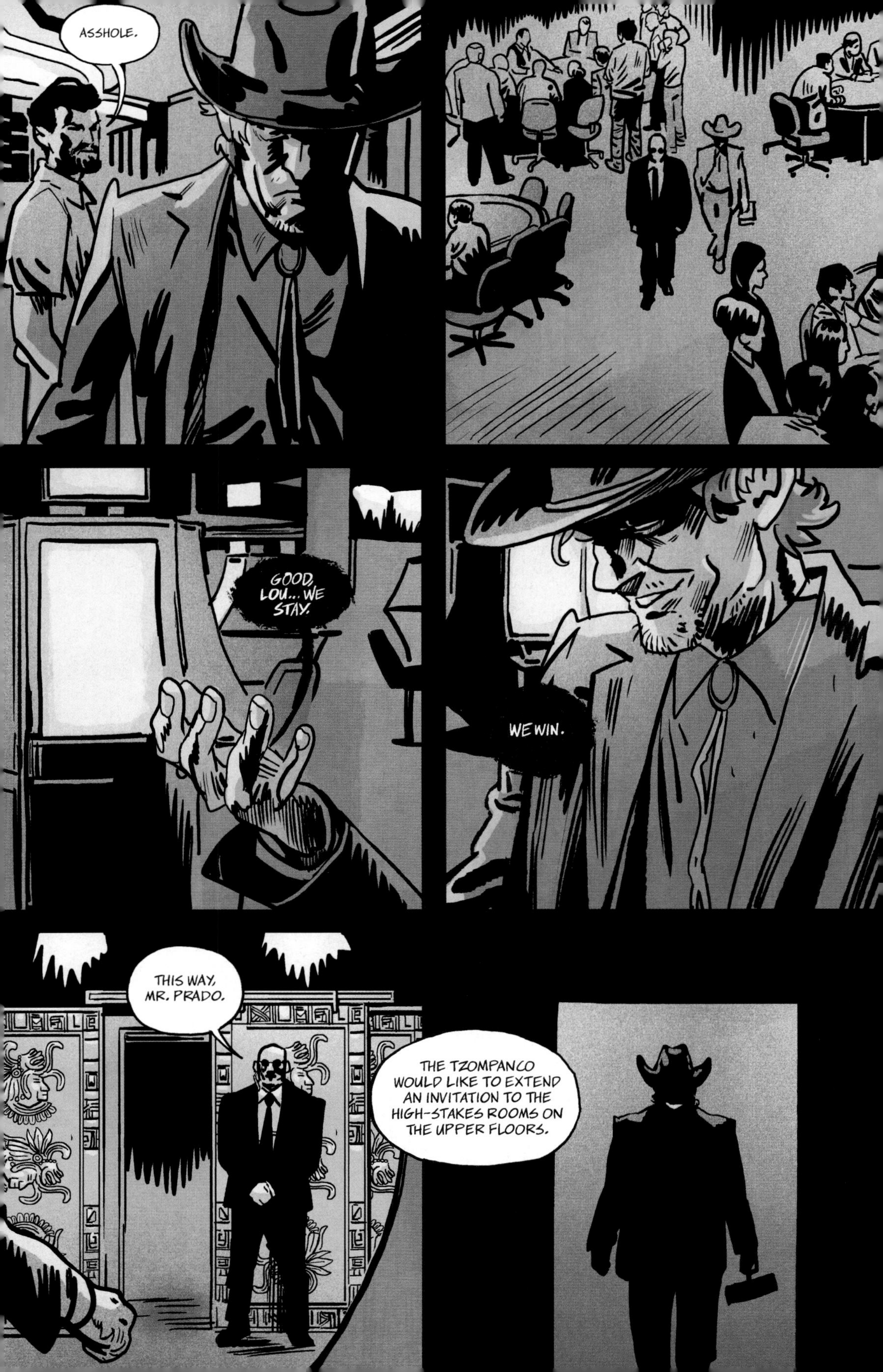
ASSHOLE.
GOOD, LOU... WE STAY.
WE WIN.
THIS WAY, MR. PRADO.
THE TZOMPANCO WOULD LIKE TO EXTEND AN INVITATION TO THE HIGH-STAKES ROOMS ON THE UPPER FLOORS.

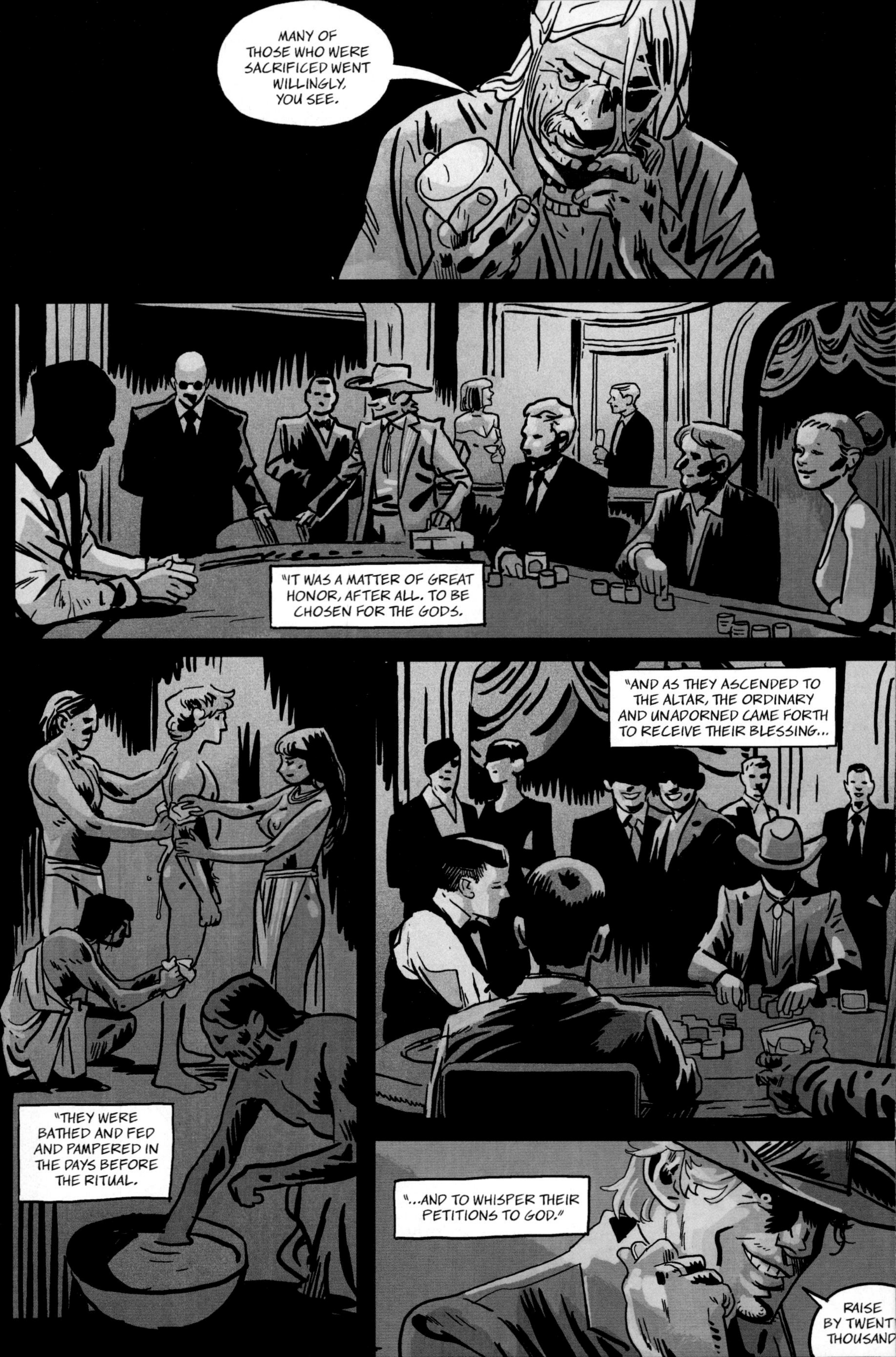
MANY OF THOSE WHO WERE SACRIFICED WENT WILLINGLY, YOU SEE.
"IT WAS A MATTER OF GREAT HONOR, AFTER ALL. TO BE CHOSEN FOR THE GODS.
"THEY WERE BATHED AND FED AND PAMPERED IN THE DAYS BEFORE THE RITUAL.
"AND AS THEY ASCENDED TO THE ALTAR, THE ORDINARY AND UNADORNED CAME FORTH TO RECEIVE THEIR BLESSING...
"...AND TO WHISPER THEIR PETITIONS TO GOD."
RAISE BY TWENT THOUSAND

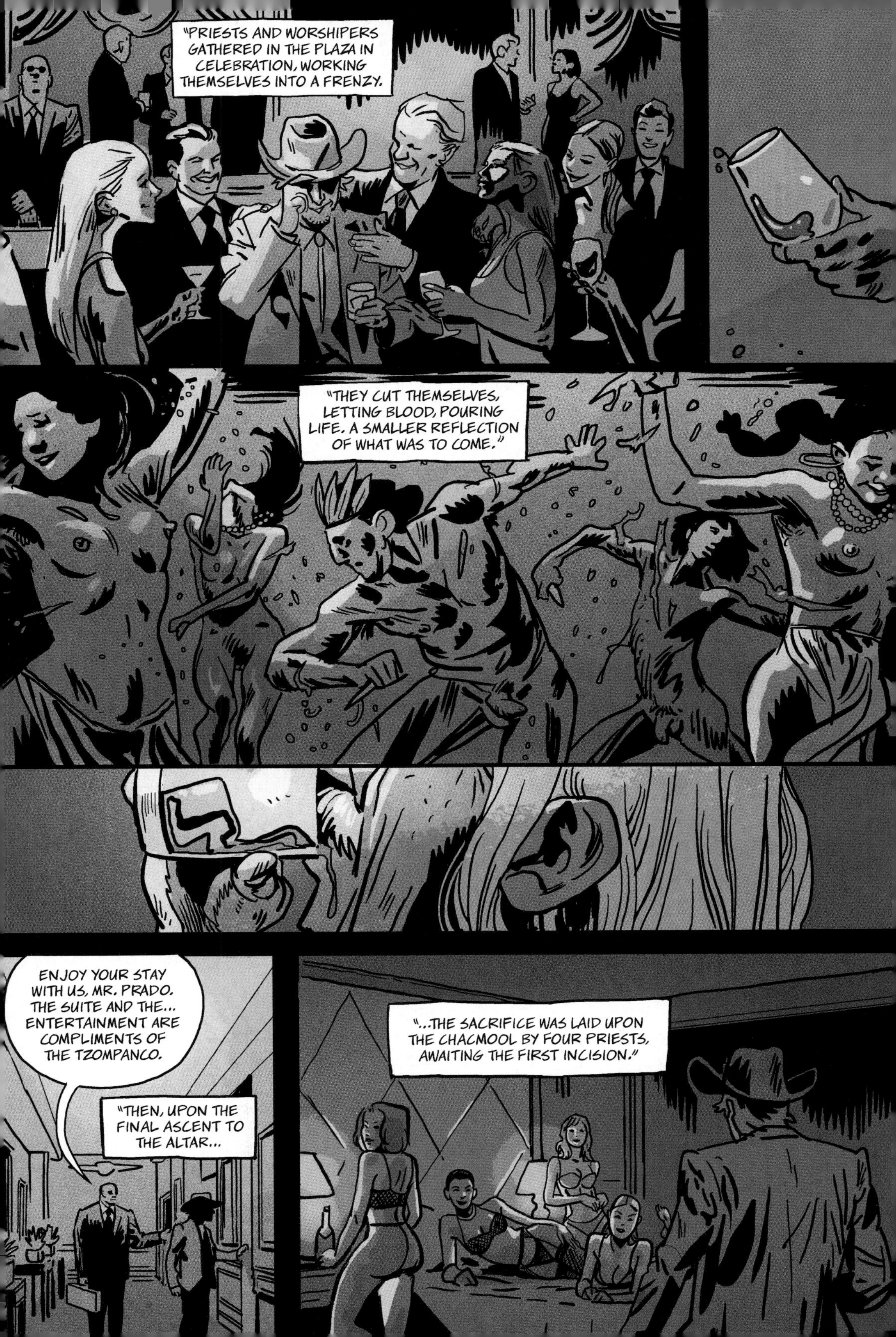
"PRIESTS AND WORSHIPERS GATHERED IN THE PLAZA IN CELEBRATION, WORKING THEMSELVES INTO A FRENZY.
"THEY CUT THEMSELVES, LETTING BLOOD, POURING LIFE. A SMALLER REFLECTION OF WHAT WAS TO COME."
ENJOY YOUR STAY WITH US, MR. PRADO. THE SUITE AND THE... ENTERTAINMENT ARE COMPLIMENTS OF THE TZOMPANCO.
"THEN, UPON THE FINAL ASCENT TO THE ALTAR...
"...THE SACRIFICE WAS LAID UPON THE CHACMOOL BY FOUR PRIESTS, AWAITING THE FIRST INCISION."

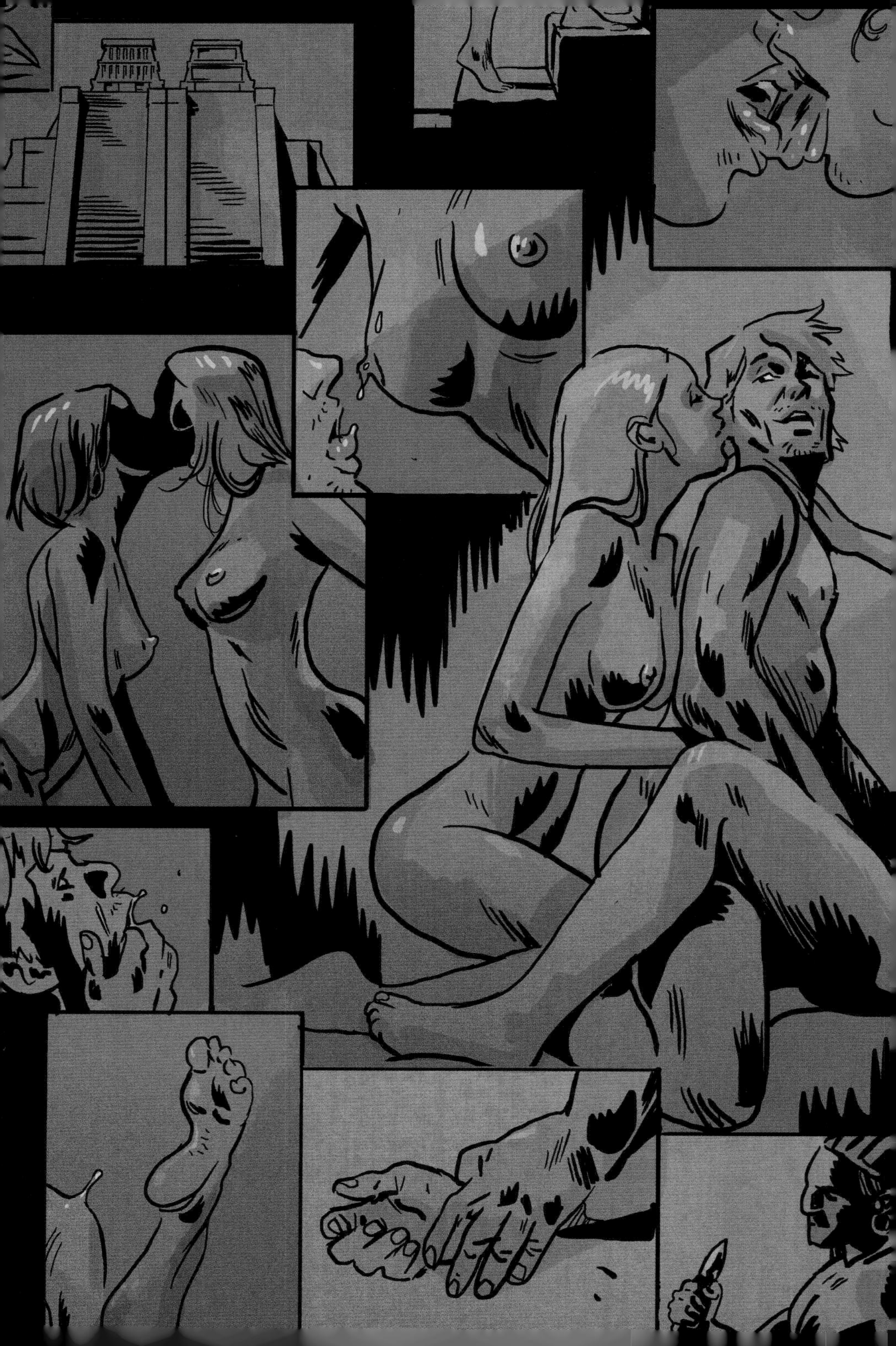

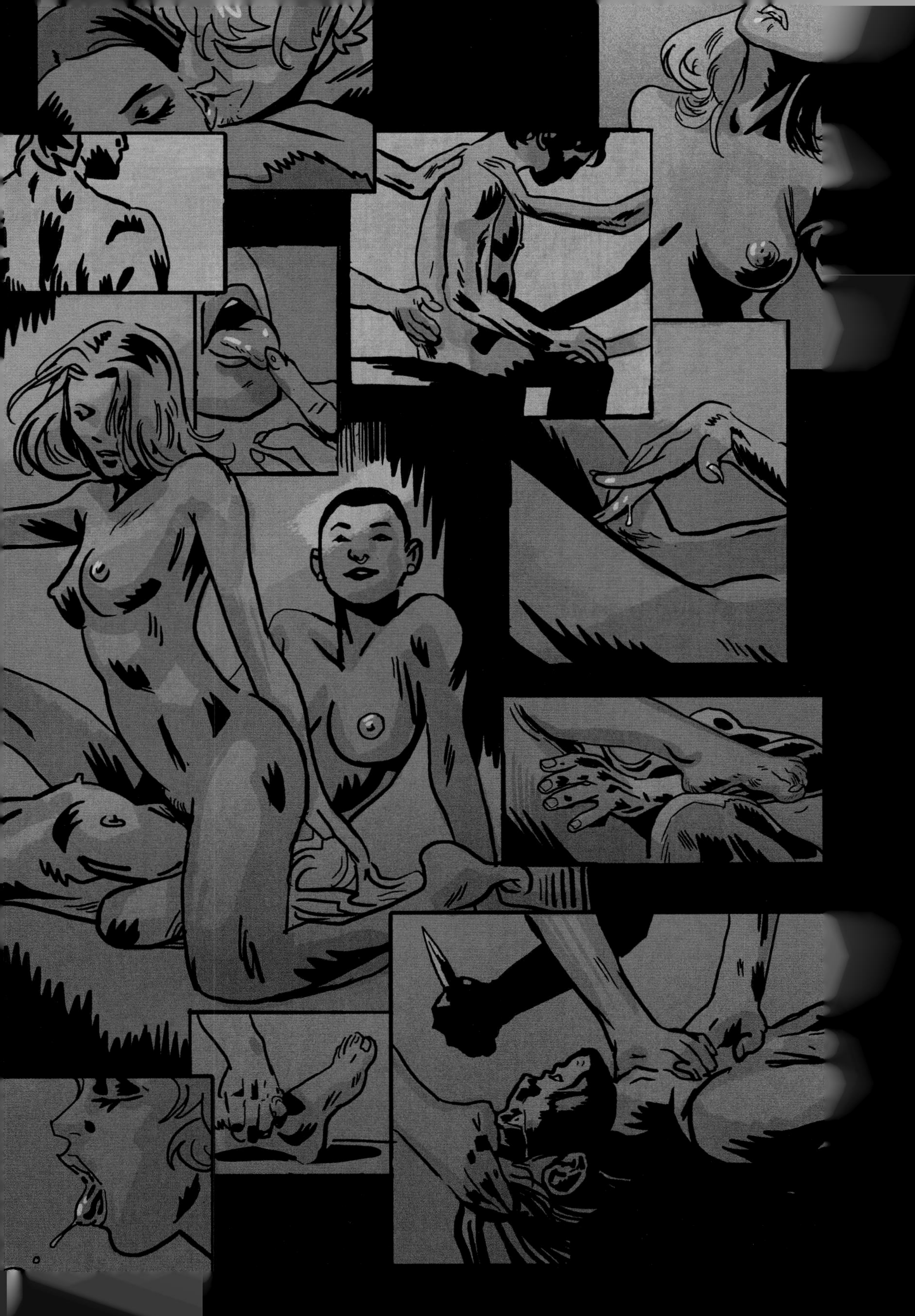

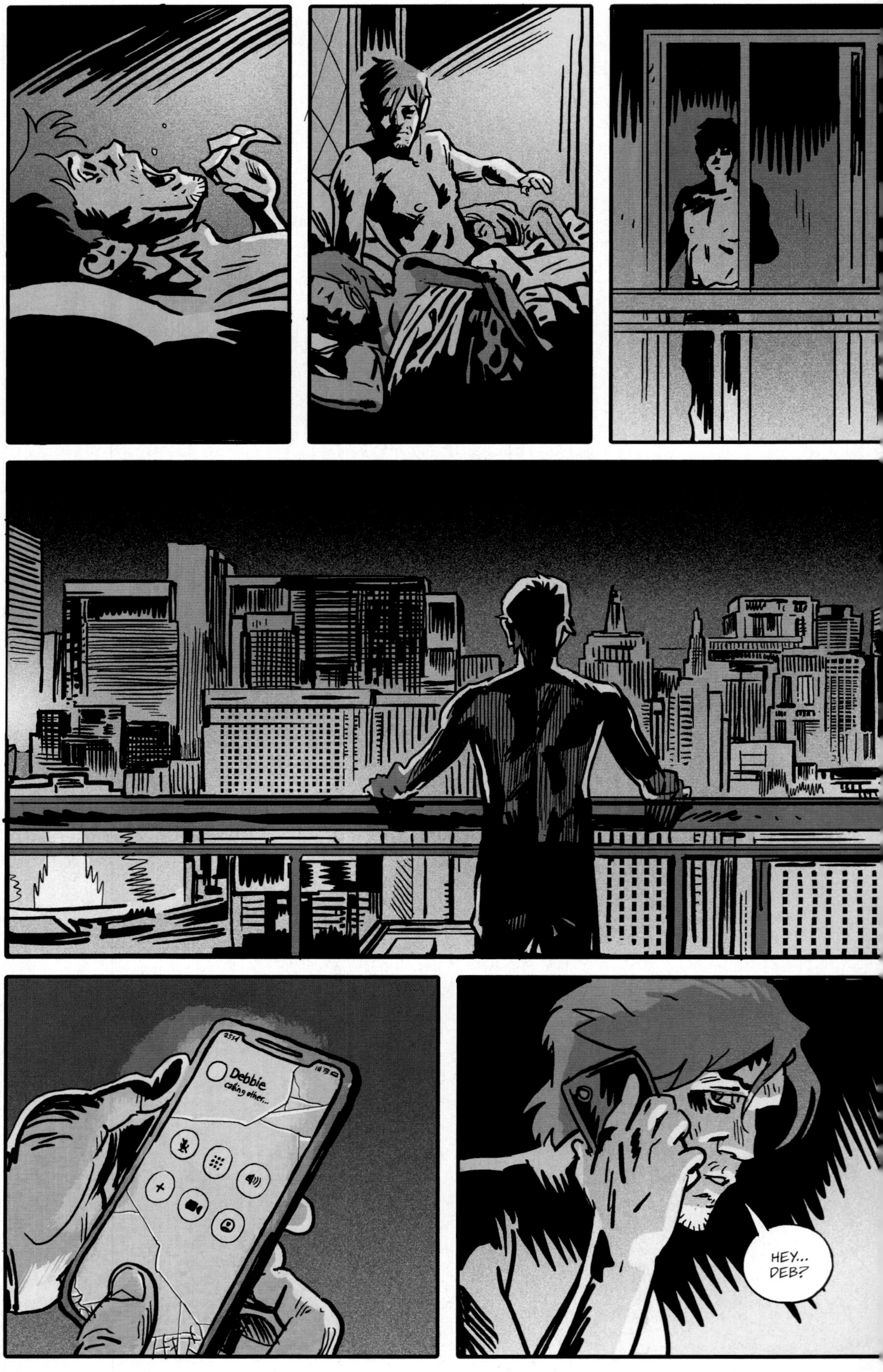
Debbie
calling other...
HEY... DEB?

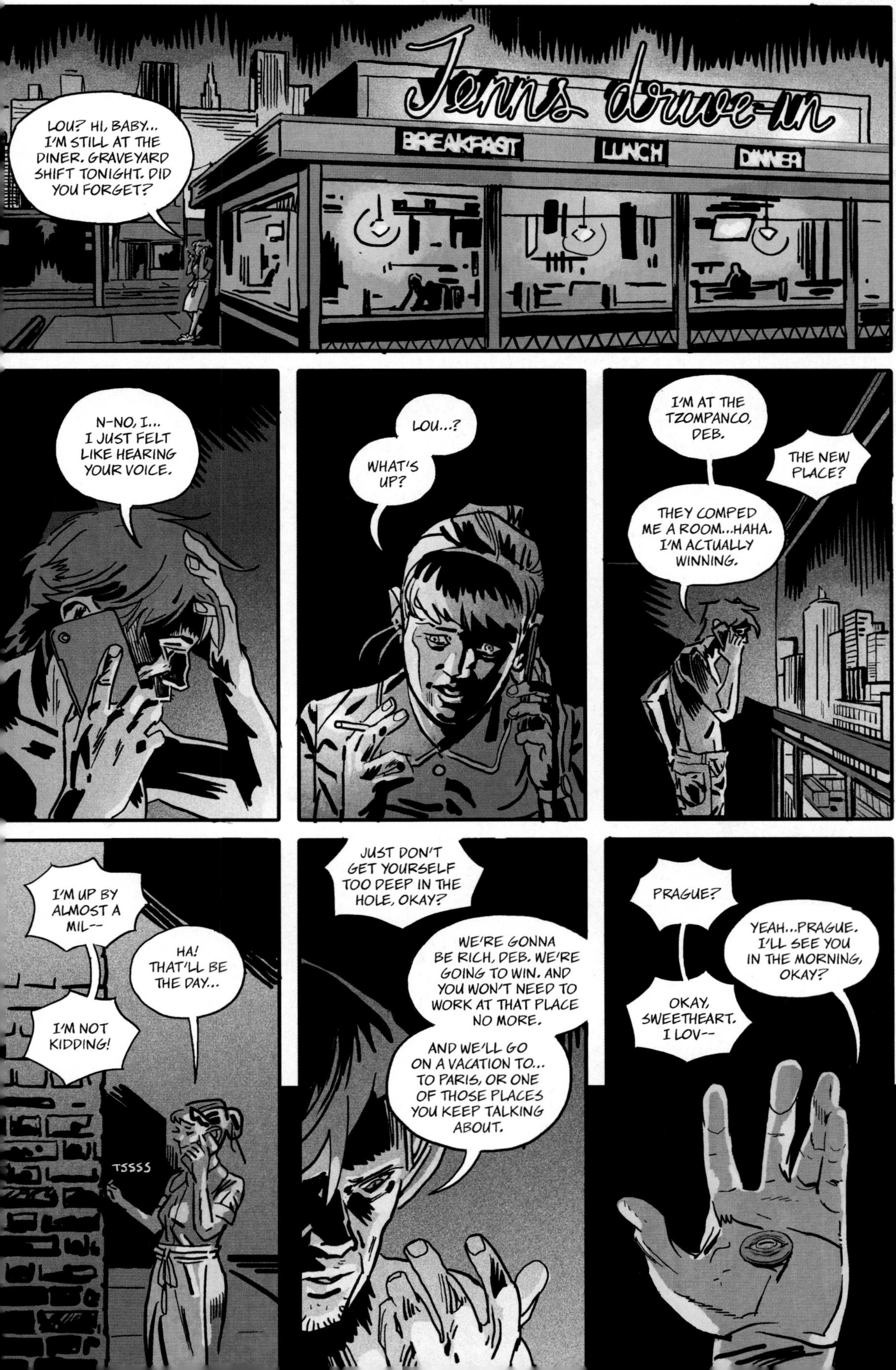
Jenns drive-in
BREAKFAST
LUNCH
DINNER
LOU? HI, BABY... I'M STILL AT THE DINER. GRAVEYARD SHIFT TONIGHT. DID YOU FORGET?
N-NO, I... I JUST FELT LIKE HEARING YOUR VOICE.
LOU...?
WHAT'S UP?
I'M AT THE TZOMPANCO, DEB.
THE NEW PLACE?
THEY COMPED ME A ROOM...HAHA. I'M ACTUALLY WINNING.
I'M UP BY ALMOST A MIL--
HA! THAT'LL BE THE DAY...
I'M NOT KIDDING!
TSSSS
JUST DON'T GET YOURSELF TOO DEEP IN THE HOLE, OKAY?
WE'RE GONNA BE RICH, DEB. WE'RE GOING TO WIN. AND YOU WON'T NEED TO WORK AT THAT PLACE NO MORE.
AND WE'LL GO ON A VACATION TO... TO PARIS, OR ONE OF THOSE PLACES YOU KEEP TALKING ABOUT.
PRAGUE?
YEAH...PRAGUE. I'LL SEE YOU IN THE MORNING, OKAY?
OKAY, SWEETHEART. I LOV--

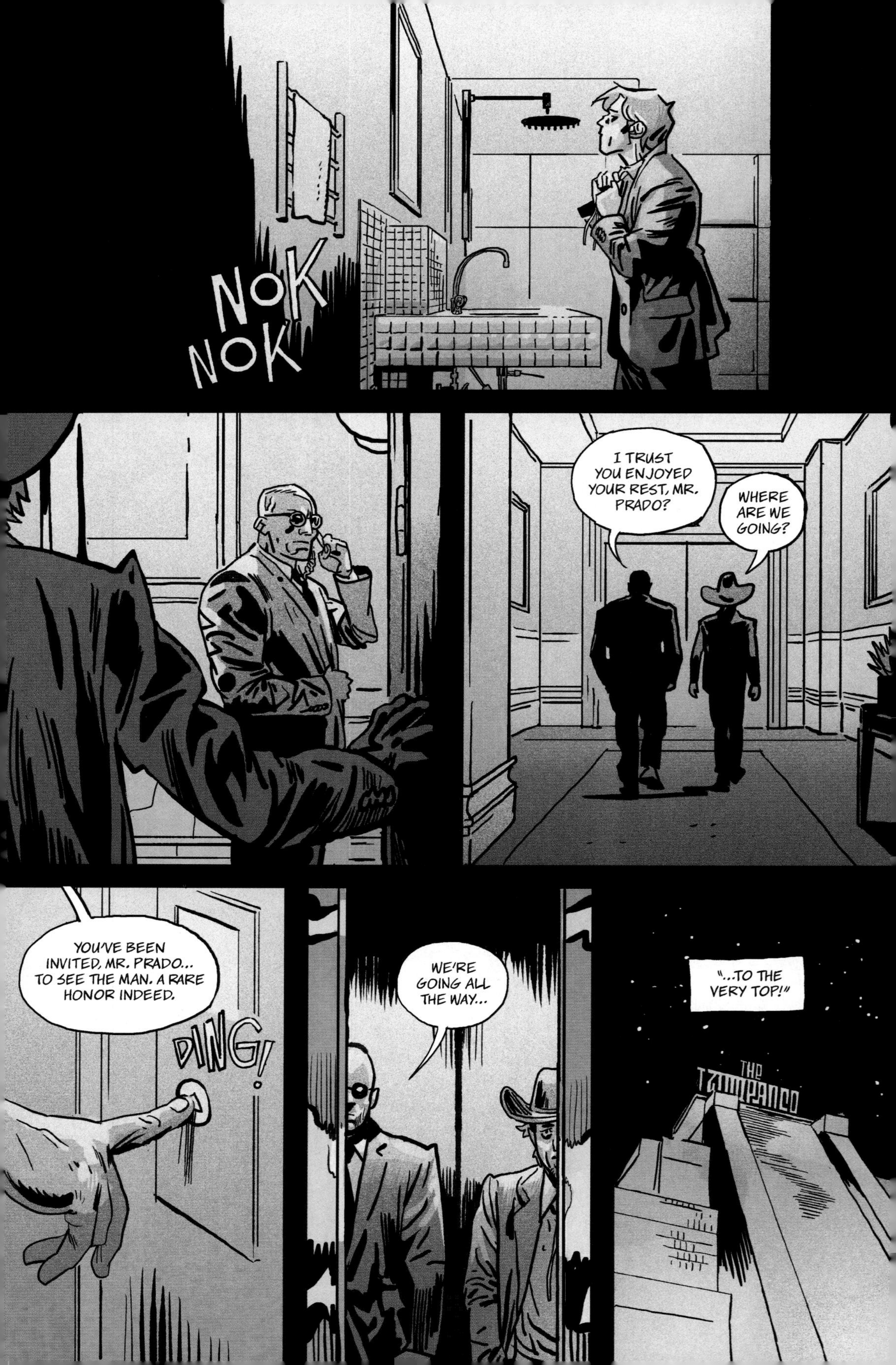
NOK NOK
I TRUST YOU ENJOYED YOUR REST, MR. PRADO?
WHERE ARE WE GOING?
YOU'VE BEEN INVITED, MR. PRADO... TO SEE THE MAN. A RARE HONOR INDEED.
DING!
WE'RE GOING ALL THE WAY...
"...TO THE VERY TOP!"

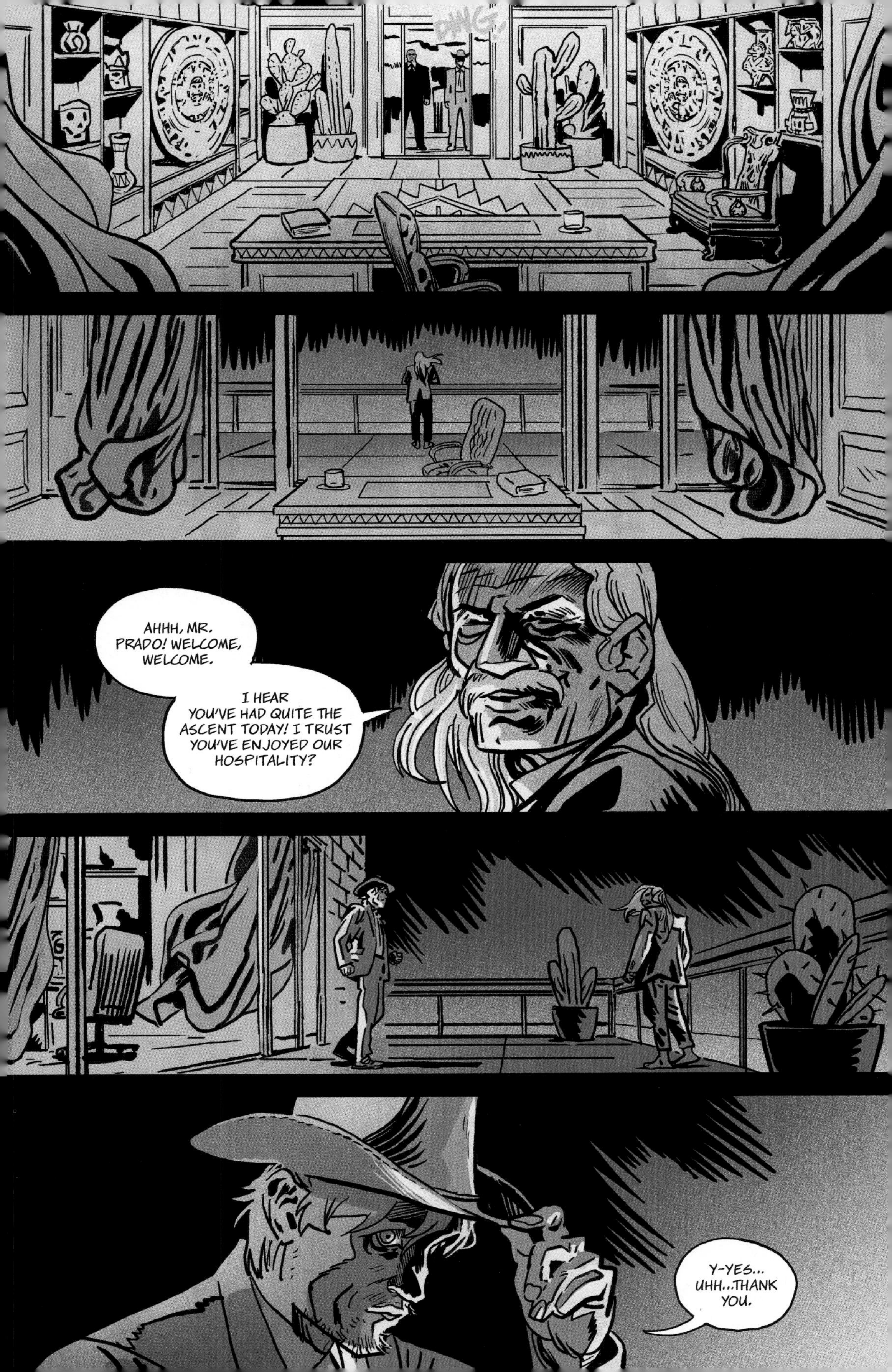
DING!
AHHH, MR. PRADO! WELCOME, WELCOME.
I HEAR YOU'VE HAD QUITE THE ASCENT TODAY! I TRUST YOU'VE ENJOYED OUR HOSPITALITY?
Y-YES... UHH...THANK YOU.

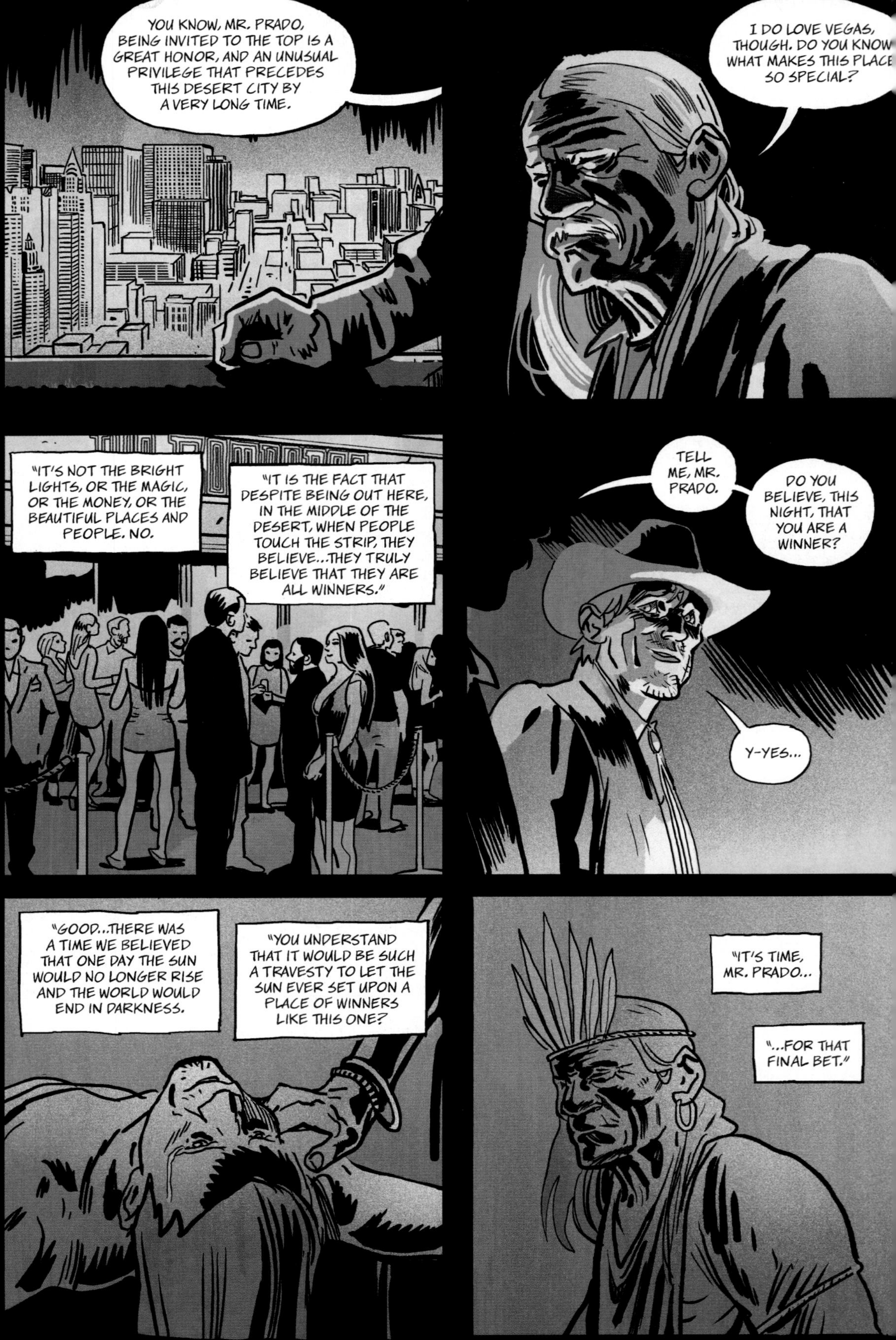
YOU KNOW, MR. PRADO, BEING INVITED TO THE TOP IS A GREAT HONOR, AND AN UNUSUAL PRIVILEGE THAT PRECEDES THIS DESERT CITY BY A VERY LONG TIME.
I DO LOVE VEGAS, THOUGH. DO YOU KNOW WHAT MAKES THIS PLACE SO SPECIAL?
"IT'S NOT THE BRIGHT LIGHTS, OR THE MAGIC, OR THE MONEY, OR THE BEAUTIFUL PLACES AND PEOPLE. NO.
"IT IS THE FACT THAT DESPITE BEING OUT HERE, IN THE MIDDLE OF THE DESERT, WHEN PEOPLE TOUCH THE STRIP, THEY BELIEVE...THEY TRULY BELIEVE THAT THEY ARE ALL WINNERS."
TELL ME, MR. PRADO.
DO YOU BELIEVE, THIS NIGHT, THAT YOU ARE A WINNER?
Y-YES...
"GOOD...THERE WAS A TIME WE BELIEVED THAT ONE DAY THE SUN WOULD NO LONGER RISE AND THE WORLD WOULD END IN DARKNESS.
"YOU UNDERSTAND THAT IT WOULD BE SUCH A TRAVESTY TO LET THE SUN EVER SET UPON A PLACE OF WINNERS LIKE THIS ONE?
"IT'S TIME, MR. PRADO...
"...FOR THAT FINAL BET."

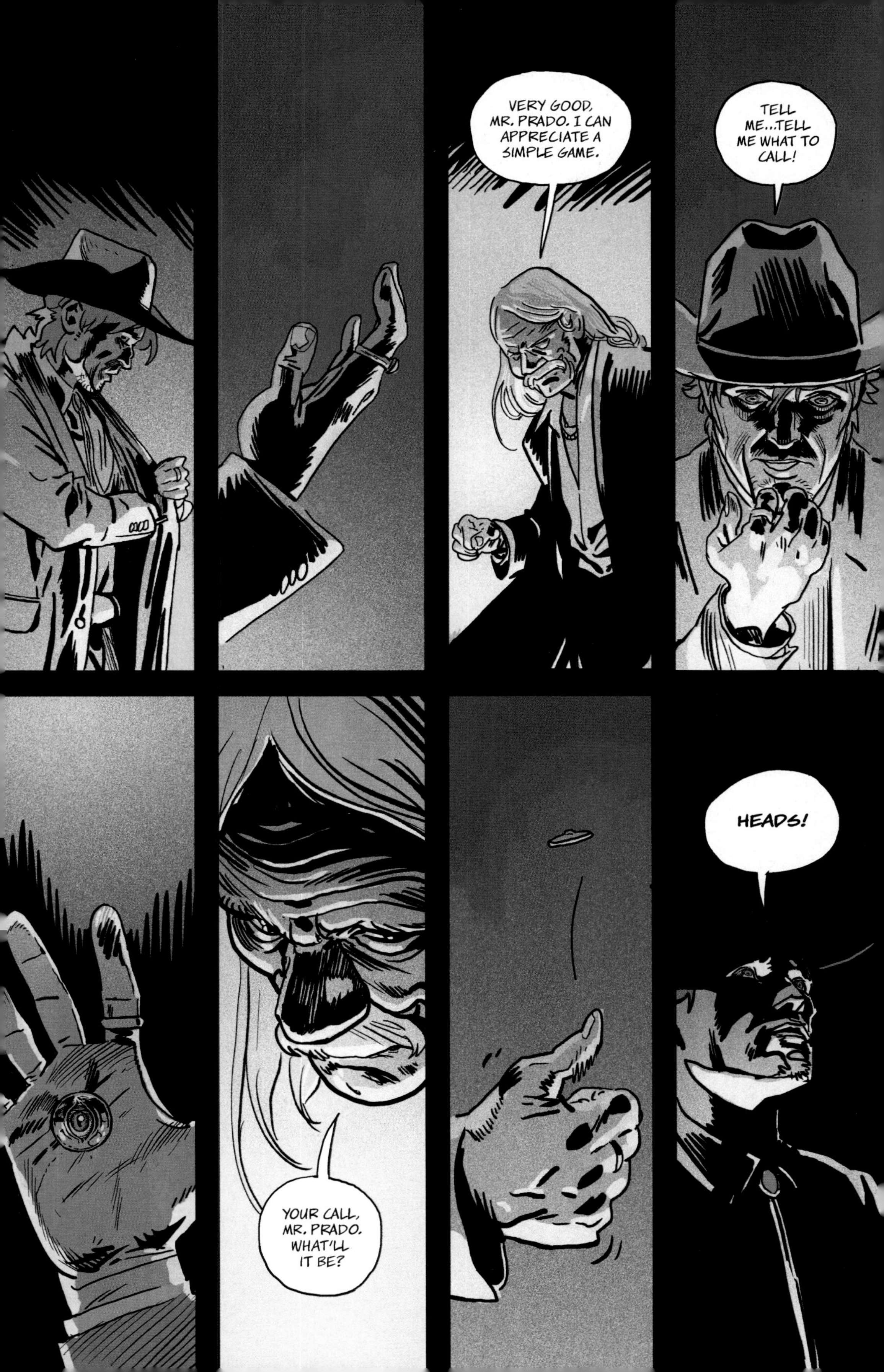
VERY GOOD, MR. PRADO. I CAN APPRECIATE A SIMPLE GAME.
TELL ME...TELL ME WHAT TO CALL!
YOUR CALL, MR. PRADO. WHAT'LL IT BE?
HEADS!

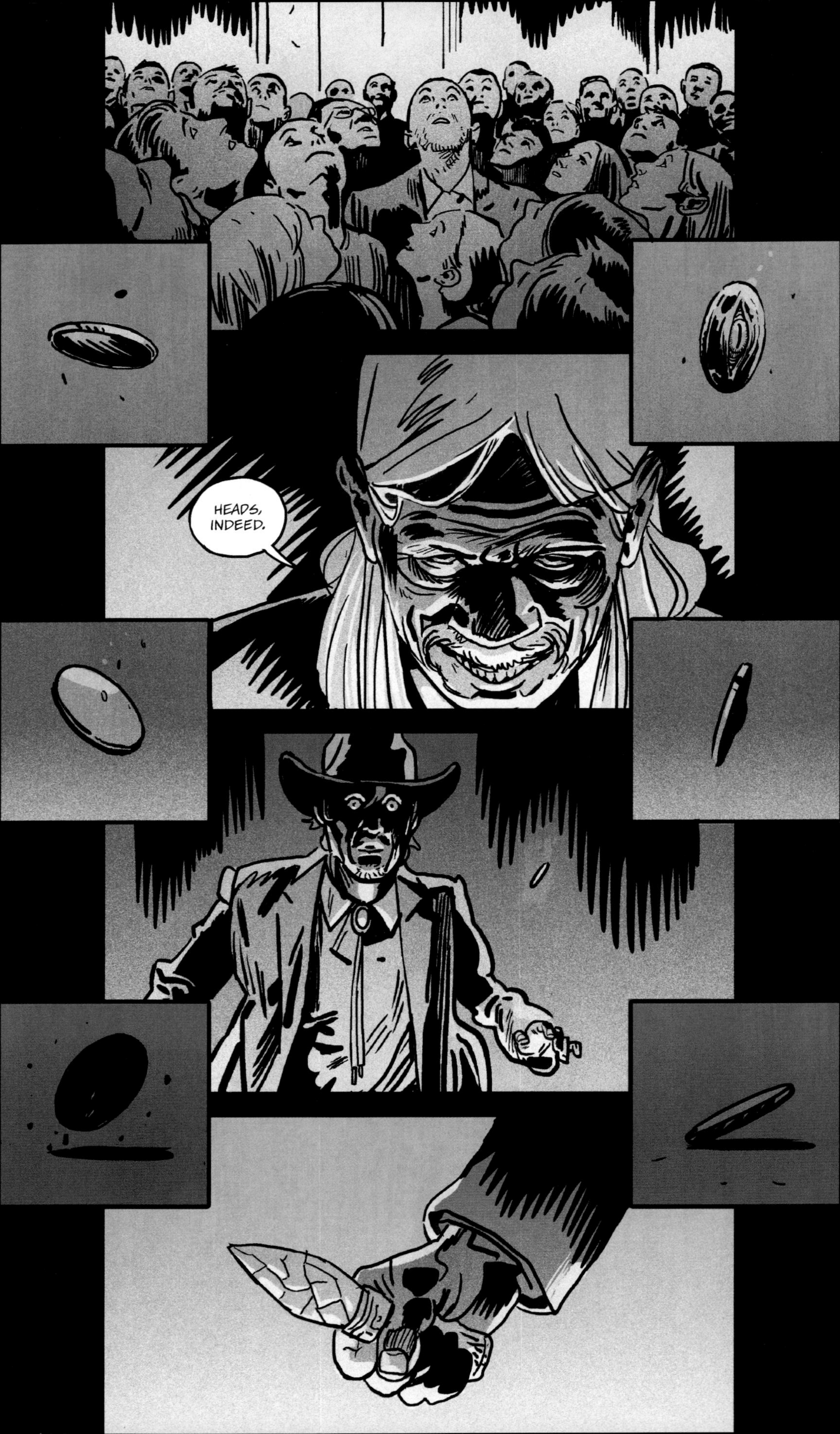
HEADS, INDEED.

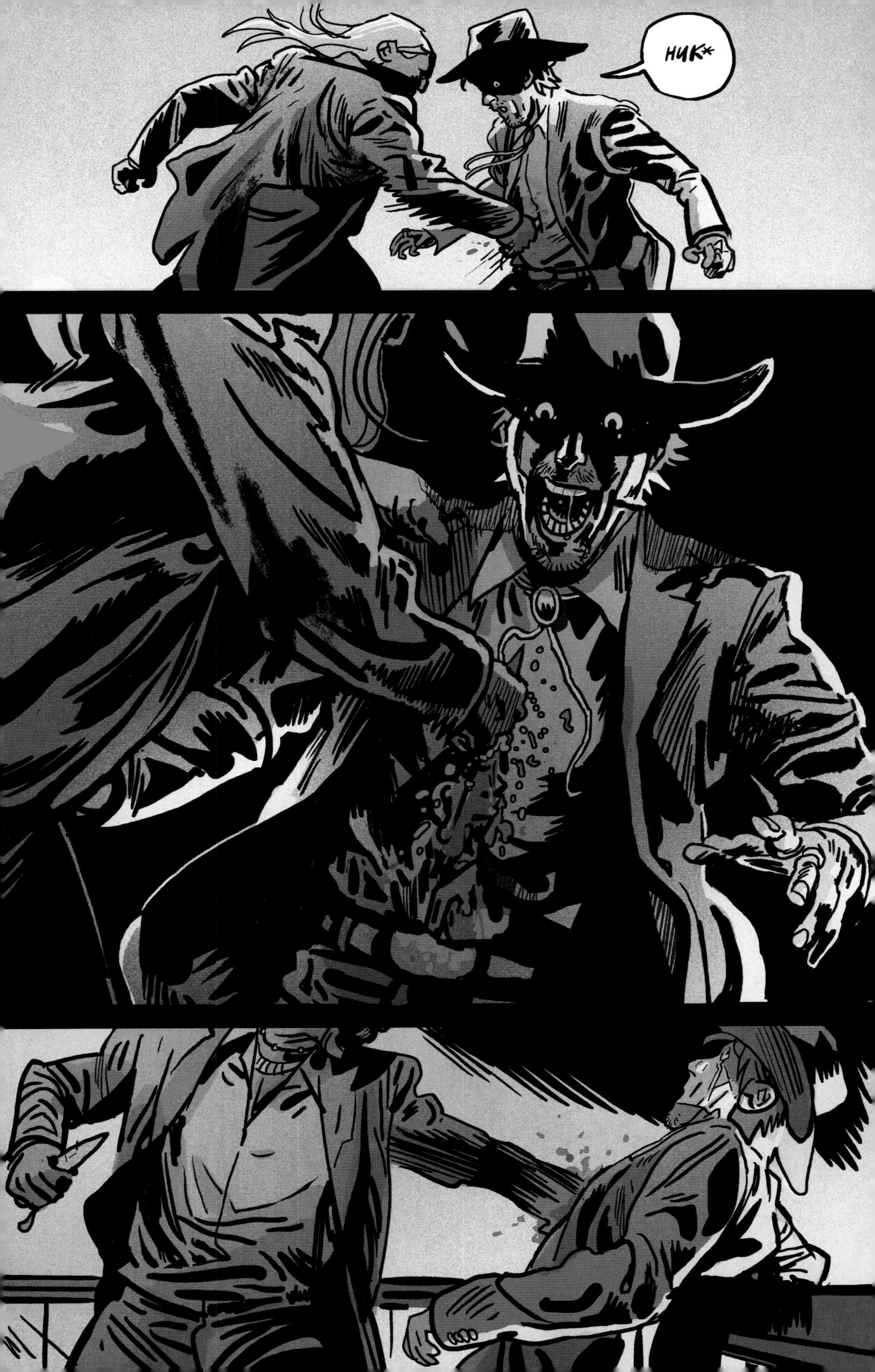
HUK*

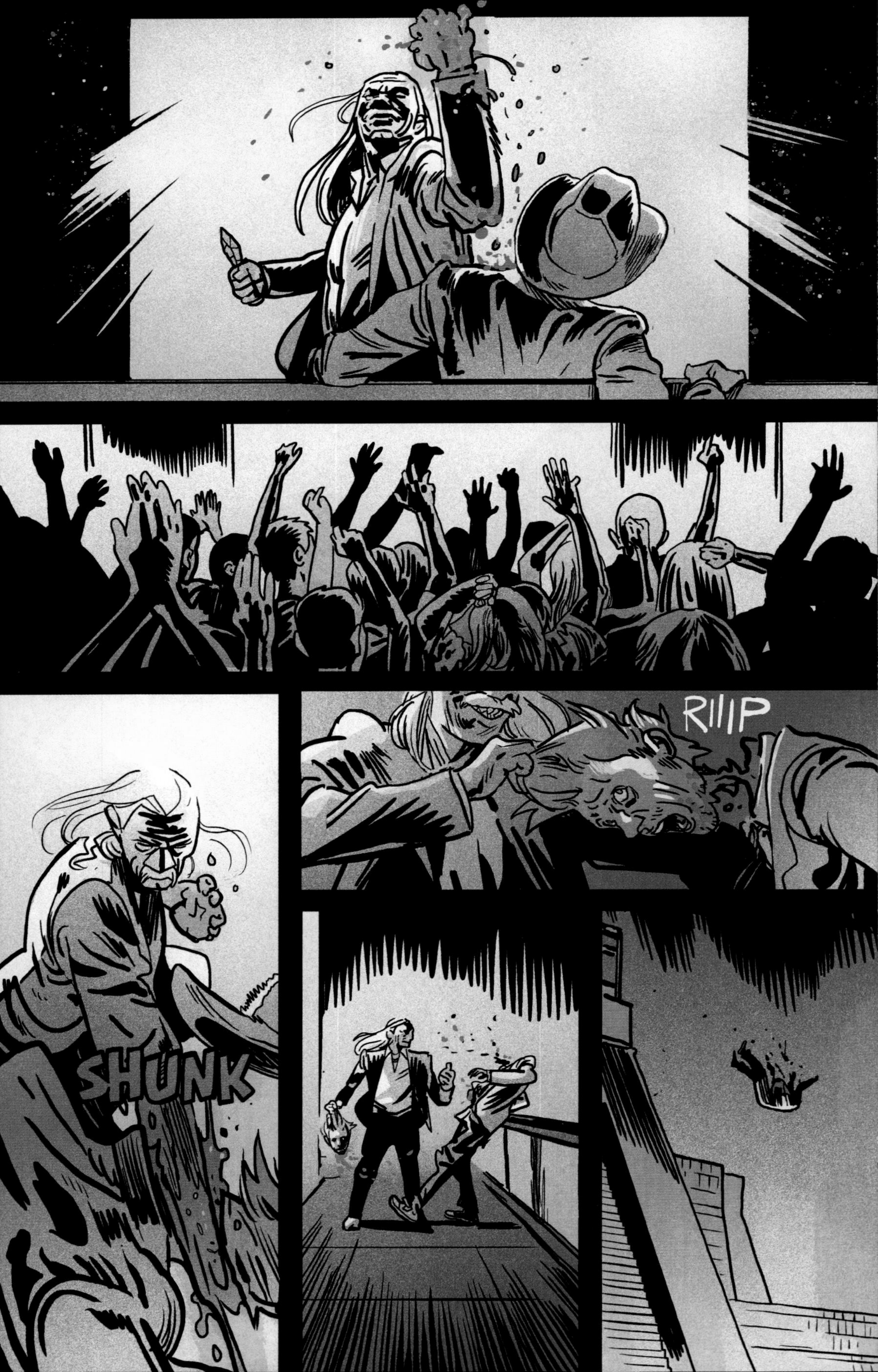
RIIIP
SHUNK

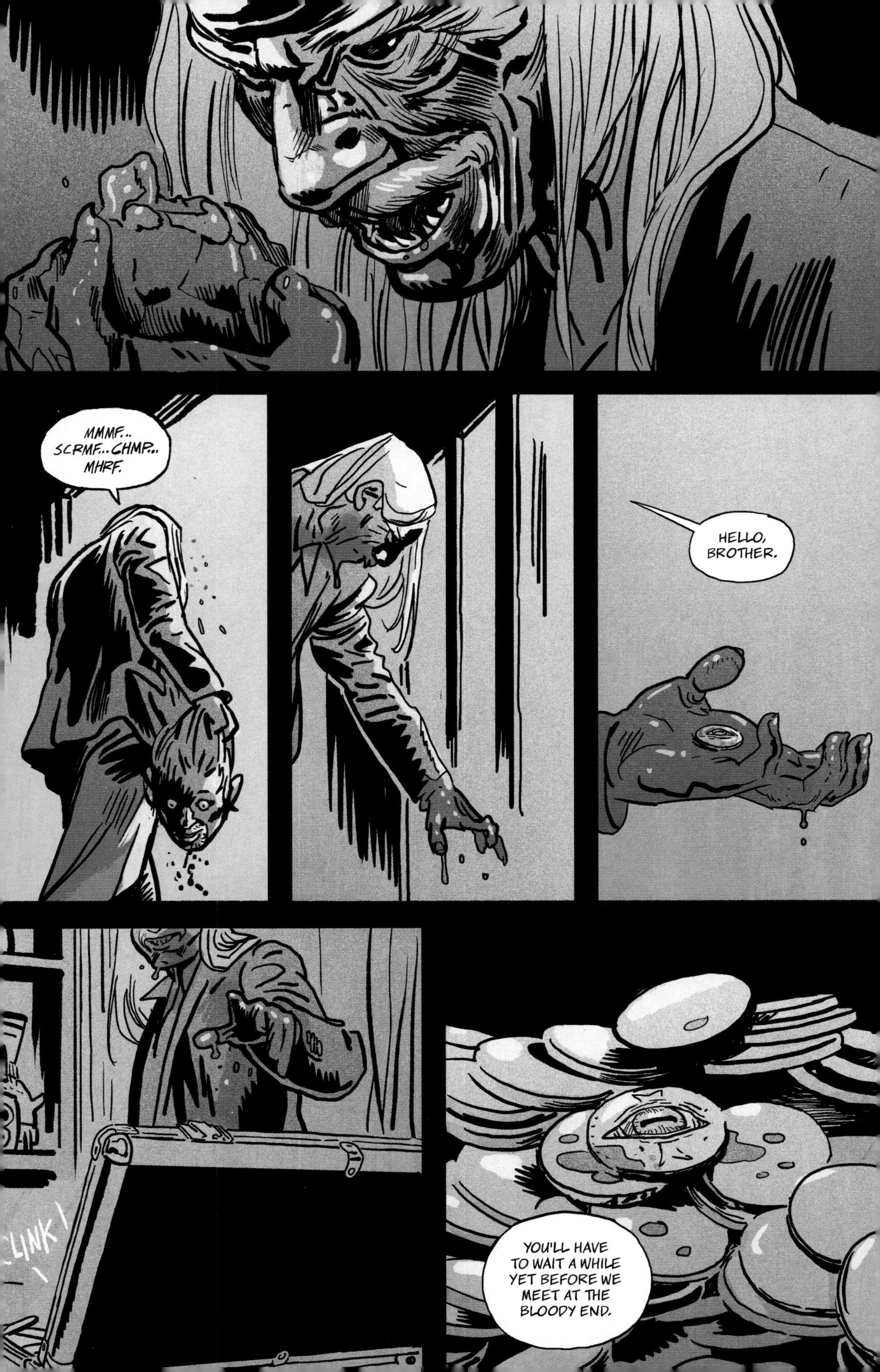
MMMF.. SCRMF...CHMP... MHRF.
HELLO, BROTHER.
LINK!
YOU'LL HAVE TO WAIT A WHILE YET BEFORE WE MEET AT THE BLOODY END.

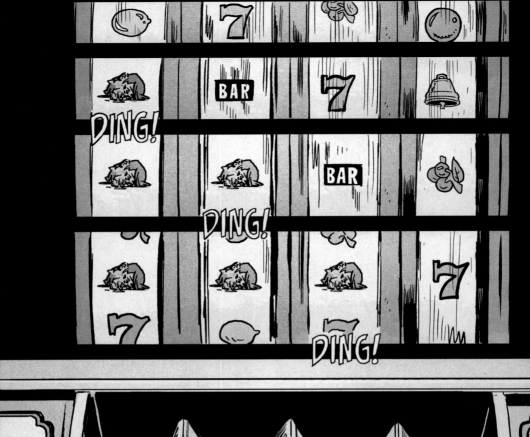

DING!

DING!

DING!

NG!DING!DING!DING!DING!DING!DING!DING!DING!DING!D

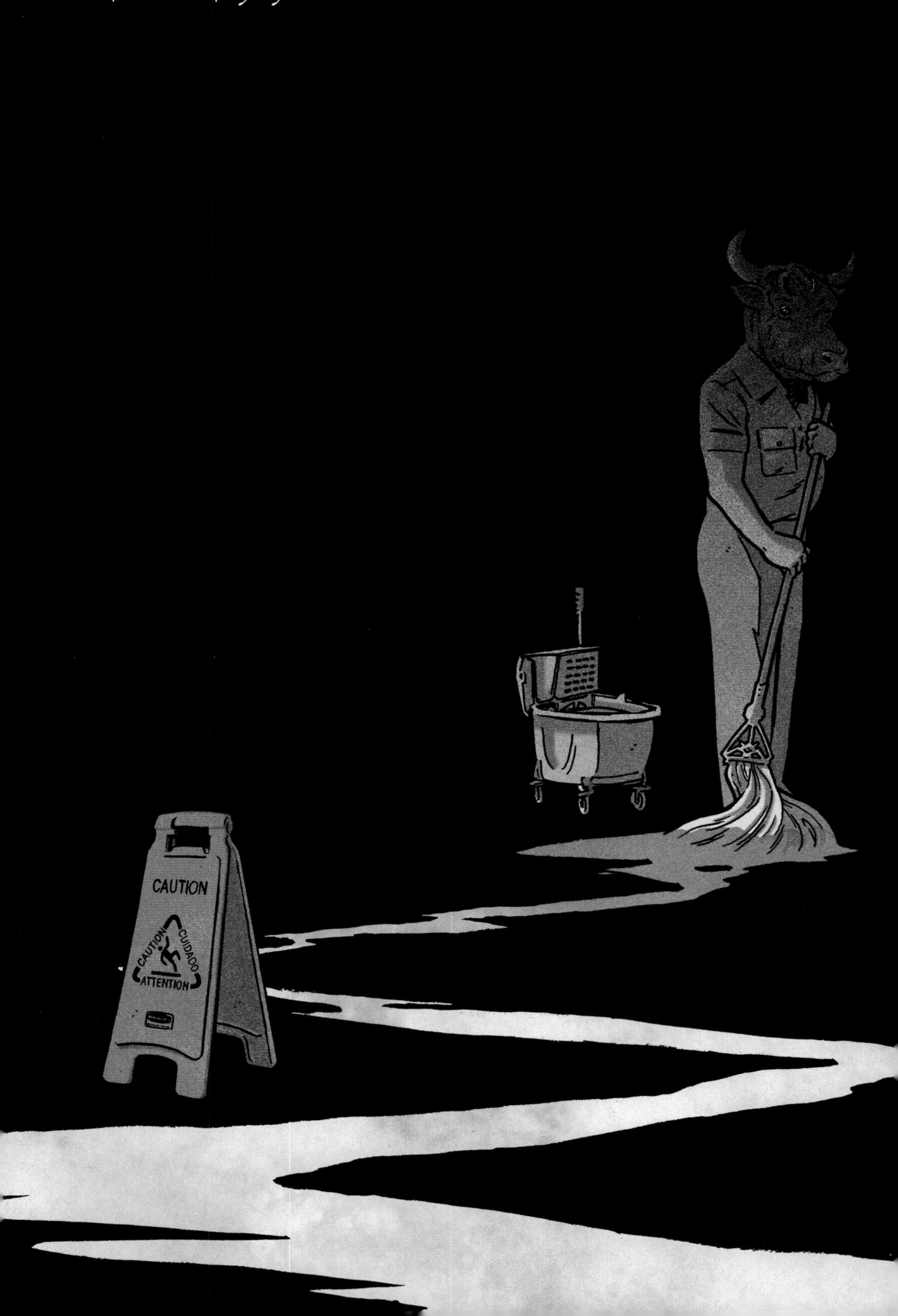
CAUTION
CAUTION
CUIDADO
ATTENTION

Rising and Falling in America

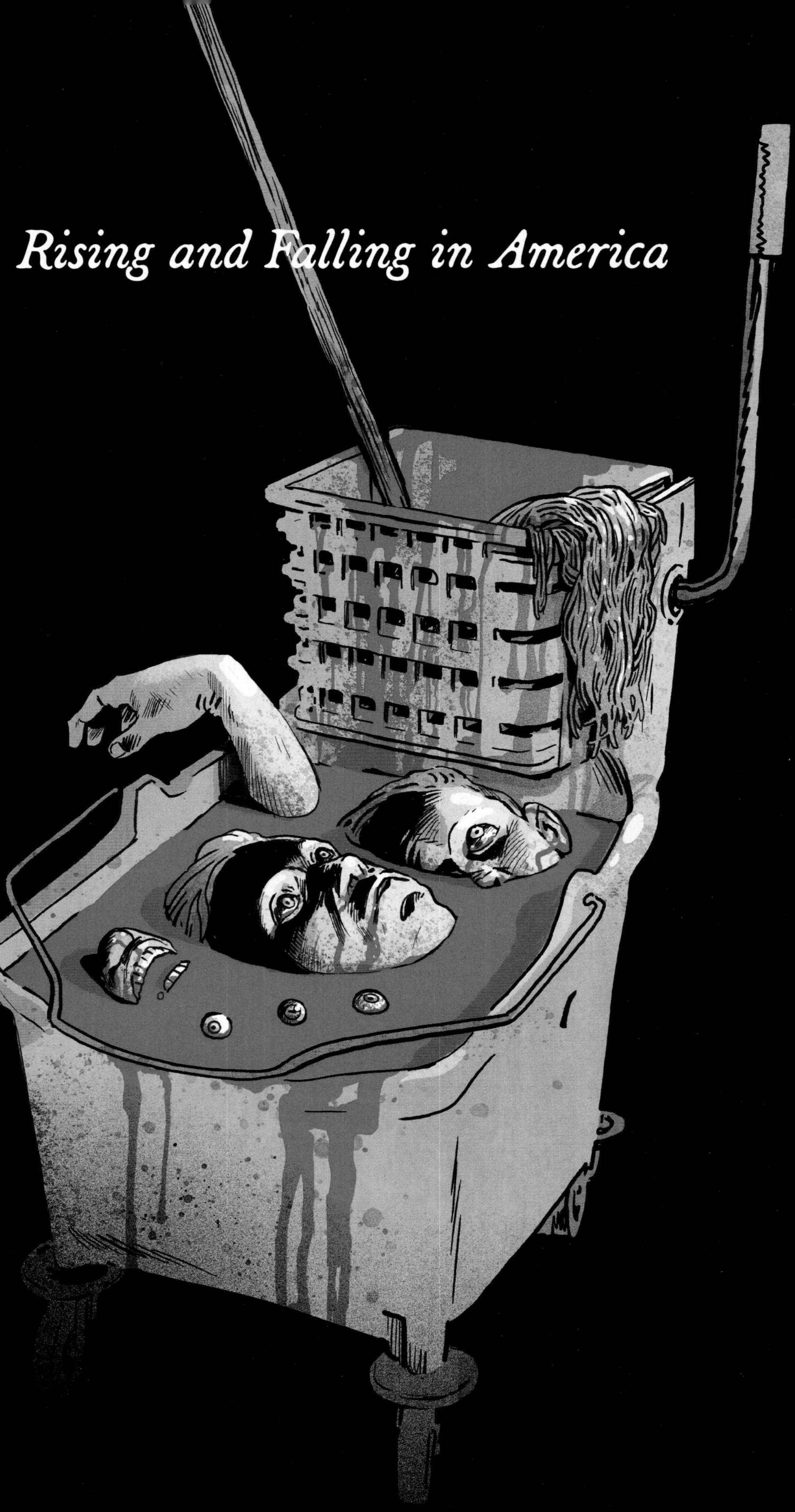

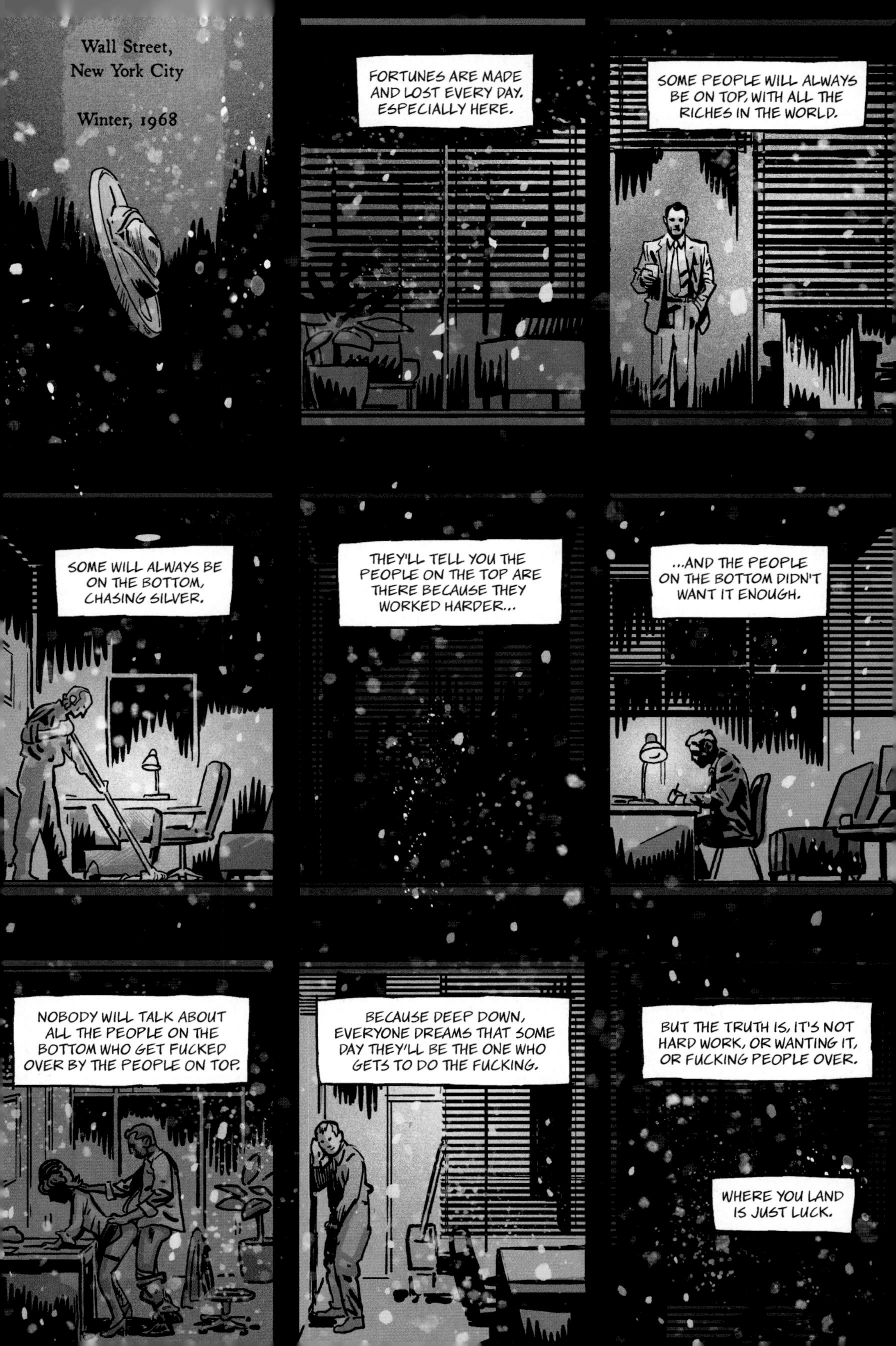
Wall Street,
New York City
Winter, 1968
FORTUNES ARE MADE AND LOST EVERY DAY. ESPECIALLY HERE.
SOME PEOPLE WILL ALWAYS BE ON TOP, WITH ALL THE RICHES IN THE WORLD.
SOME WILL ALWAYS BE ON THE BOTTOM, CHASING SILVER.
THEY'LL TELL YOU THE PEOPLE ON THE TOP ARE THERE BECAUSE THEY WORKED HARDER...
...AND THE PEOPLE ON THE BOTTOM DIDN'T WANT IT ENOUGH.
NOBODY WILL TALK ABOUT ALL THE PEOPLE ON THE BOTTOM WHO GET FUCKED OVER BY THE PEOPLE ON TOP.
BECAUSE DEEP DOWN, EVERYONE DREAMS THAT SOME DAY THEY'LL BE THE ONE WHO GETS TO DO THE FUCKING.
BUT THE TRUTH IS, IT'S NOT HARD WORK, OR WANTING IT, OR FUCKING PEOPLE OVER.
WHERE YOU LAND IS JUST LUCK.

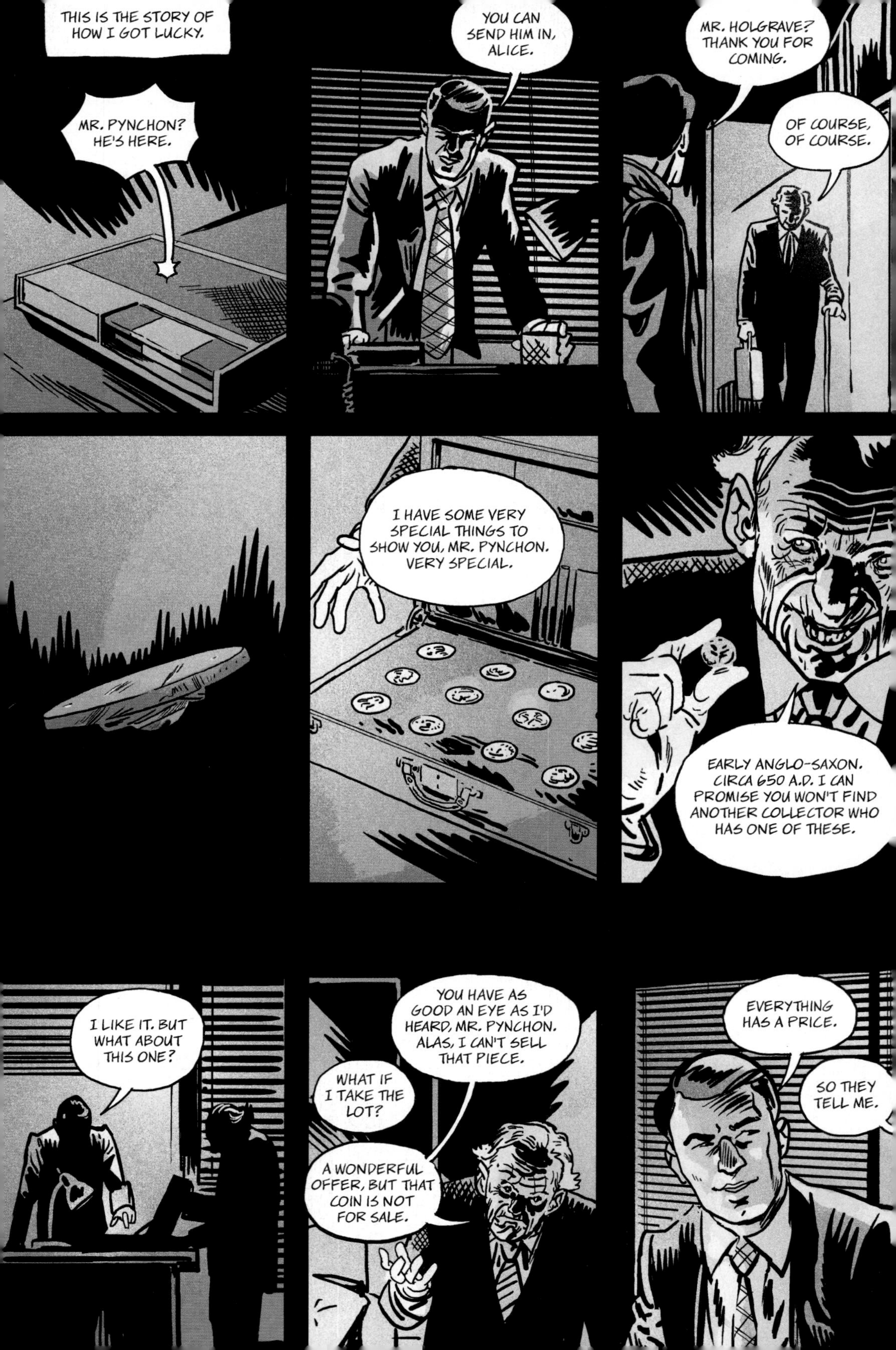
THIS IS THE STORY OF HOW I GOT LUCKY.
MR. PYNCHON? HE'S HERE.
YOU CAN SEND HIM IN, ALICE.
MR. HOLGRAVE? THANK YOU FOR COMING.
OF COURSE, OF COURSE.
I HAVE SOME VERY SPECIAL THINGS TO SHOW YOU, MR. PYNCHON. VERY SPECIAL.
EARLY ANGLO-SAXON. CIRCA 650 A.D. I CAN PROMISE YOU WON'T FIND ANOTHER COLLECTOR WHO HAS ONE OF THESE.
I LIKE IT. BUT WHAT ABOUT THIS ONE?
YOU HAVE AS GOOD AN EYE AS I'D HEARD, MR. PYNCHON. ALAS, I CAN'T SELL THAT PIECE.
WHAT IF I TAKE THE LOT?
A WONDERFUL OFFER, BUT THAT COIN IS NOT FOR SALE.
EVERYTHING HAS A PRICE.
SO THEY TELL ME.

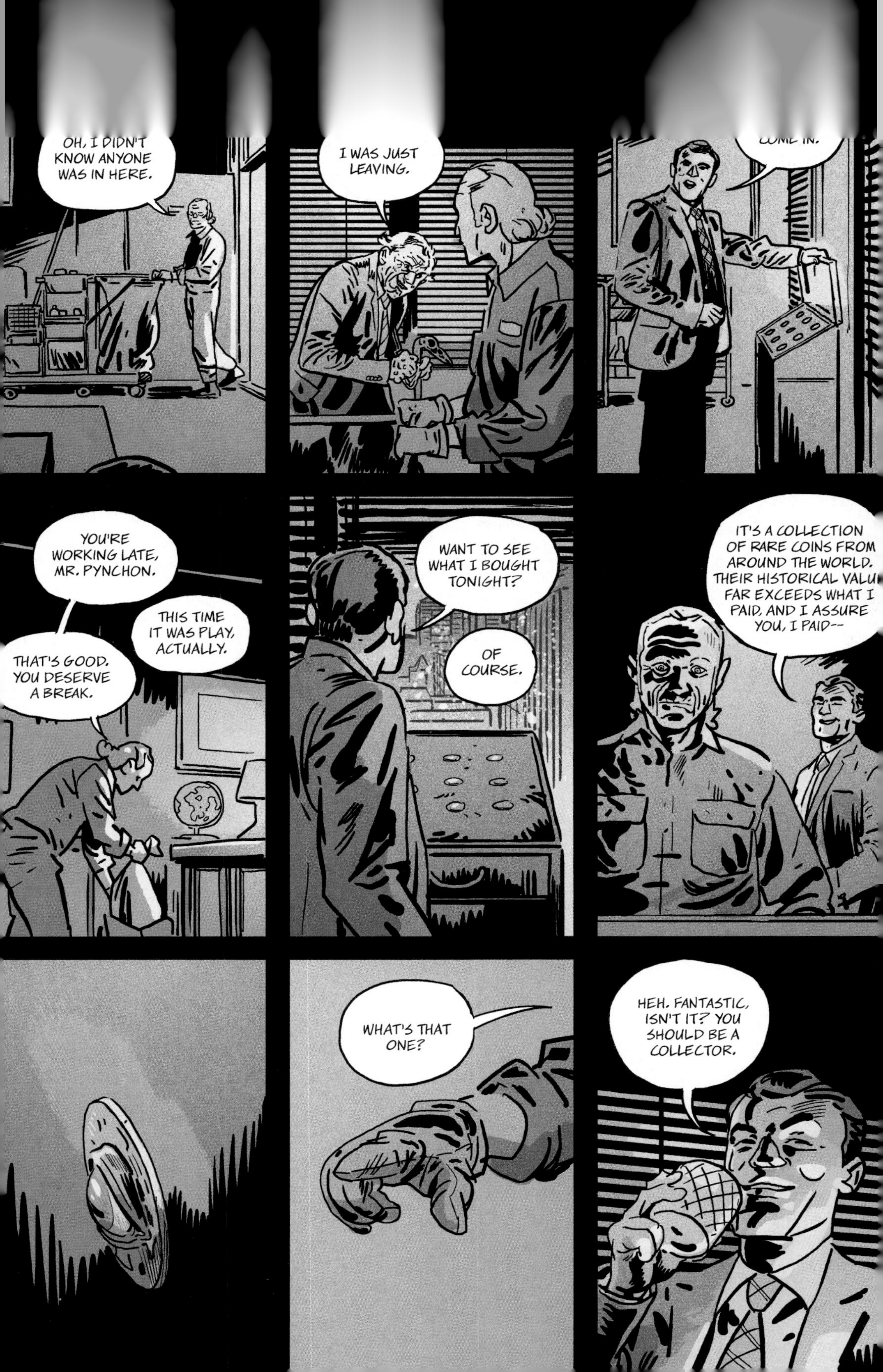
OH, I DIDN'T KNOW ANYONE WAS IN HERE.
I WAS JUST LEAVING.
YOU'RE WORKING LATE, MR. PYNCHON.
THIS TIME IT WAS PLAY, ACTUALLY.
THAT'S GOOD. YOU DESERVE A BREAK.
WANT TO SEE WHAT I BOUGHT TONIGHT?
OF COURSE.
IT'S A COLLECTION OF RARE COINS FROM AROUND THE WORLD. THEIR HISTORICAL VALU FAR EXCEEDS WHAT I PAID, AND I ASSURE YOU, I PAID--
WHAT'S THAT ONE?
HEH. FANTASTIC, ISN'T IT? YOU SHOULD BE A COLLECTOR.

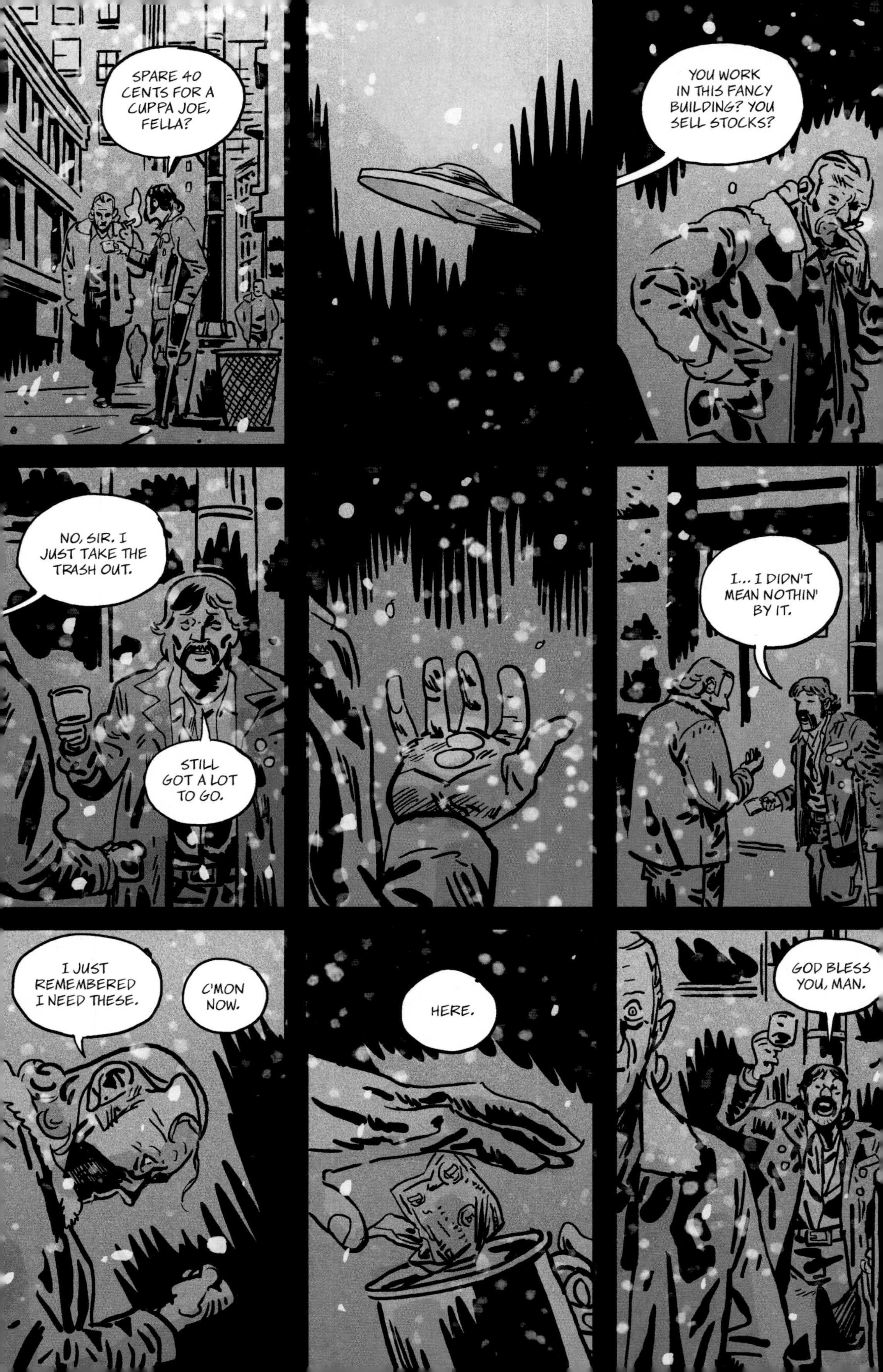
SPARE 40 CENTS FOR A CUPPA JOE, FELLA?
YOU WORK IN THIS FANCY BUILDING? YOU SELL STOCKS?
NO, SIR. I JUST TAKE THE TRASH OUT.
STILL GOT A LOT TO GO.
I... I DIDN'T MEAN NOTHIN' BY IT.
I JUST REMEMBERED I NEED THESE.
C'MON NOW.
HERE.
GOD BLESS YOU, MAN.

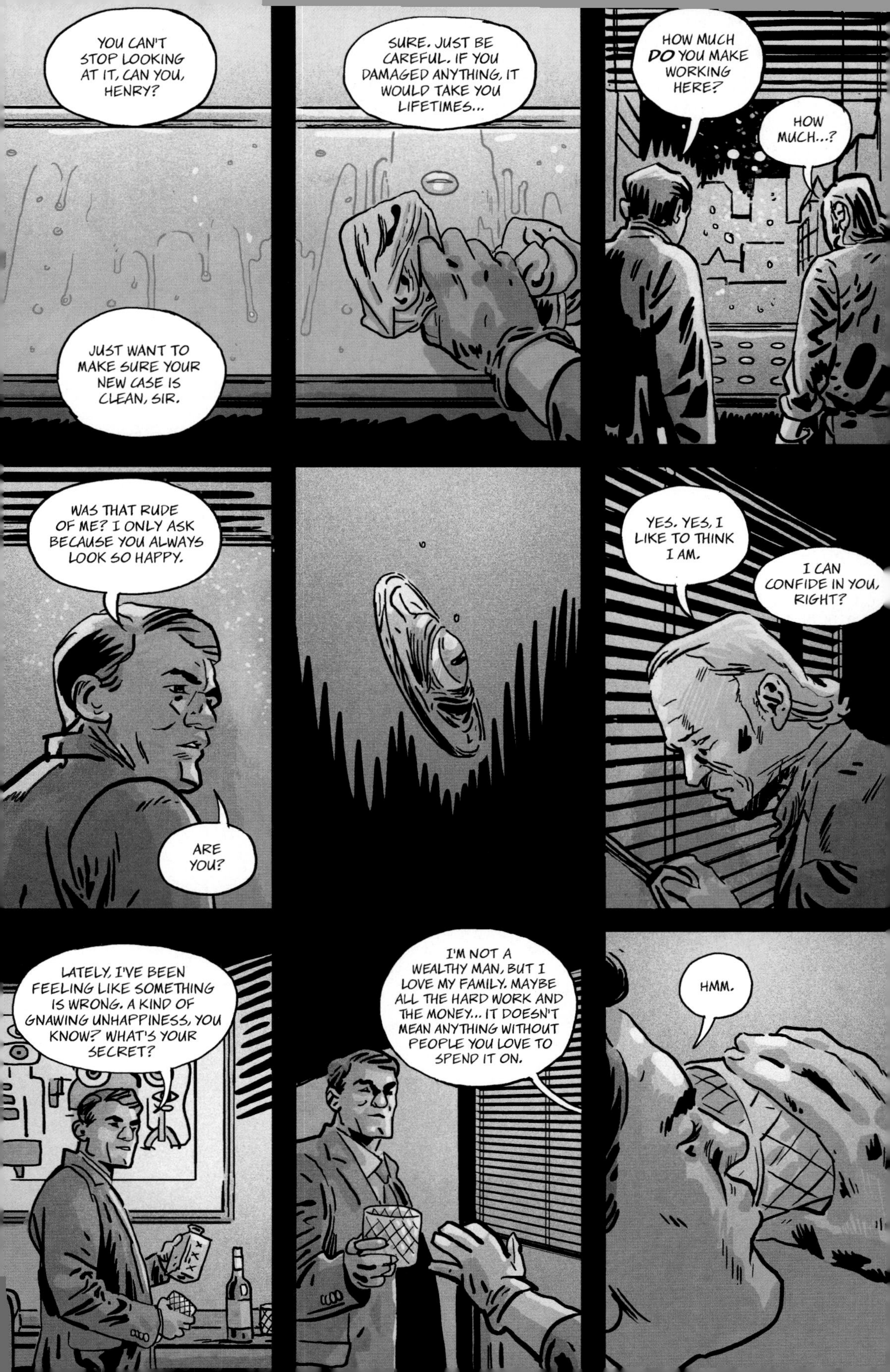
YOU CAN'T STOP LOOKING AT IT, CAN YOU, HENRY?
JUST WANT TO MAKE SURE YOUR NEW CASE IS CLEAN, SIR.
SURE. JUST BE CAREFUL. IF YOU DAMAGED ANYTHING, IT WOULD TAKE YOU LIFETIMES...
HOW MUCH **DO** YOU MAKE WORKING HERE?
HOW MUCH...?
WAS THAT RUDE OF ME? I ONLY ASK BECAUSE YOU ALWAYS LOOK SO HAPPY.
ARE YOU?
YES. YES, I LIKE TO THINK I AM.
I CAN CONFIDE IN YOU, RIGHT?
LATELY, I'VE BEEN FEELING LIKE SOMETHING IS WRONG. A KIND OF GNAWING UNHAPPINESS, YOU KNOW? WHAT'S YOUR SECRET?
I'M NOT A WEALTHY MAN, BUT I LOVE MY FAMILY. MAYBE ALL THE HARD WORK AND THE MONEY... IT DOESN'T MEAN ANYTHING WITHOUT PEOPLE YOU LOVE TO SPEND IT ON.
HMM.

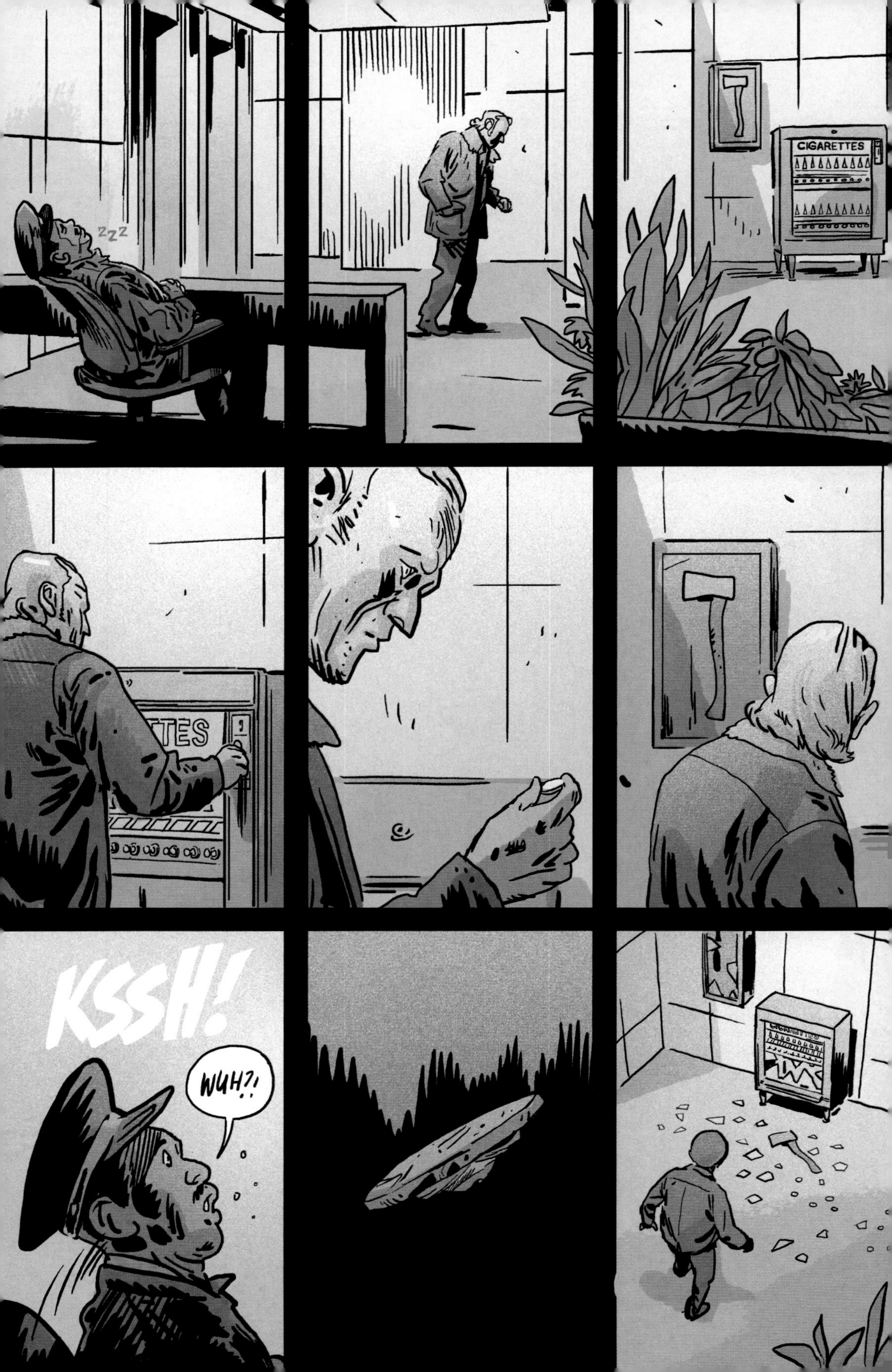
ZZZ
CIGARETTES
TTES
KSSH!
WUH?!

HENRY, MAY I HAVE A WORD?

HELLO, ALICE. HOW'S PHOEBE?

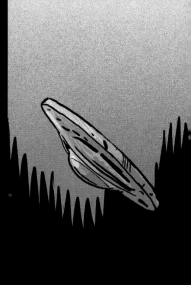

SHE'S GOOD, THANK YOU. BUT, HENRY, LISTEN. LOUIS WILL BE CLEANING THIS FLOOR FROM NOW ON.

THIS IS A MISTAKE. LOUIS HANDLES EVERYTHING BELOW 20. THIS IS MY FLOOR.

WE'RE CHANGING THAT.

WHY WOULD YOU DO THAT TO ME?

THIS IS A GOOD THING. YOU'LL BE HOME TO YOUR FAMILY SOONER.

WHY?

THERE WERE... SOME COMPLAINTS.

WHO COMPLAINED?

I THINK IT'S BEST IF YOU GO NOW, HENRY. LOTS OF OTHER FLOORS TO CLEAN TONIGHT.

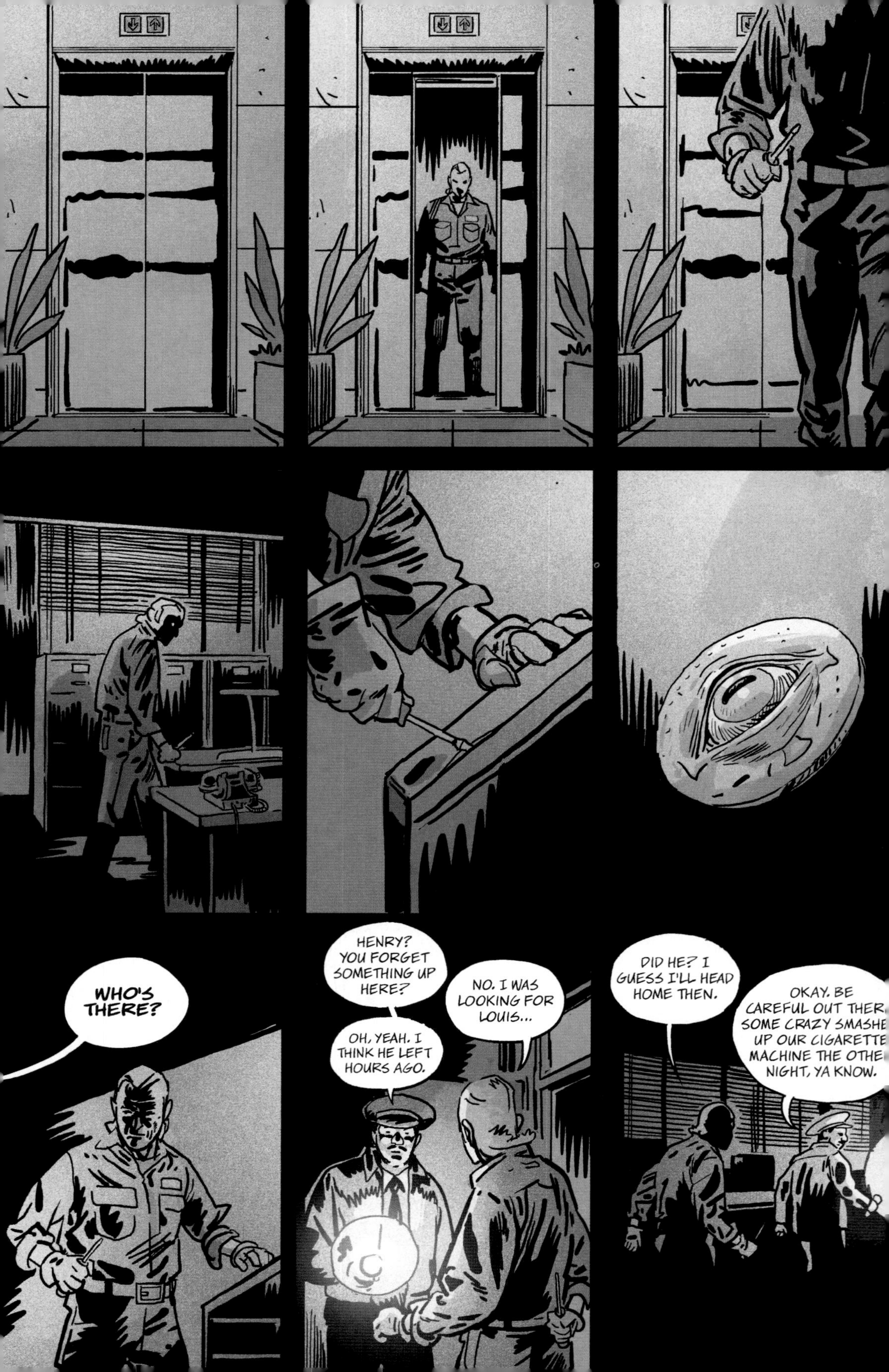
WHO'S THERE?
HENRY? YOU FORGET SOMETHING UP HERE?
NO. I WAS LOOKING FOR LOUIS...
OH, YEAH. I THINK HE LEFT HOURS AGO.
DID HE? I GUESS I'LL HEAD HOME THEN.
OKAY. BE CAREFUL OUT THER SOME CRAZY SMASHE UP OUR CIGARETTE MACHINE THE OTHE NIGHT, YA KNOW.

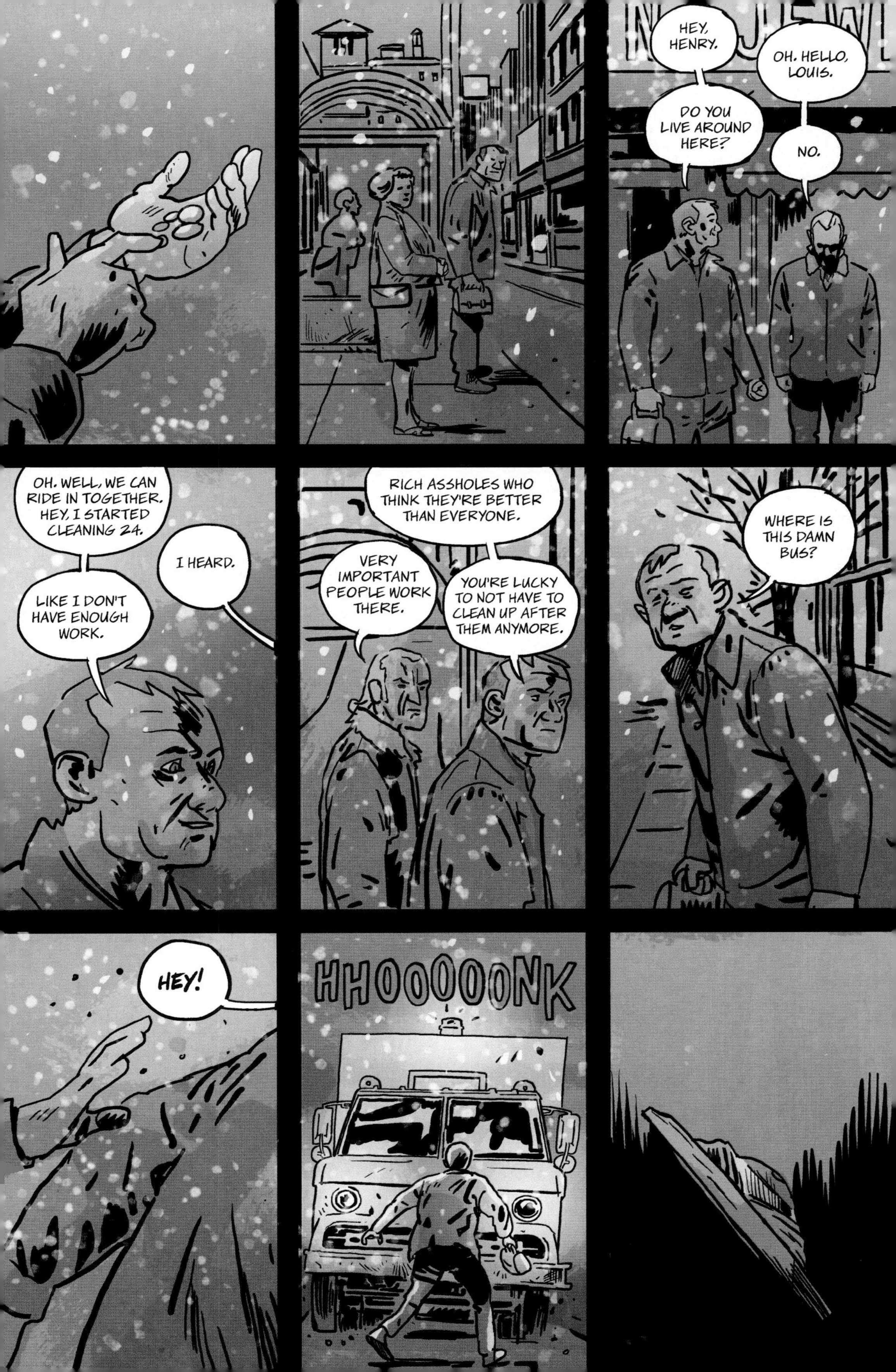
HEY, HENRY.
OH. HELLO, LOUIS.
DO YOU LIVE AROUND HERE?
NO.
OH. WELL, WE CAN RIDE IN TOGETHER. HEY, I STARTED CLEANING 24.
I HEARD.
LIKE I DON'T HAVE ENOUGH WORK.
RICH ASSHOLES WHO THINK THEY'RE BETTER THAN EVERYONE.
VERY IMPORTANT PEOPLE WORK THERE.
YOU'RE LUCKY TO NOT HAVE TO CLEAN UP AFTER THEM ANYMORE.
WHERE IS THIS DAMN BUS?
HEY!
HHOOOOONK

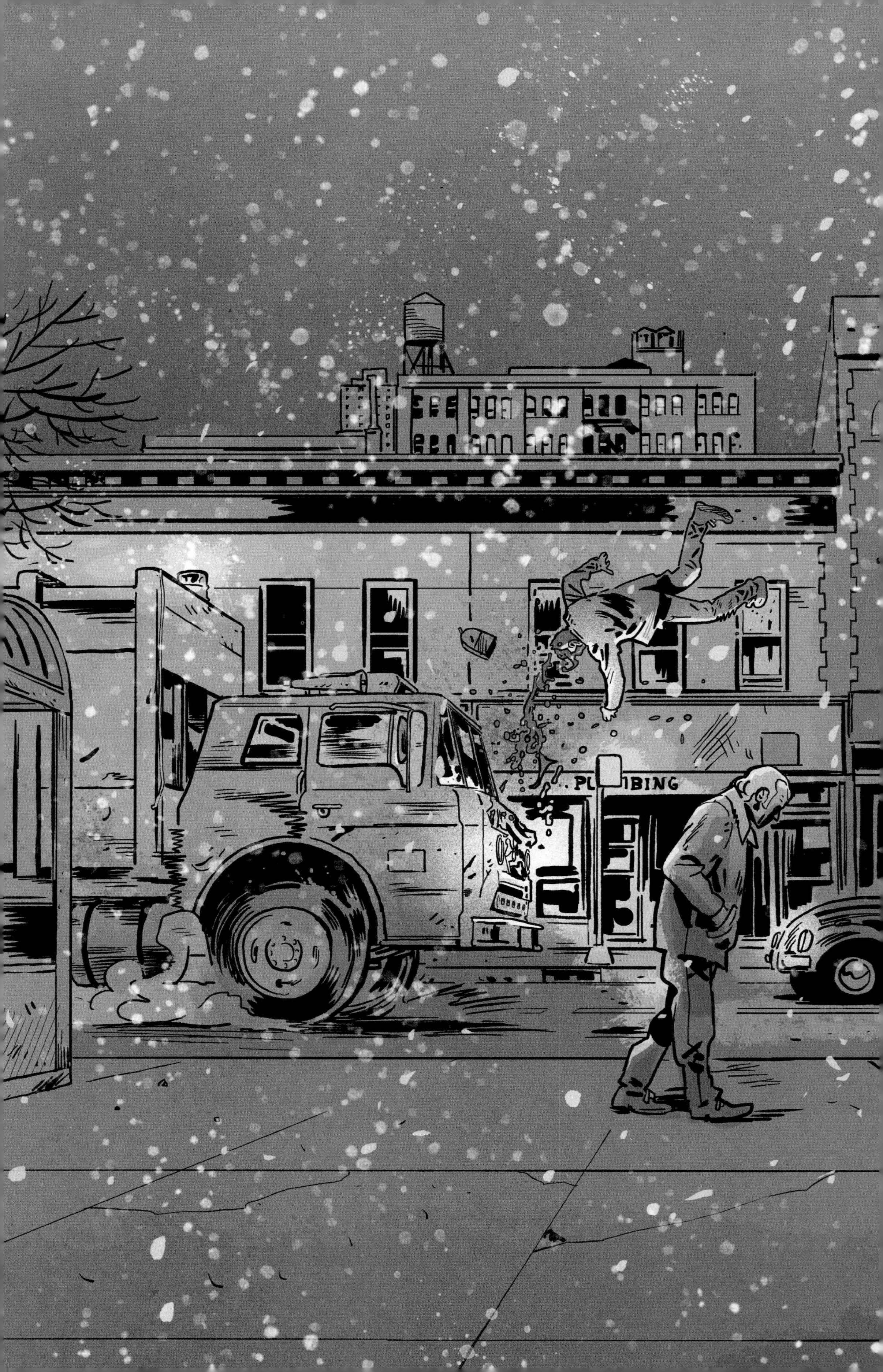
PL
BING

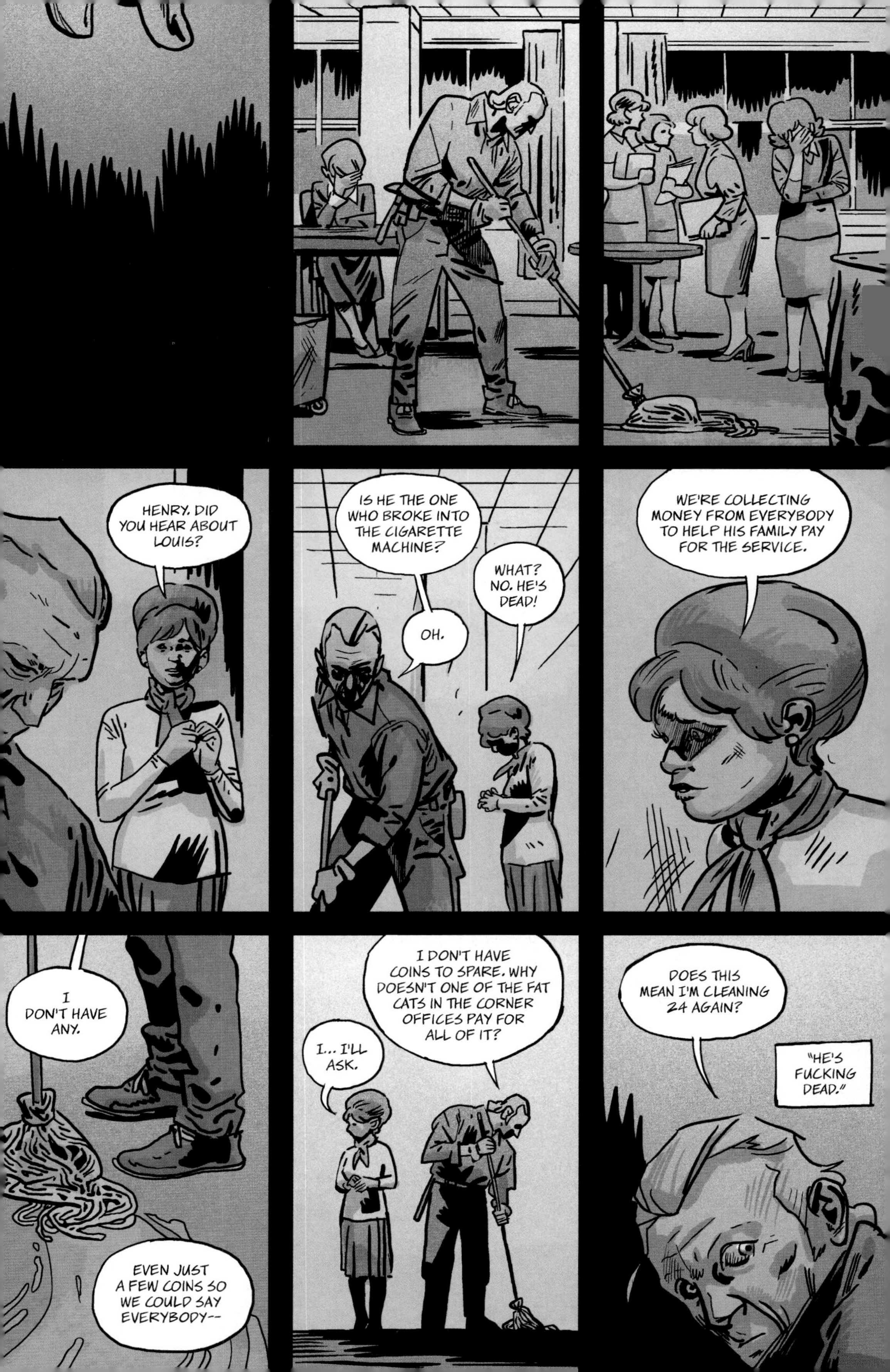
HENRY. DID YOU HEAR ABOUT LOUIS?
IS HE THE ONE WHO BROKE INTO THE CIGARETTE MACHINE?
WHAT? NO. HE'S DEAD!
OH.
WE'RE COLLECTING MONEY FROM EVERYBODY TO HELP HIS FAMILY PAY FOR THE SERVICE.
I DON'T HAVE ANY.
EVEN JUST A FEW COINS SO WE COULD SAY EVERYBODY--
I DON'T HAVE COINS TO SPARE. WHY DOESN'T ONE OF THE FAT CATS IN THE CORNER OFFICES PAY FOR ALL OF IT?
I... I'LL ASK.
DOES THIS MEAN I'M CLEANING 24 AGAIN?
"HE'S FUCKING DEAD."

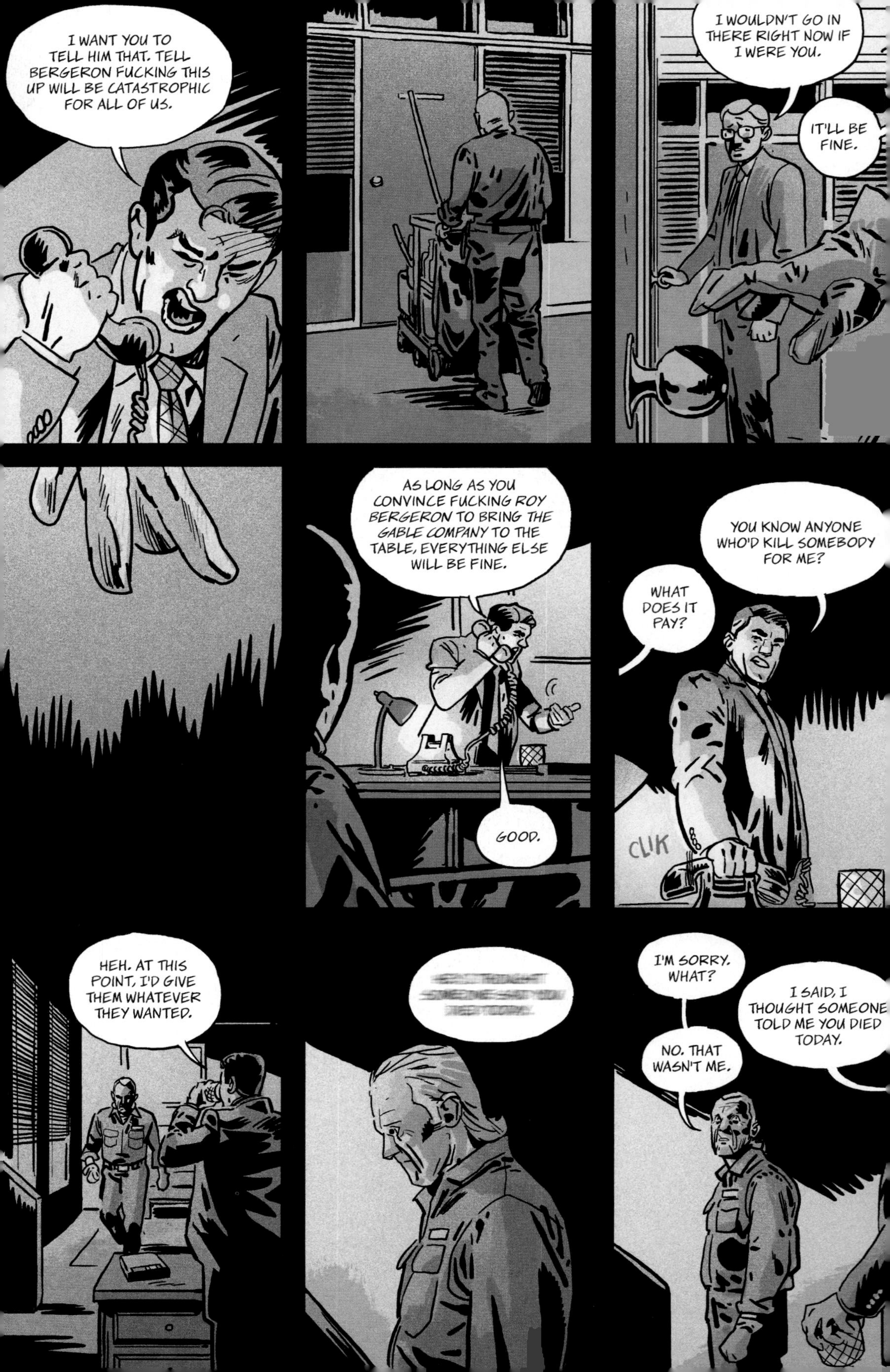
I WANT YOU TO TELL HIM THAT. TELL BERGERON FUCKING THIS UP WILL BE CATASTROPHIC FOR ALL OF US.
I WOULDN'T GO IN THERE RIGHT NOW IF I WERE YOU.
IT'LL BE FINE.
AS LONG AS YOU CONVINCE FUCKING ROY BERGERON TO BRING THE GABLE COMPANY TO THE TABLE, EVERYTHING ELSE WILL BE FINE.
GOOD.
YOU KNOW ANYONE WHO'D KILL SOMEBODY FOR ME?
WHAT DOES IT PAY?
CLIK
HEH. AT THIS POINT, I'D GIVE THEM WHATEVER THEY WANTED.
I'M SORRY. WHAT?
I SAID, I THOUGHT SOMEONE TOLD ME YOU DIED TODAY.
NO. THAT WASN'T ME.

"HOW'S YOUR FAMILY?"

"THEY'RE GOOD."

"EXCELLENT. BECAUSE, AS YOU SAID, FAMILY IS EVERYTHING, RIGHT?"

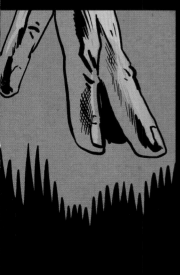

HELLO, OPERATOR? I'M LOOKING FOR THE ADDRESS OF A MR. ROY BERGERON... IN MANHATTAN, I BELIEVE.

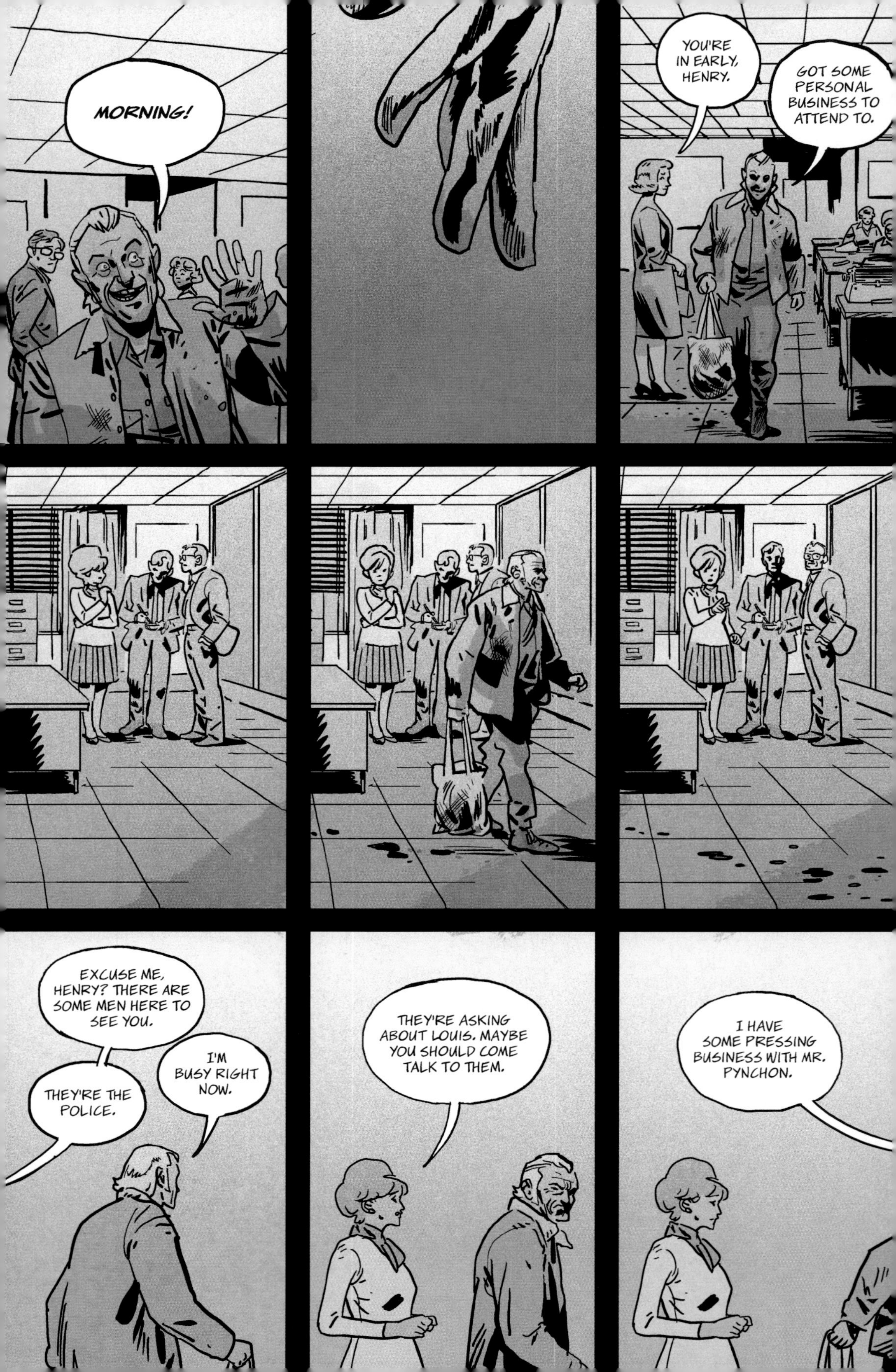
MORNING!
YOU'RE IN EARLY, HENRY.
GOT SOME PERSONAL BUSINESS TO ATTEND TO.
EXCUSE ME, HENRY? THERE ARE SOME MEN HERE TO SEE YOU.
THEY'RE THE POLICE.
I'M BUSY RIGHT NOW.
THEY'RE ASKING ABOUT LOUIS. MAYBE YOU SHOULD COME TALK TO THEM.
I HAVE SOME PRESSING BUSINESS WITH MR. PYNCHON.

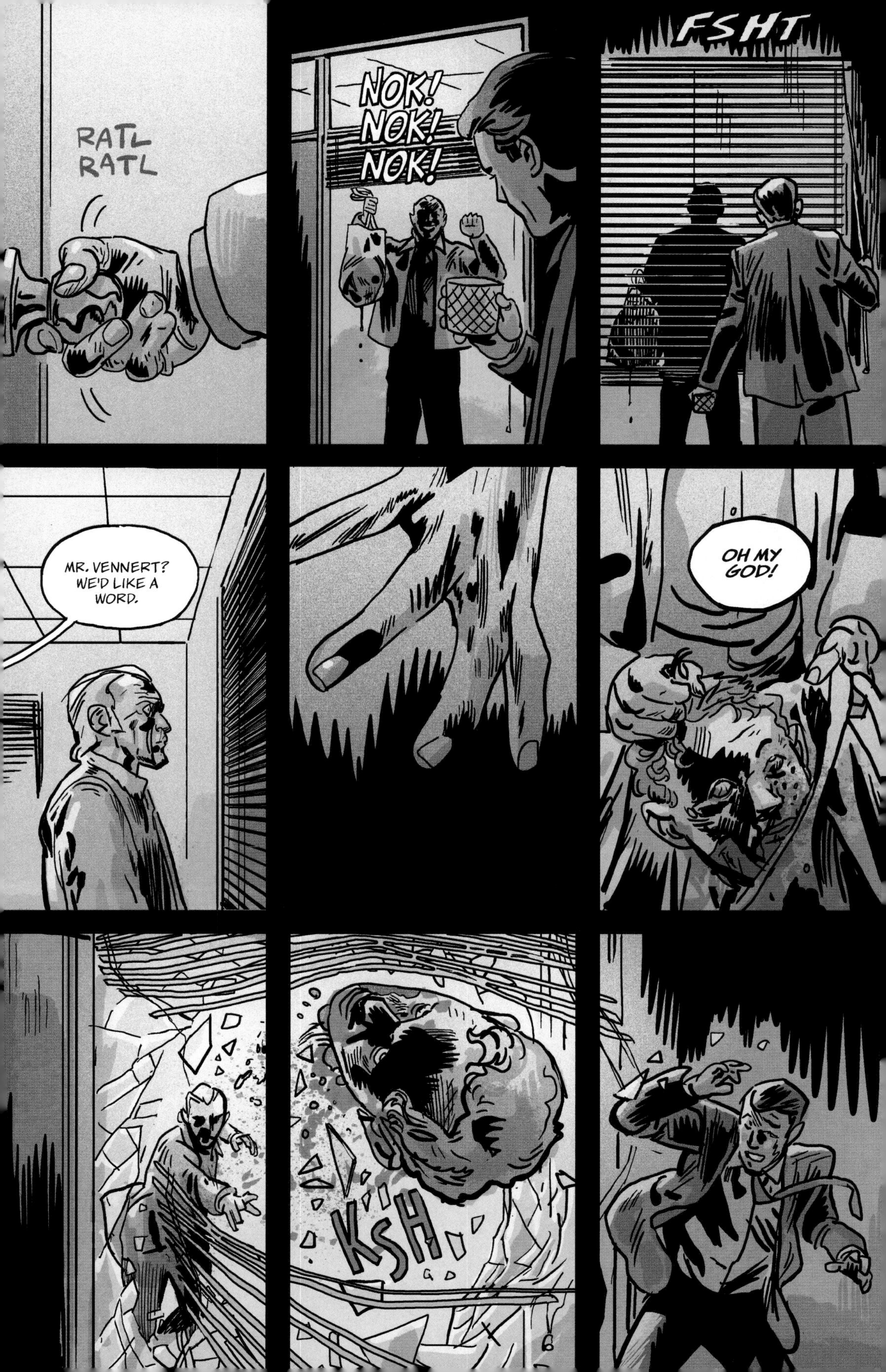
RATL
RATL
NOK!
NOK!
NOK!
FSHT
MR. VENNERT? WE'D LIKE A WORD.
OH MY GOD!
KSH

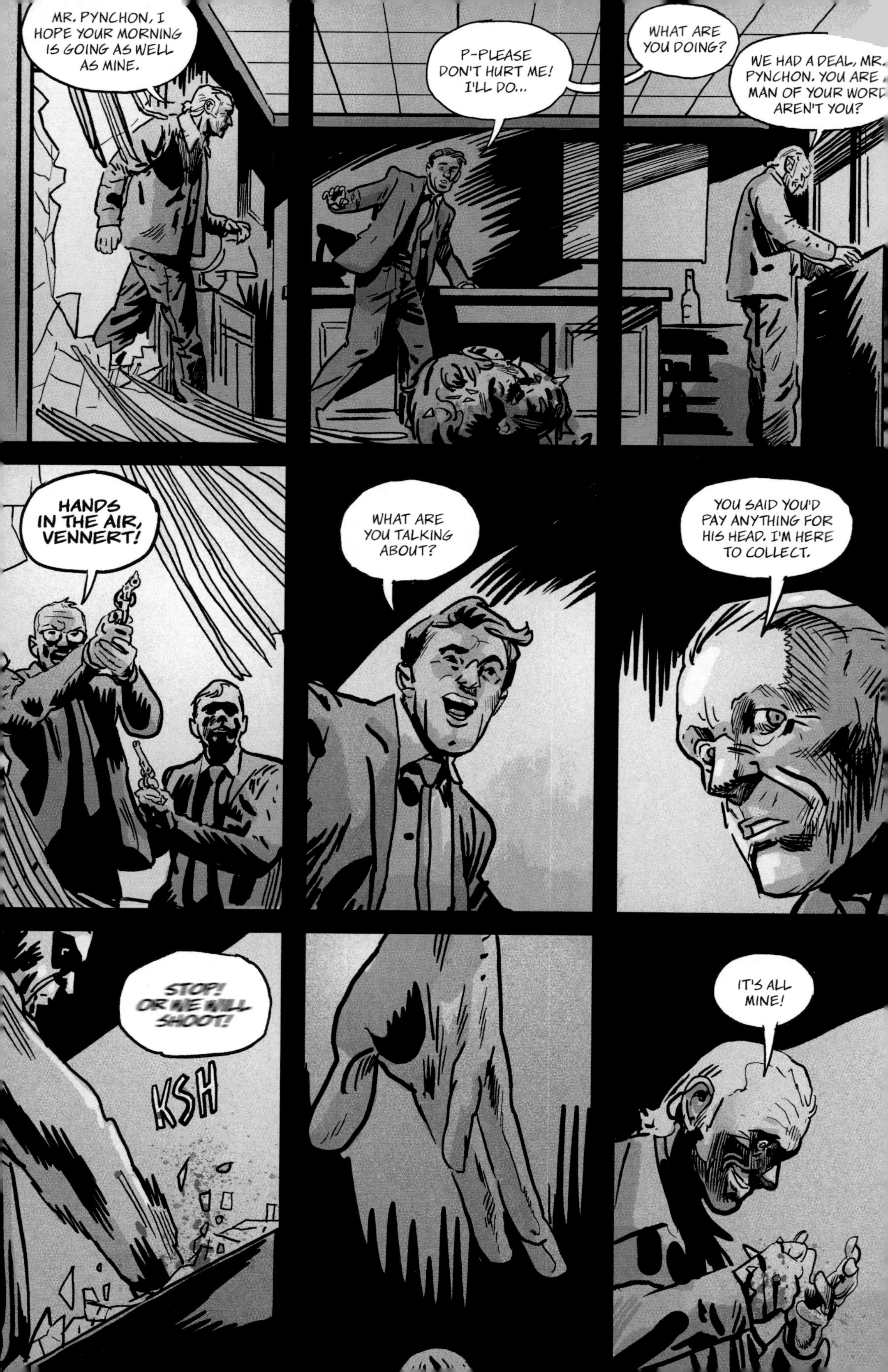
MR. PYNCHON, I HOPE YOUR MORNING IS GOING AS WELL AS MINE.
P-PLEASE DON'T HURT ME! I'LL DO...
WHAT ARE YOU DOING?
WE HAD A DEAL, MR. PYNCHON. YOU ARE MAN OF YOUR WORD AREN'T YOU?
HANDS IN THE AIR, VENNERT!
WHAT ARE YOU TALKING ABOUT?
YOU SAID YOU'D PAY ANYTHING FOR HIS HEAD. I'M HERE TO COLLECT.
STOP! OR WE WILL SHOOT!
KSH
IT'S ALL MINE!

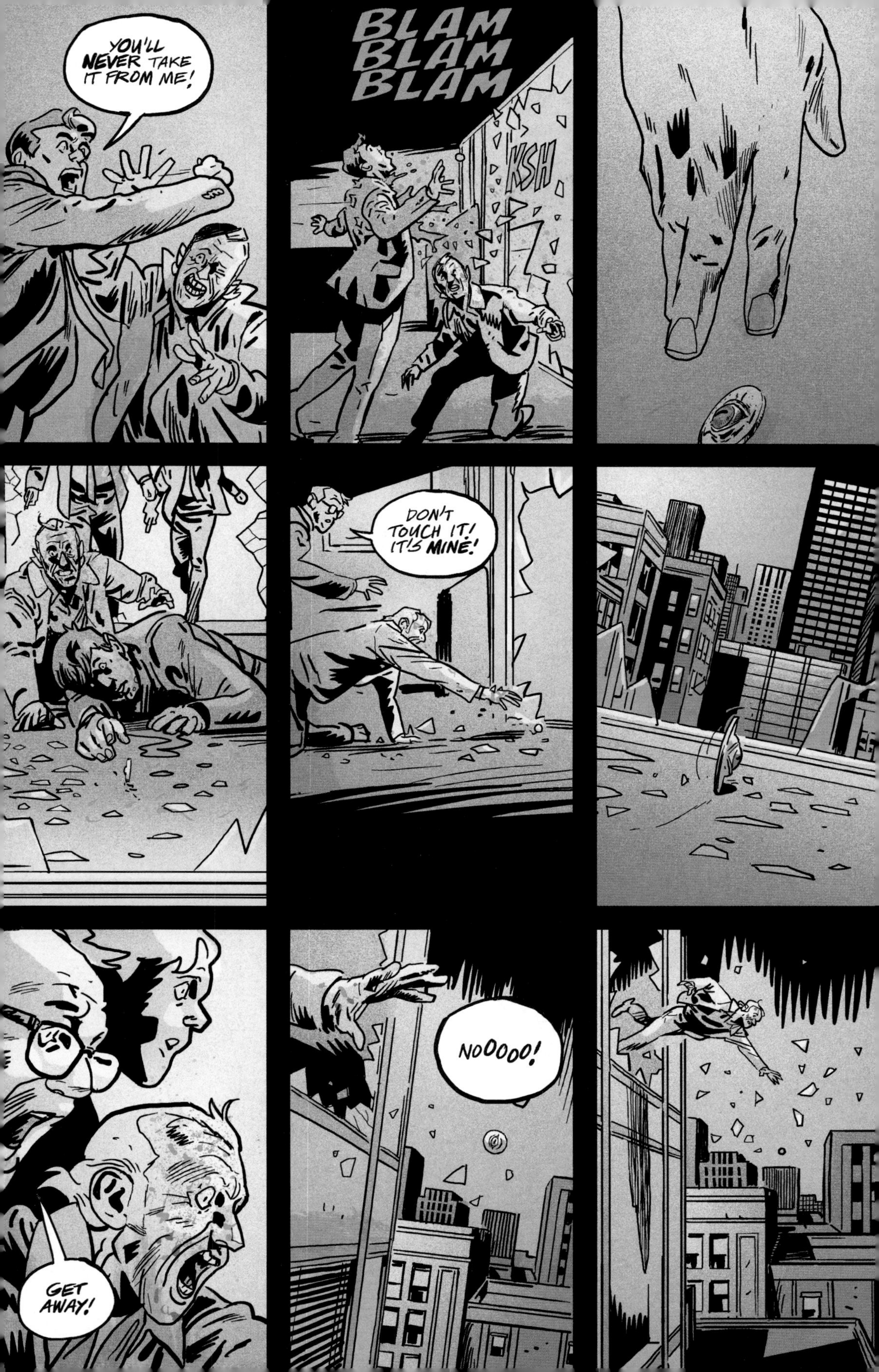
YOU'LL NEVER TAKE IT FROM ME!
BLAM BLAM BLAM
KSH
DON'T TOUCH IT! IT'S MINE!
GET AWAY!
NOOOOO!

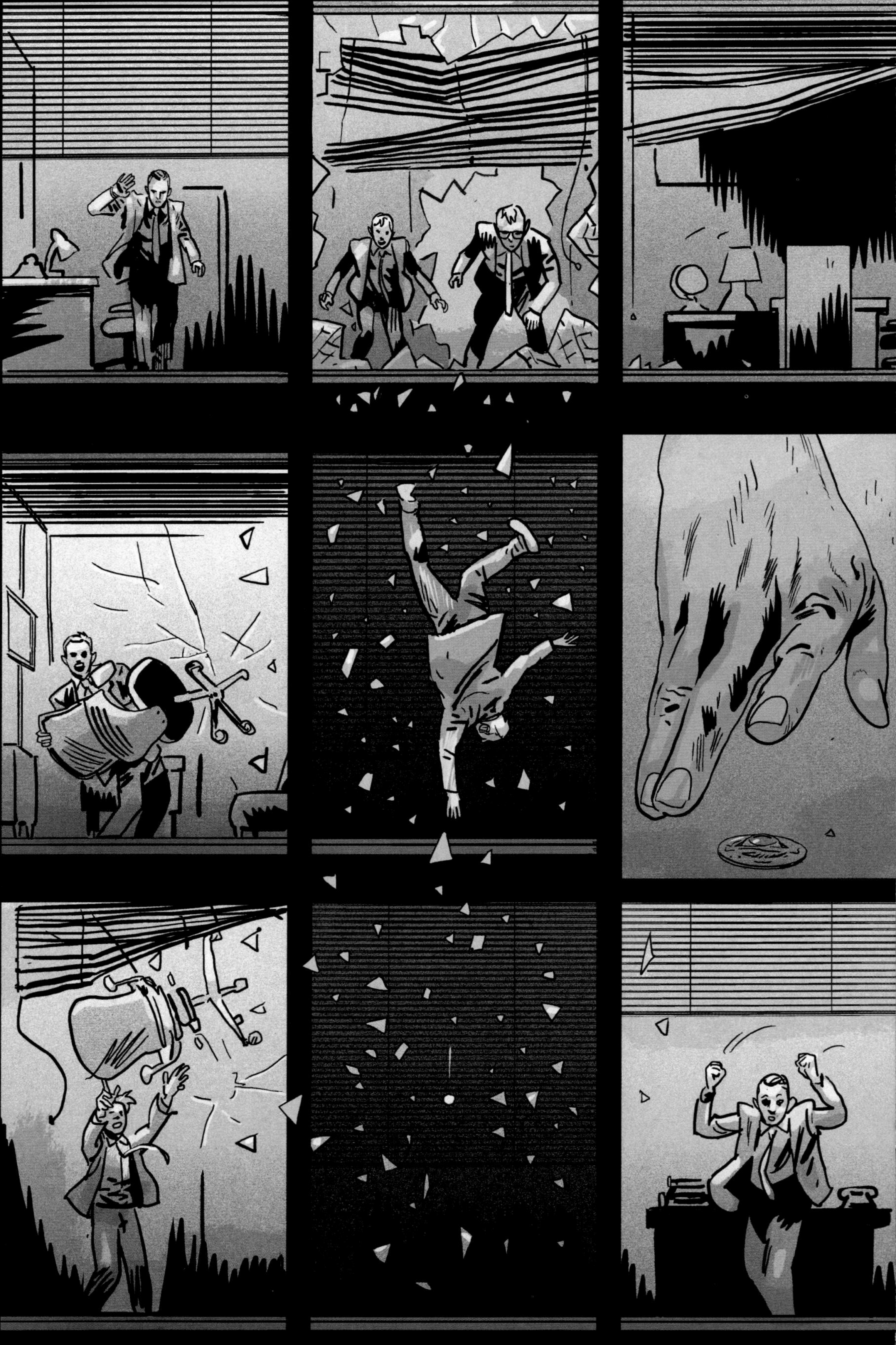

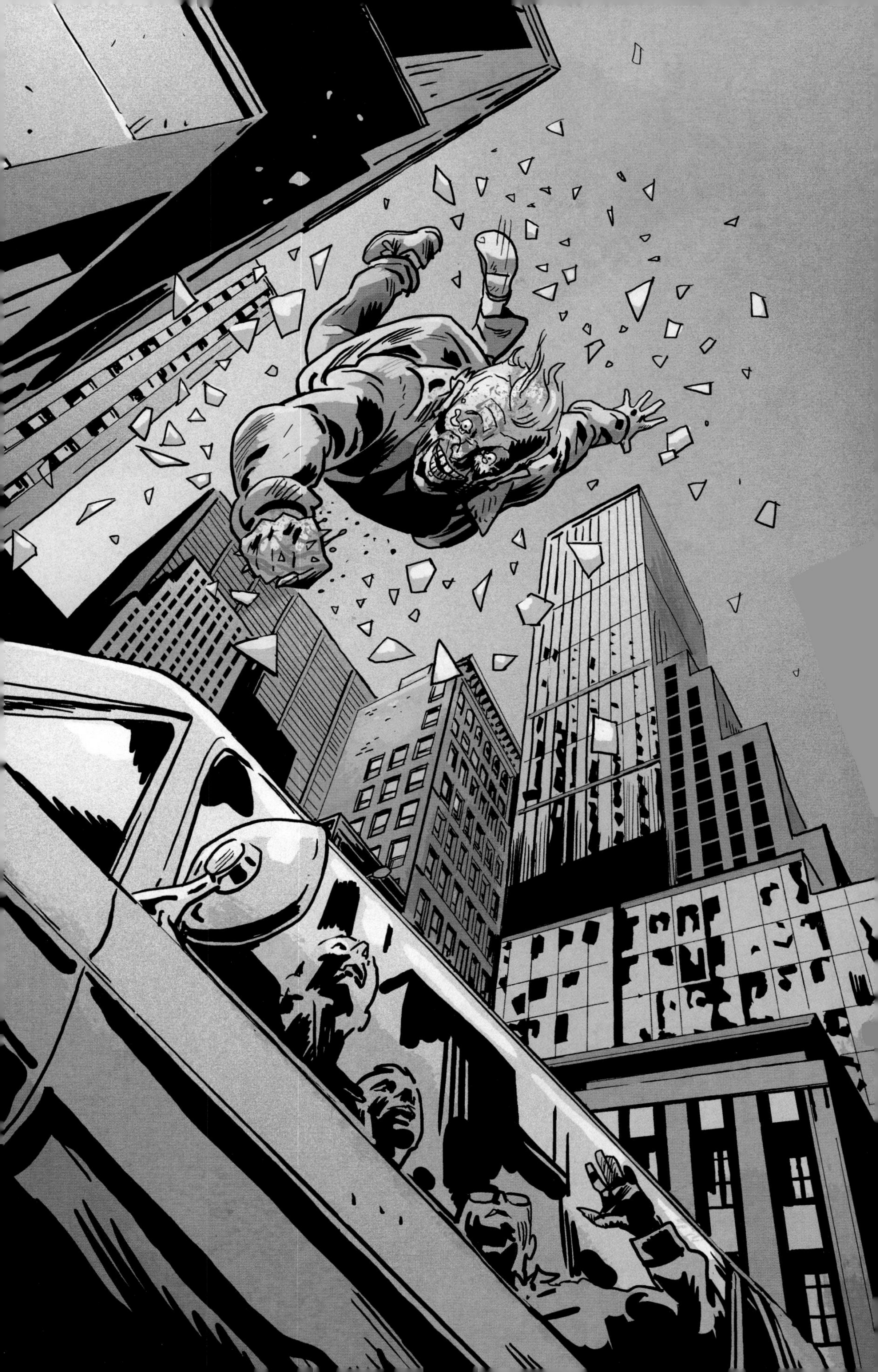

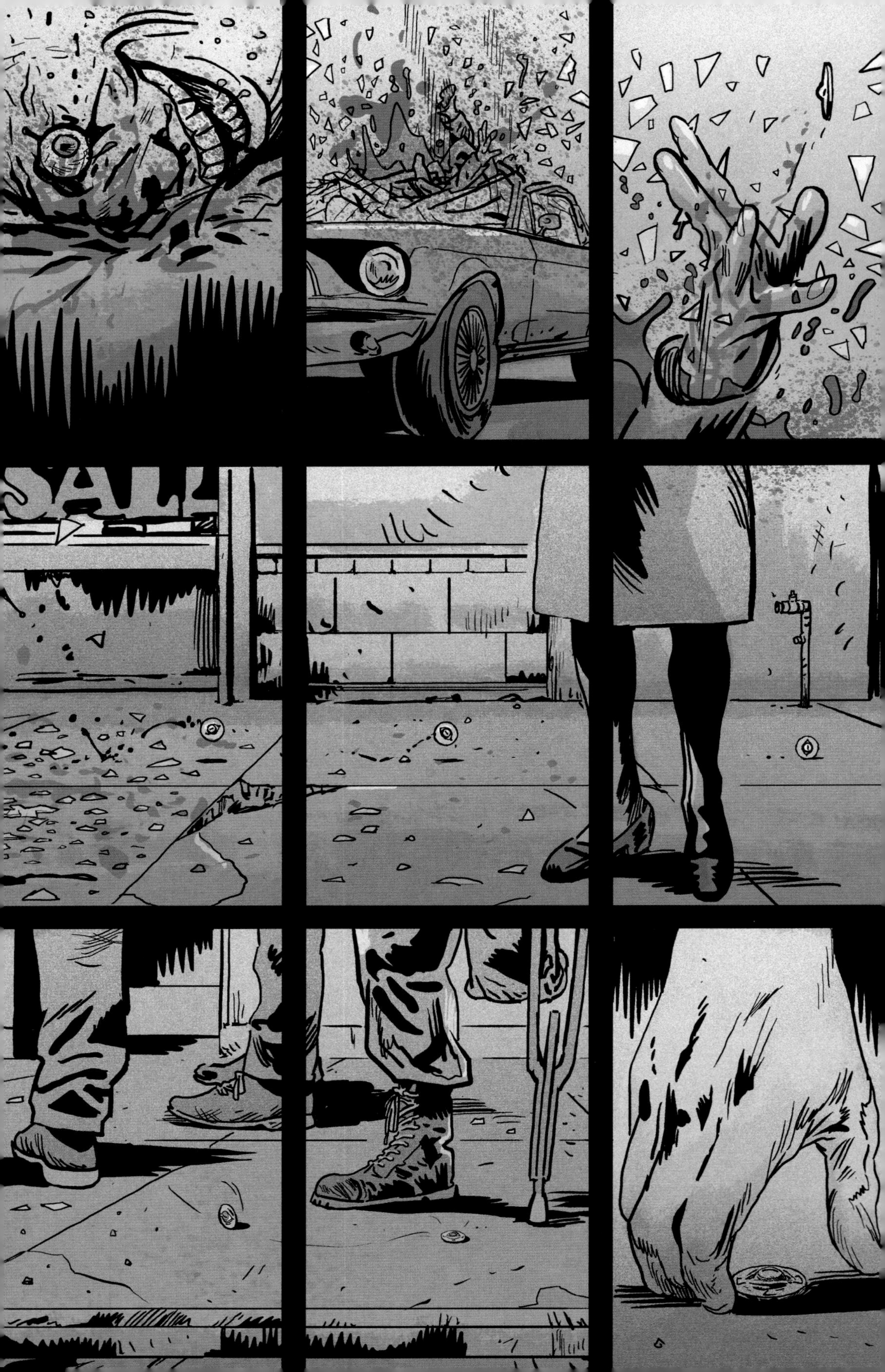

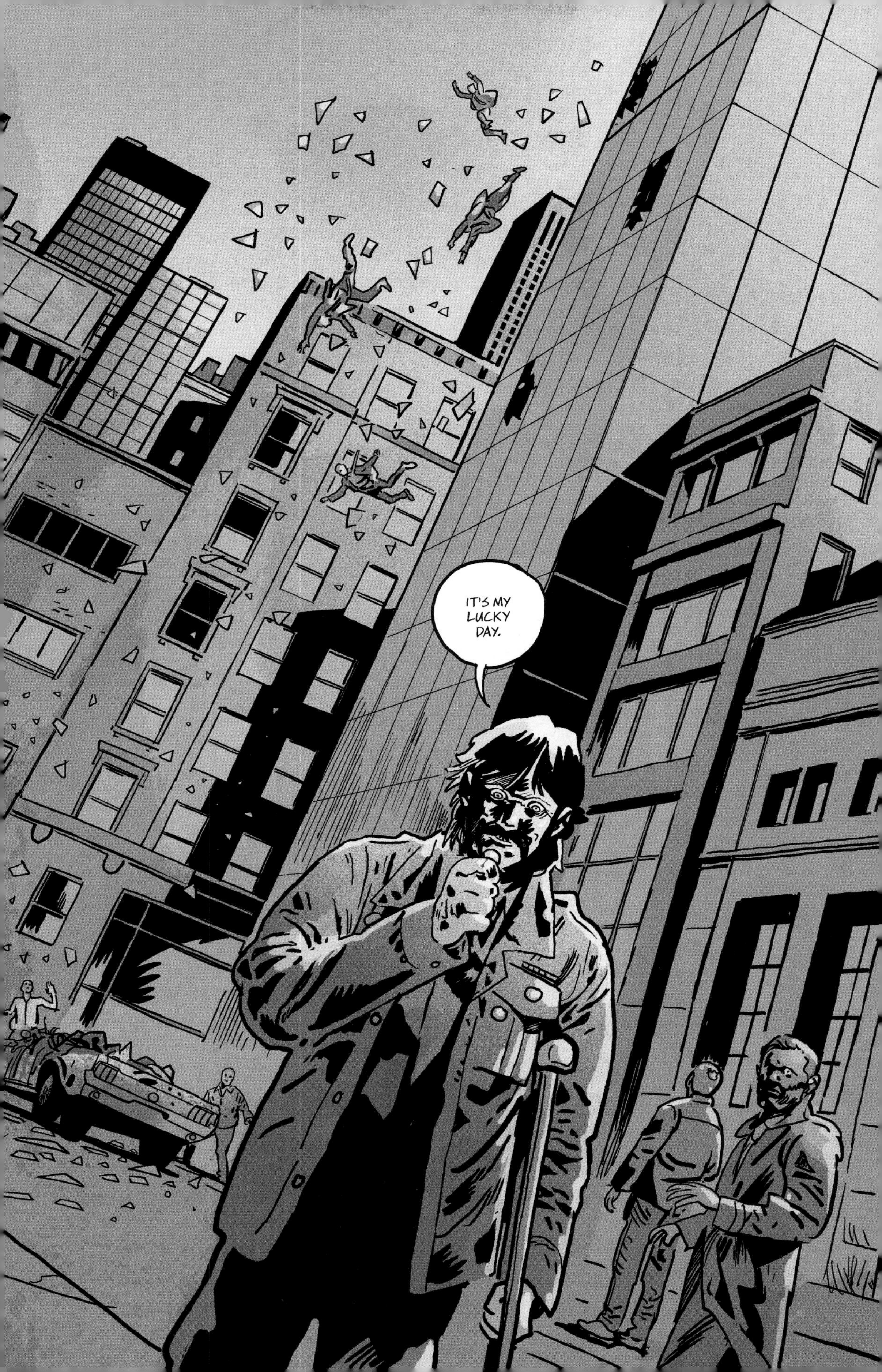
IT'S MY LUCKY DAY.

The Dancer

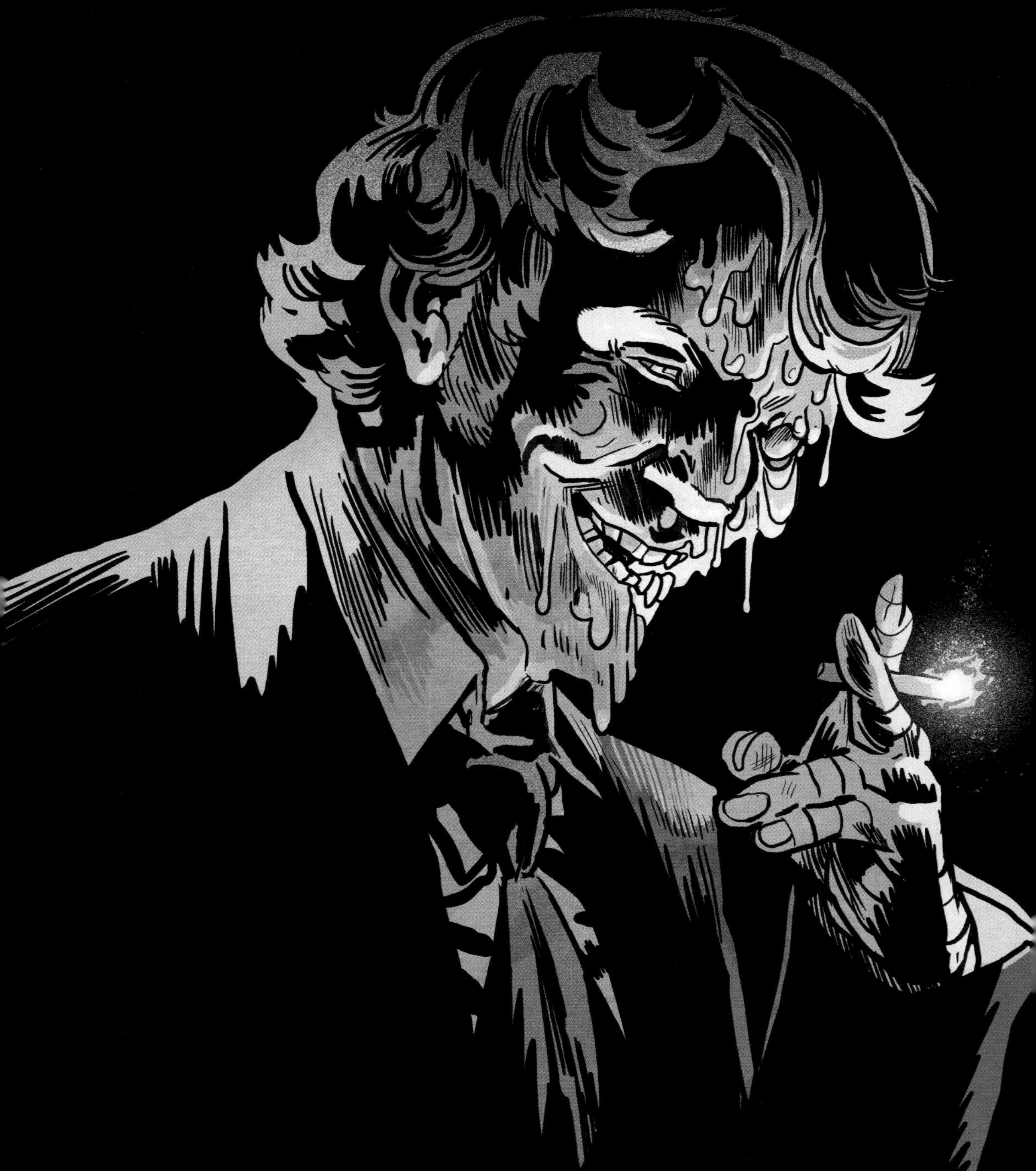

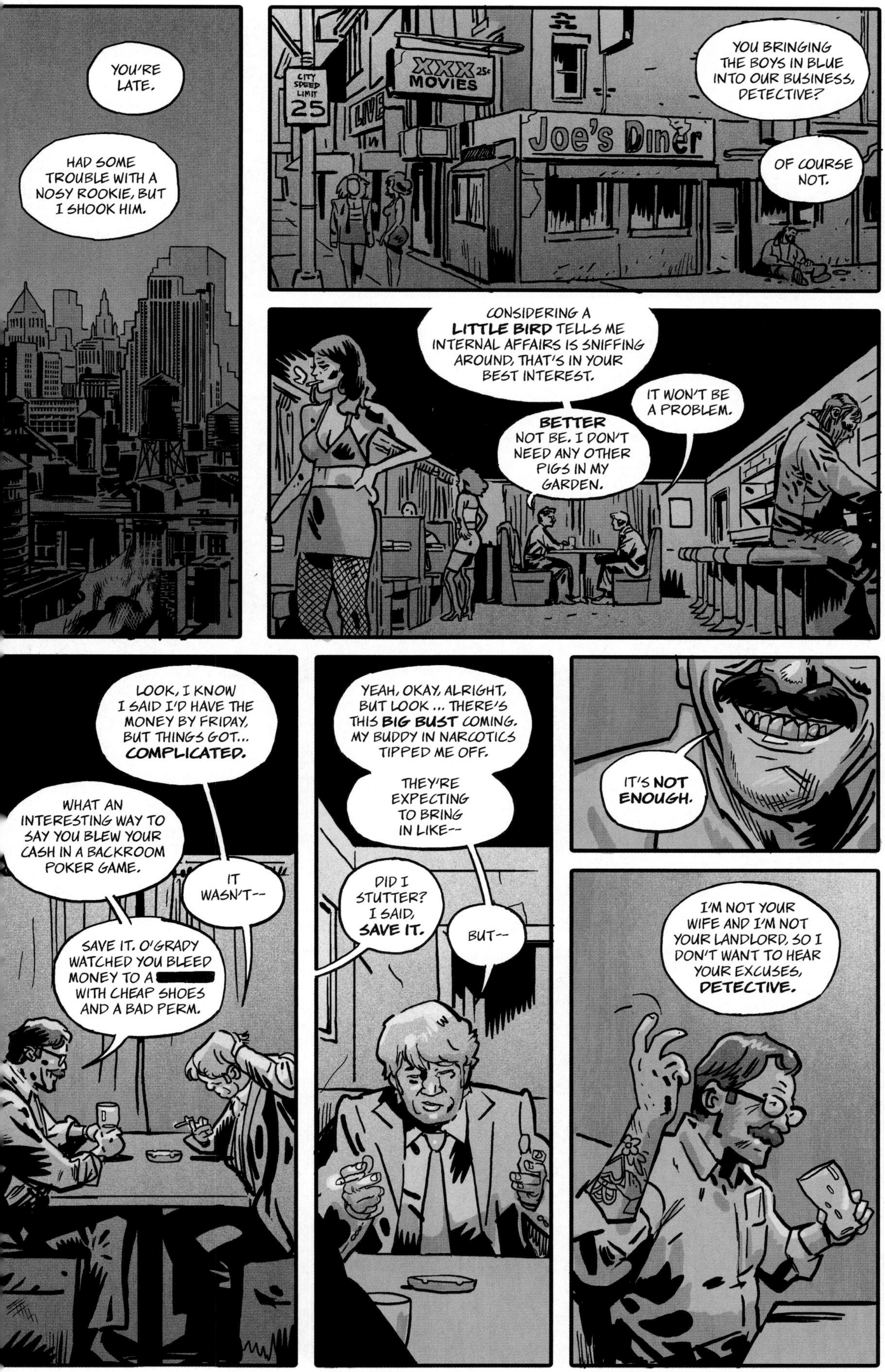
YOU'RE LATE.
HAD SOME TROUBLE WITH A NOSY ROOKIE, BUT I SHOOK HIM.
CITY SPEED LIMIT 25
XXX 25¢ MOVIES
LIVE
Joe's Diner
YOU BRINGING THE BOYS IN BLUE INTO OUR BUSINESS, DETECTIVE?
OF COURSE NOT.
CONSIDERING A **LITTLE BIRD** TELLS ME INTERNAL AFFAIRS IS SNIFFING AROUND, THAT'S IN YOUR BEST INTEREST.
IT WON'T BE A PROBLEM.
BETTER NOT BE. I DON'T NEED ANY OTHER PIGS IN MY GARDEN.
LOOK, I KNOW I SAID I'D HAVE THE MONEY BY FRIDAY, BUT THINGS GOT... **COMPLICATED.**
WHAT AN INTERESTING WAY TO SAY YOU BLEW YOUR CASH IN A BACKROOM POKER GAME.
IT WASN'T--
SAVE IT. O'GRADY WATCHED YOU BLEED MONEY TO A [redacted] WITH CHEAP SHOES AND A BAD PERM.
YEAH, OKAY, ALRIGHT, BUT LOOK ... THERE'S THIS **BIG BUST** COMING. MY BUDDY IN NARCOTICS TIPPED ME OFF.
THEY'RE EXPECTING TO BRING IN LIKE--
DID I STUTTER? I SAID, **SAVE IT.**
BUT--
IT'S **NOT ENOUGH.**
I'M NOT YOUR WIFE AND I'M NOT YOUR LANDLORD, SO I DON'T WANT TO HEAR YOUR EXCUSES, **DETECTIVE.**

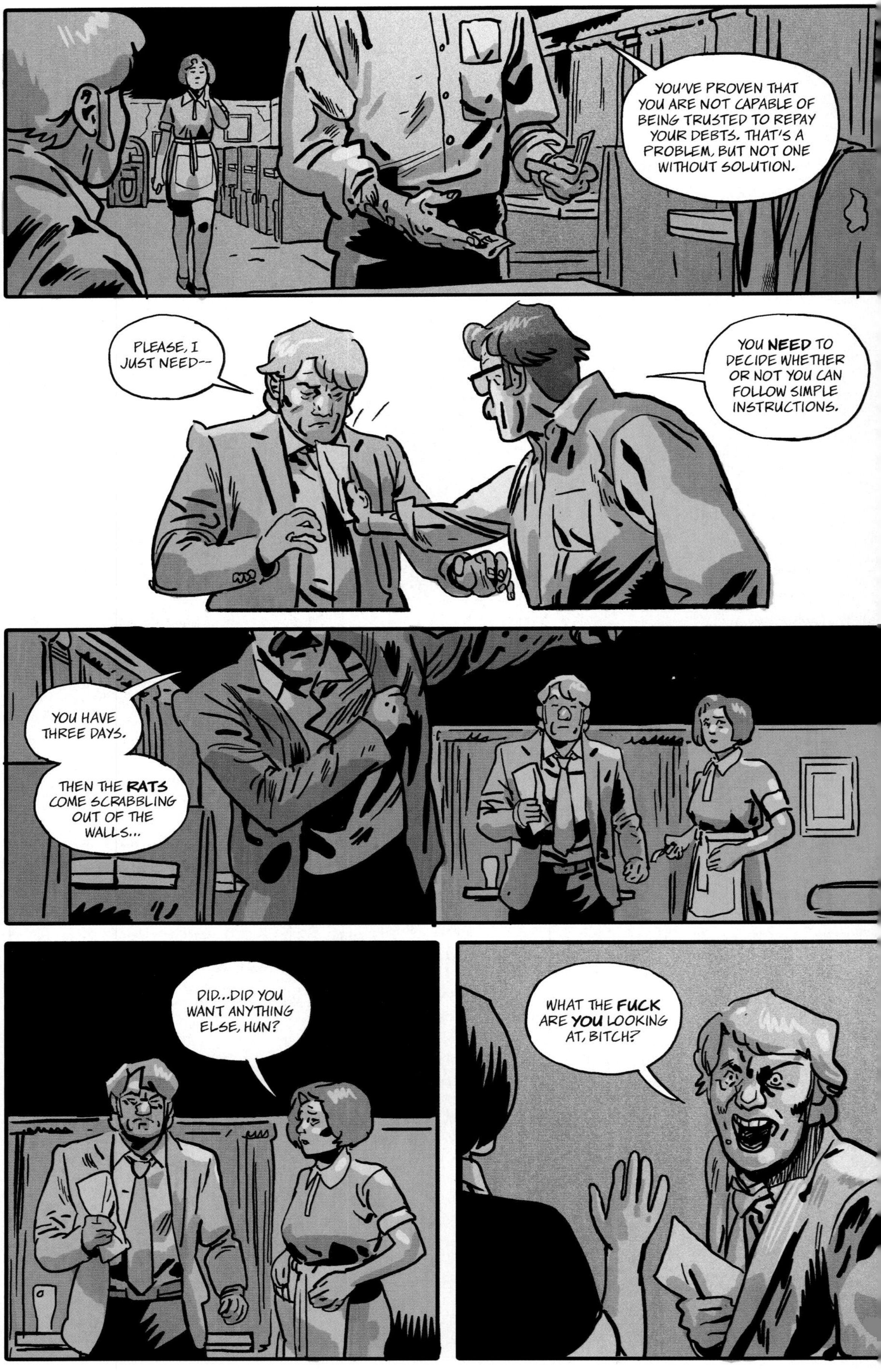
YOU'VE PROVEN THAT YOU ARE NOT CAPABLE OF BEING TRUSTED TO REPAY YOUR DEBTS. THAT'S A PROBLEM, BUT NOT ONE WITHOUT SOLUTION.
PLEASE, I JUST NEED--
YOU NEED TO DECIDE WHETHER OR NOT YOU CAN FOLLOW SIMPLE INSTRUCTIONS.
YOU HAVE THREE DAYS.
THEN THE RATS COME SCRABBLING OUT OF THE WALLS...
DID...DID YOU WANT ANYTHING ELSE, HUN?
WHAT THE FUCK ARE YOU LOOKING AT, BITCH?

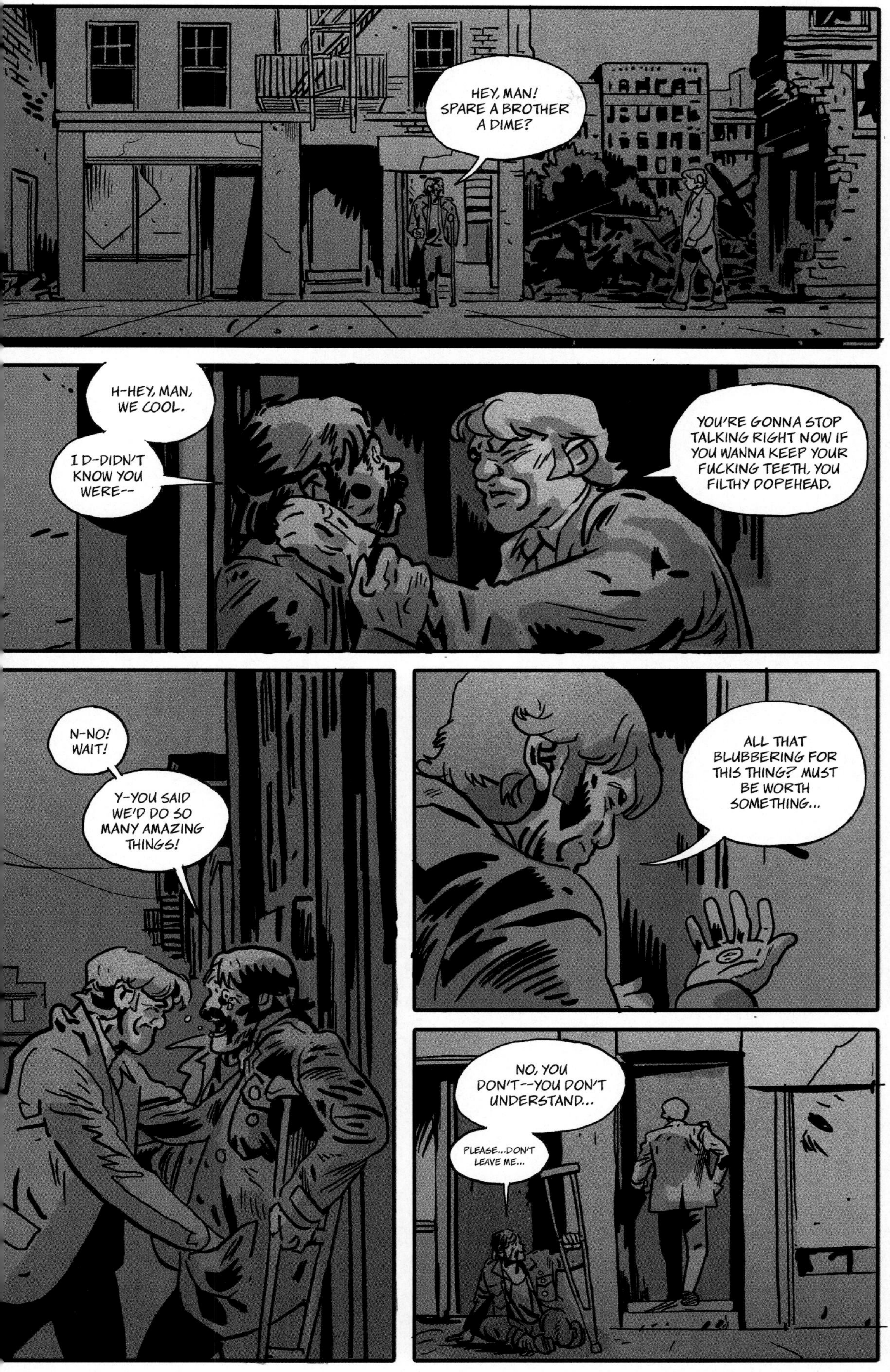
HEY, MAN! SPARE A BROTHER A DIME?
H-HEY, MAN, WE COOL.
I D-DIDN'T KNOW YOU WERE--
YOU'RE GONNA STOP TALKING RIGHT NOW IF YOU WANNA KEEP YOUR FUCKING TEETH, YOU FILTHY DOPEHEAD.
N-NO! WAIT!
Y-YOU SAID WE'D DO SO MANY AMAZING THINGS!
ALL THAT BLUBBERING FOR THIS THING? MUST BE WORTH SOMETHING...
NO, YOU DON'T--YOU DON'T UNDERSTAND...
PLEASE...DON'T LEAVE ME...

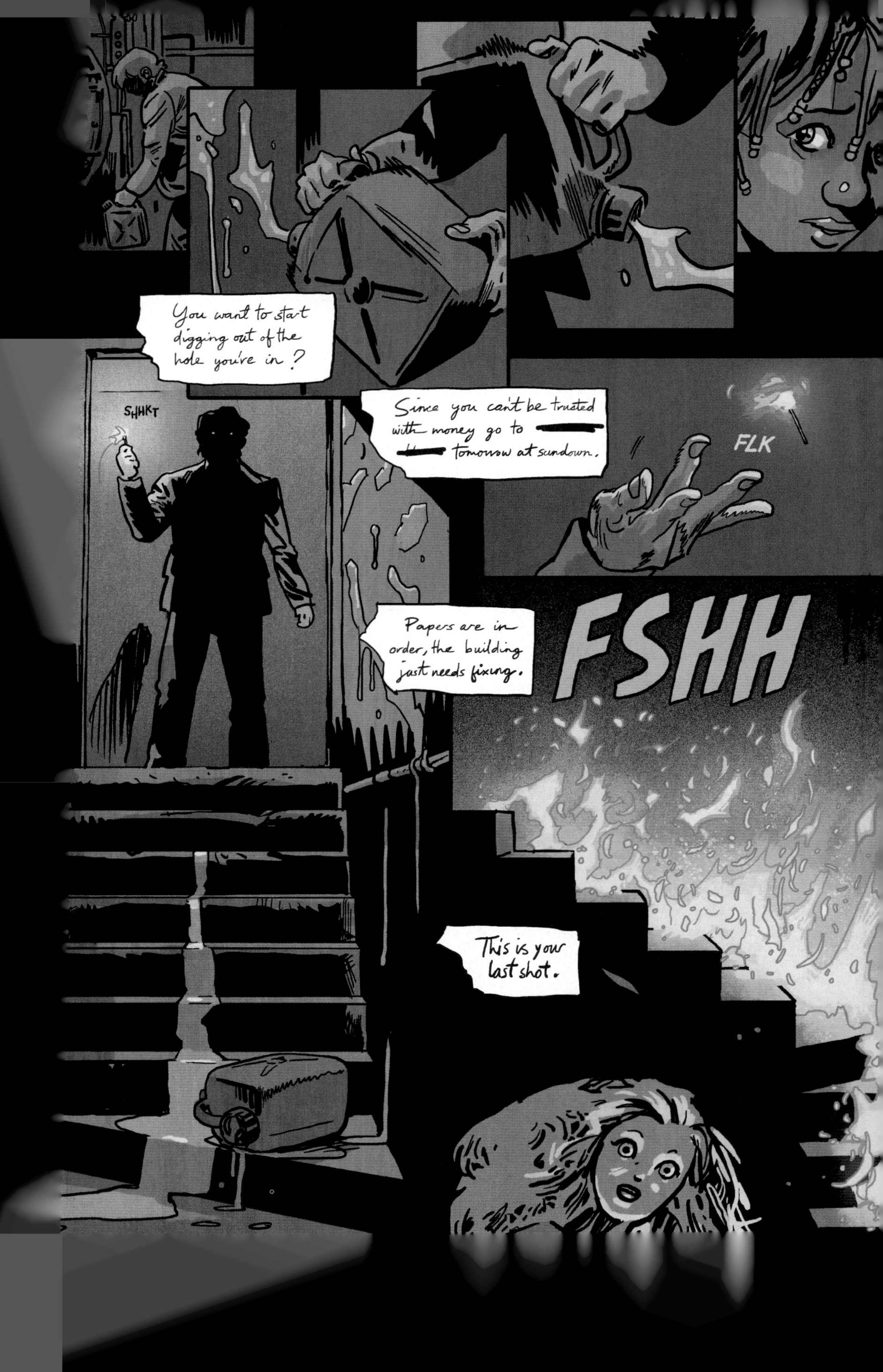
You want to start digging out of the hole you're in?
SHHKT
Since you can't be trusted with money go to [redacted] tomorrow at sundown.
FLK
Papers are in order, the building just needs fixing.
FSHH
This is your last shot.

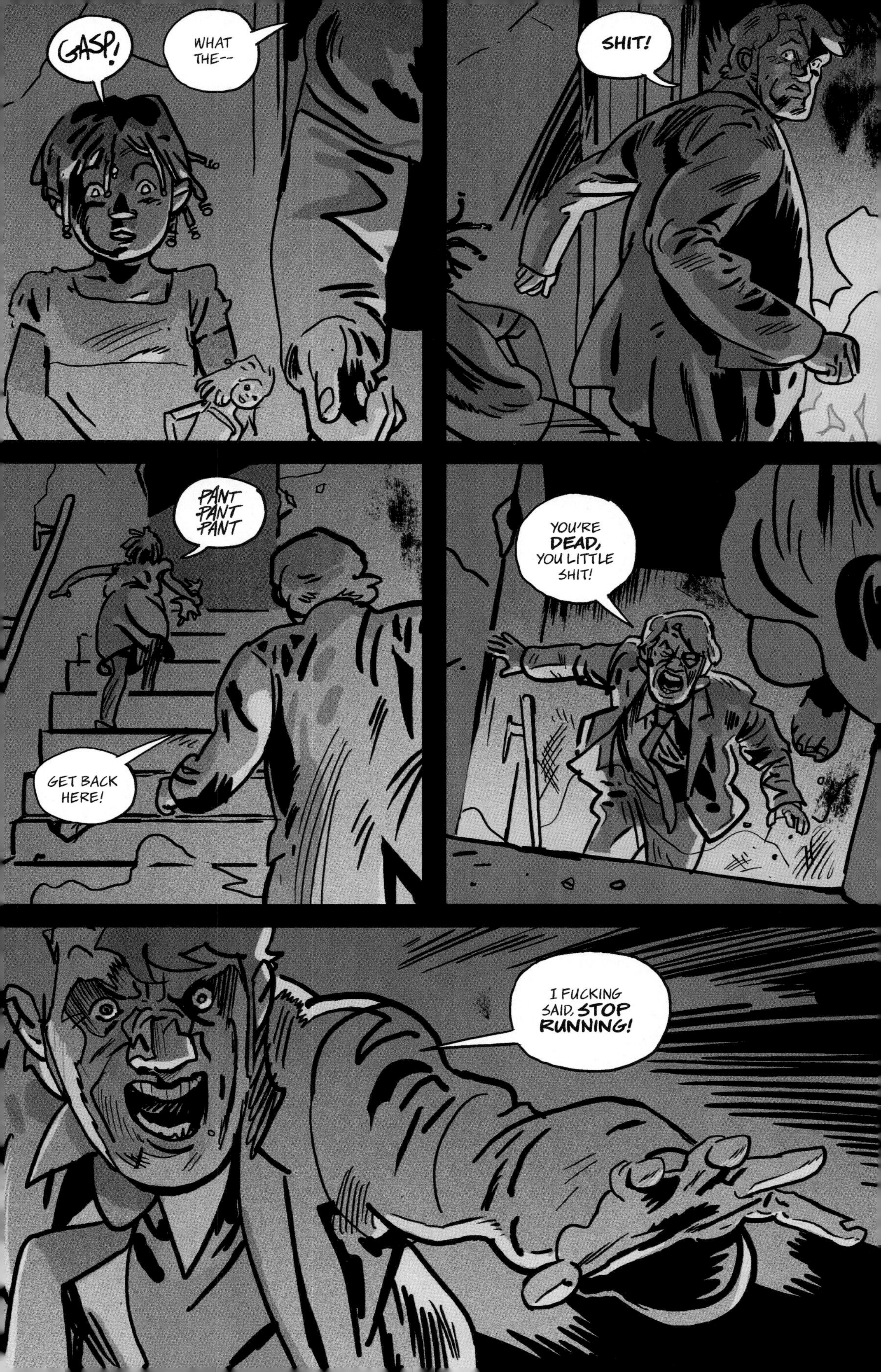
GASP!
WHAT THE--
SHIT!
PANT PANT PANT
GET BACK HERE!
YOU'RE DEAD, YOU LITTLE SHIT!
I FUCKING SAID, STOP RUNNING!

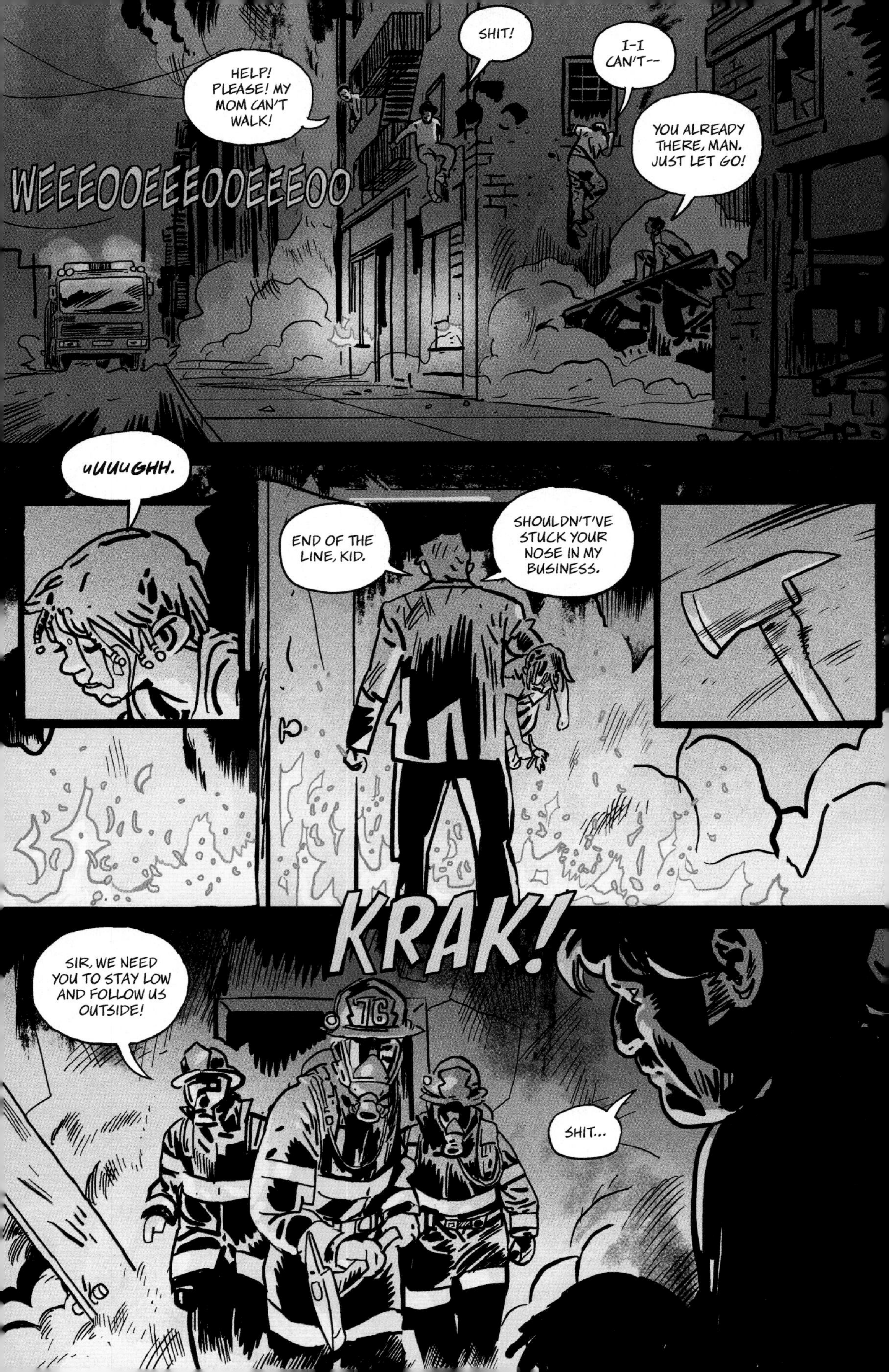
HELP! PLEASE! MY MOM CAN'T WALK!
SHIT!
I-I CAN'T--
YOU ALREADY THERE, MAN. JUST LET GO!
WEEEOOEEEOOEEEOO
uUUUGHH.
END OF THE LINE, KID.
SHOULDN'T'VE STUCK YOUR NOSE IN MY BUSINESS.
KRAK!
SIR, WE NEED YOU TO STAY LOW AND FOLLOW US OUTSIDE!
76
SHIT...

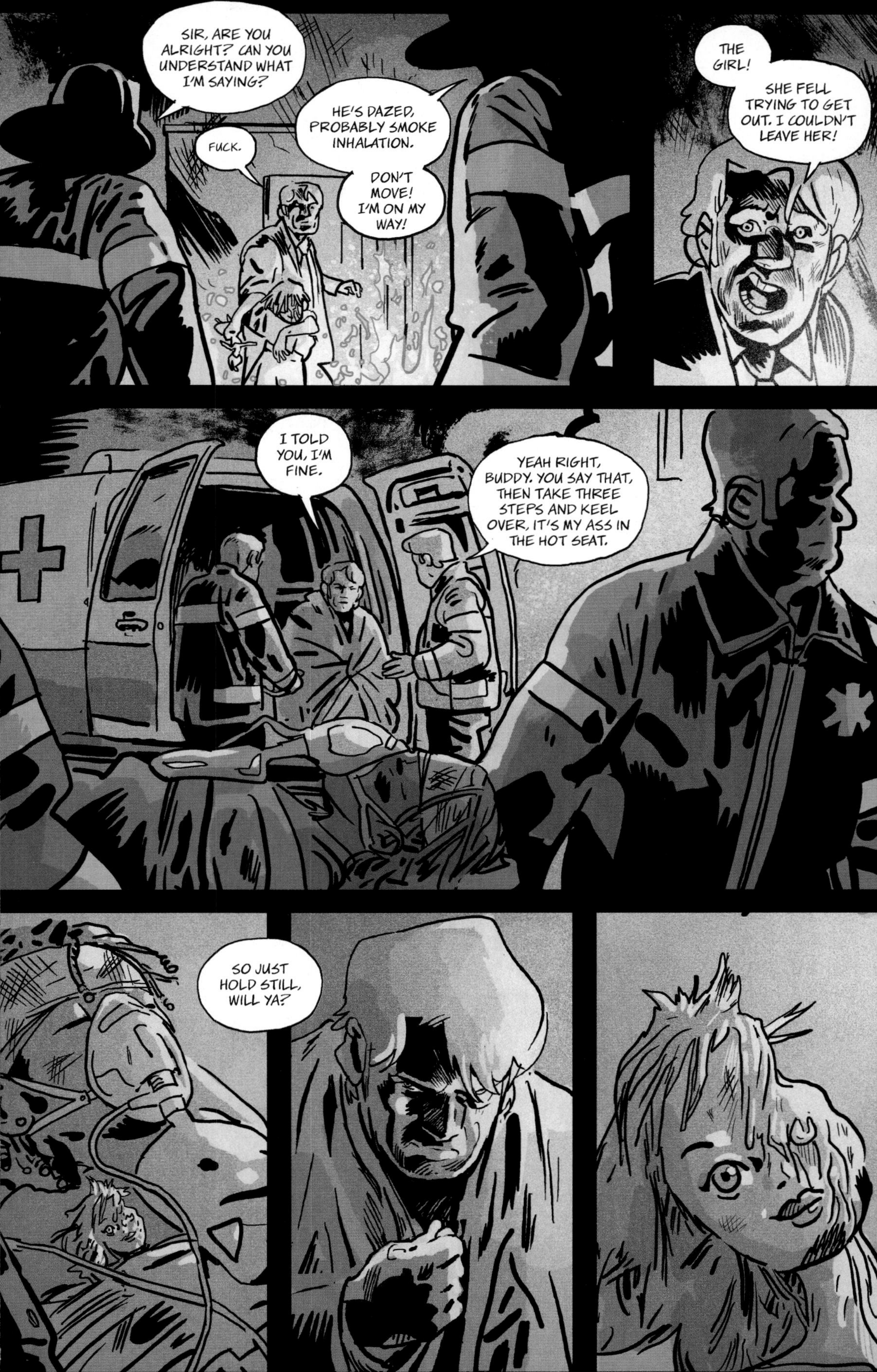
SIR, ARE YOU ALRIGHT? CAN YOU UNDERSTAND WHAT I'M SAYING?
FUCK.
HE'S DAZED, PROBABLY SMOKE INHALATION.
DON'T MOVE! I'M ON MY WAY!
THE GIRL!
SHE FELL TRYING TO GET OUT. I COULDN'T LEAVE HER!
I TOLD YOU, I'M FINE.
YEAH RIGHT, BUDDY. YOU SAY THAT, THEN TAKE THREE STEPS AND KEEL OVER, IT'S MY ASS IN THE HOT SEAT.
SO JUST HOLD STILL, WILL YA?

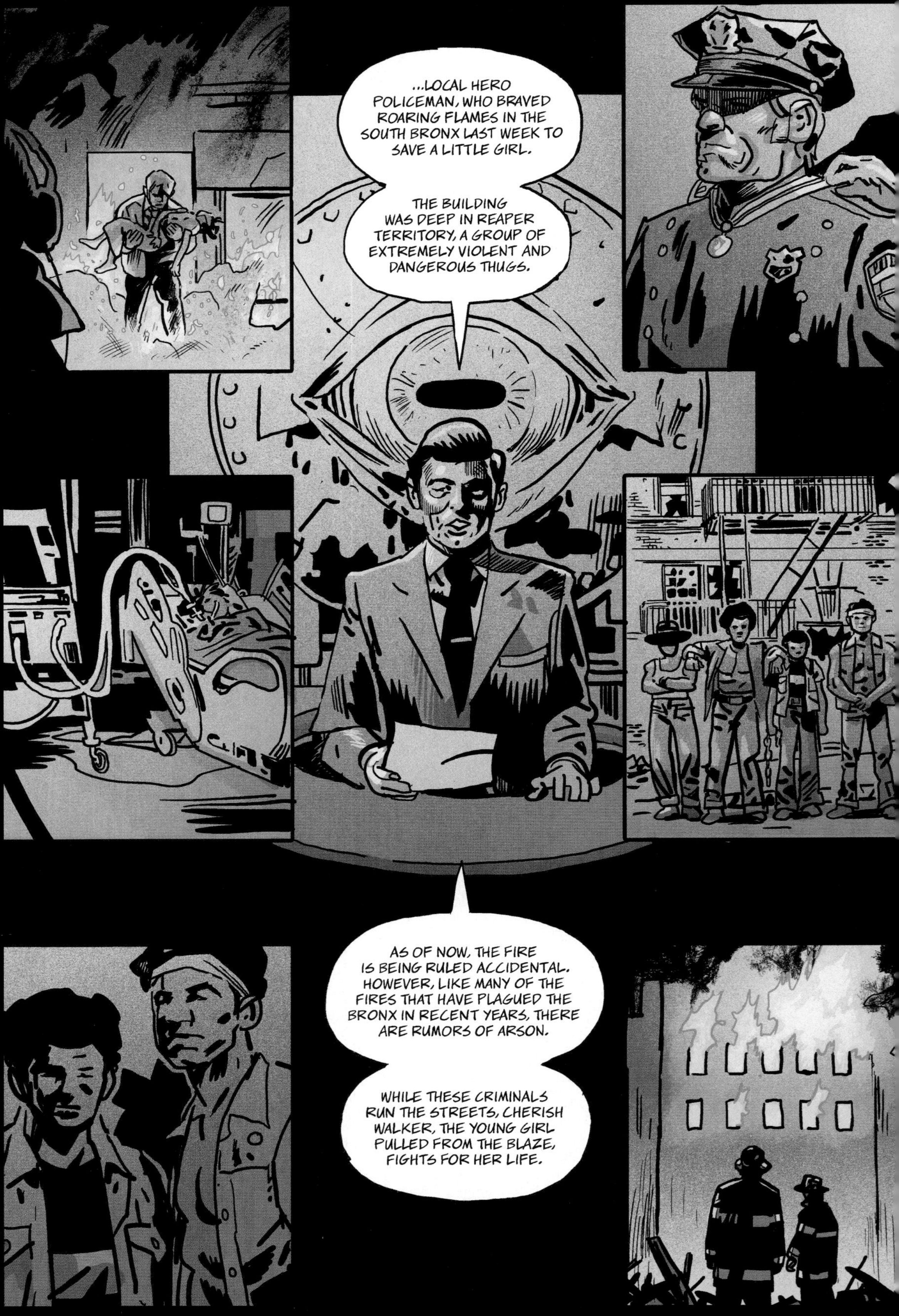
...LOCAL HERO POLICEMAN, WHO BRAVED ROARING FLAMES IN THE SOUTH BRONX LAST WEEK TO SAVE A LITTLE GIRL.
THE BUILDING WAS DEEP IN REAPER TERRITORY, A GROUP OF EXTREMELY VIOLENT AND DANGEROUS THUGS.
AS OF NOW, THE FIRE IS BEING RULED ACCIDENTAL. HOWEVER, LIKE MANY OF THE FIRES THAT HAVE PLAGUED THE BRONX IN RECENT YEARS, THERE ARE RUMORS OF ARSON.
WHILE THESE CRIMINALS RUN THE STREETS, CHERISH WALKER, THE YOUNG GIRL PULLED FROM THE BLAZE, FIGHTS FOR HER LIFE.

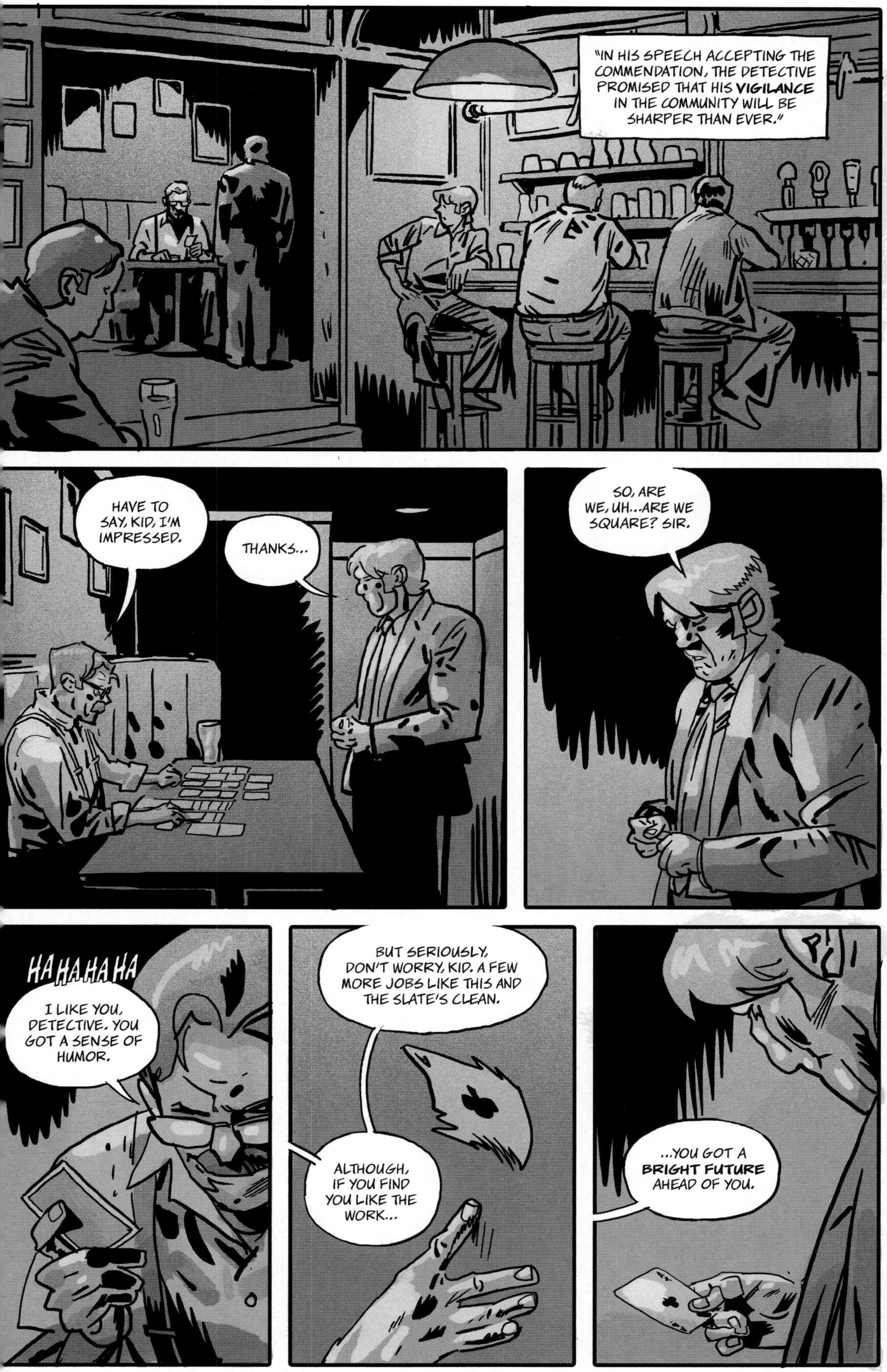
"IN HIS SPEECH ACCEPTING THE COMMENDATION, THE DETECTIVE PROMISED THAT HIS **VIGILANCE** IN THE COMMUNITY WILL BE SHARPER THAN EVER."
HAVE TO SAY, KID, I'M IMPRESSED.
THANKS...
SO, ARE WE, UH...ARE WE SQUARE? SIR.
HA HA HA HA HA
I LIKE YOU, DETECTIVE. YOU GOT A SENSE OF HUMOR.
BUT SERIOUSLY, DON'T WORRY, KID. A FEW MORE JOBS LIKE THIS AND THE SLATE'S CLEAN.
ALTHOUGH, IF YOU FIND YOU LIKE THE WORK...
...YOU GOT A **BRIGHT FUTURE** AHEAD OF YOU.

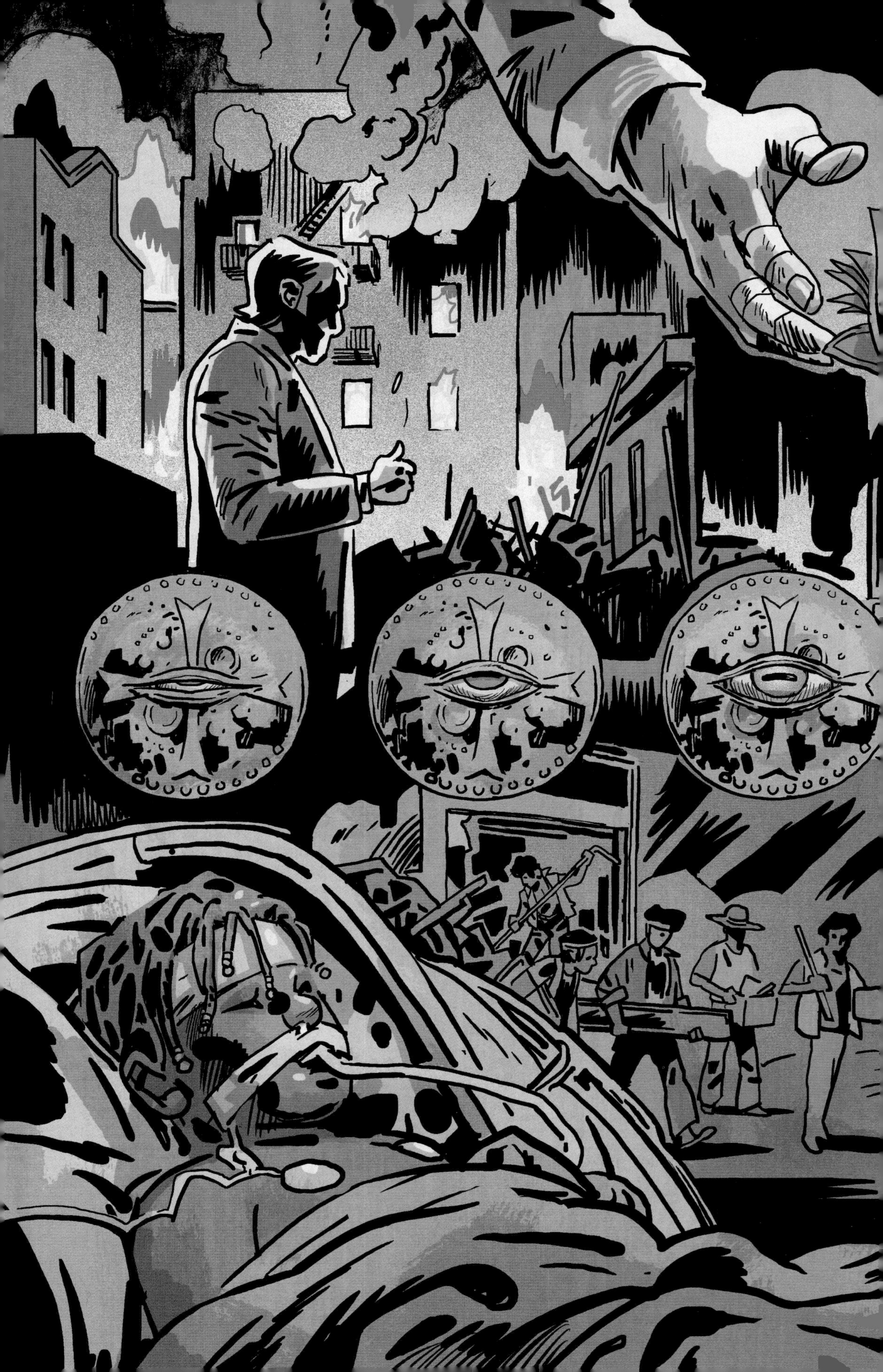

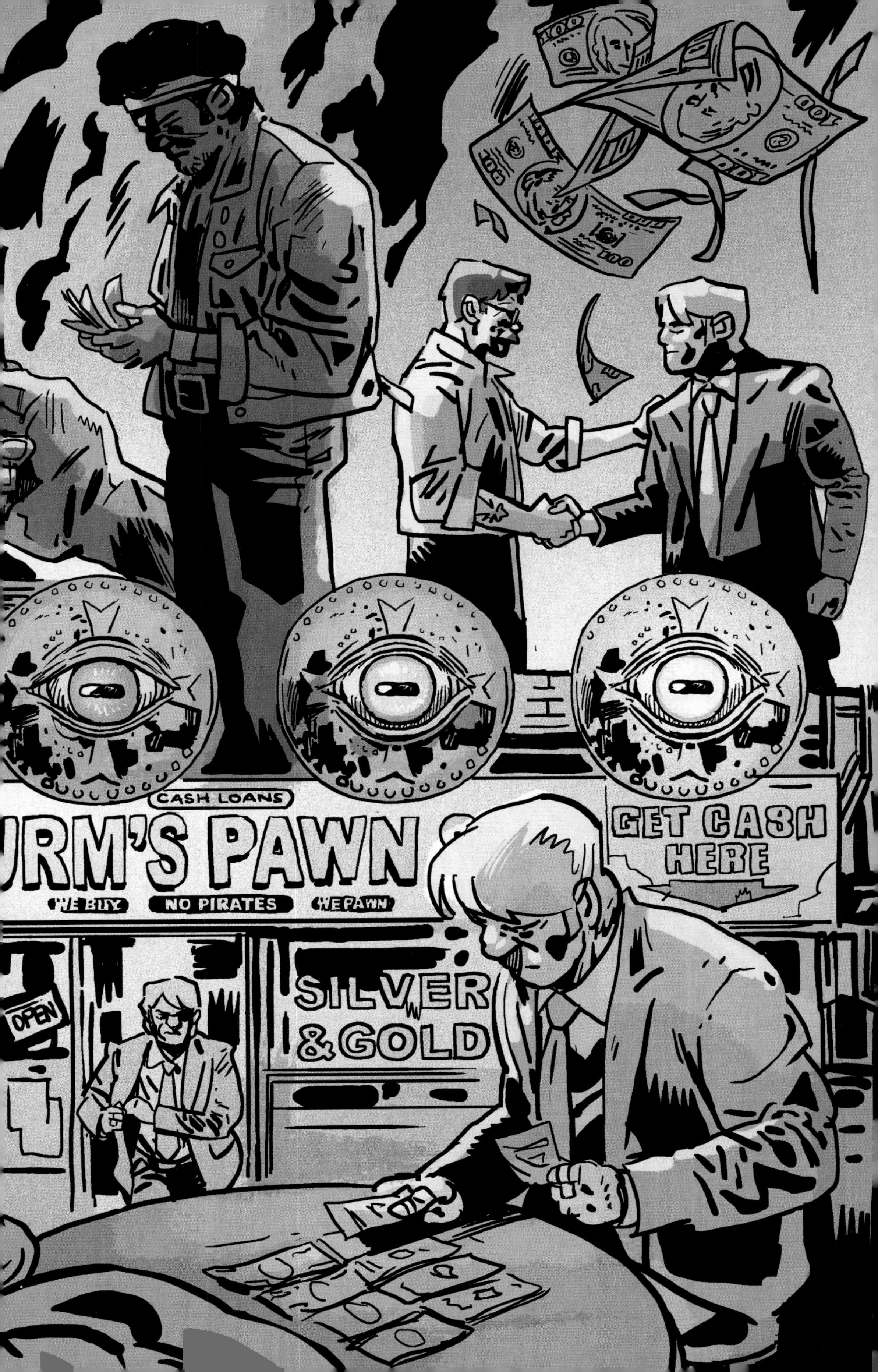

CASH LOANS
URM'S PAWN
WE BUY
NO PIRATES
WE PAWN
GET CASH HERE
OPEN
SILVER &GOLD

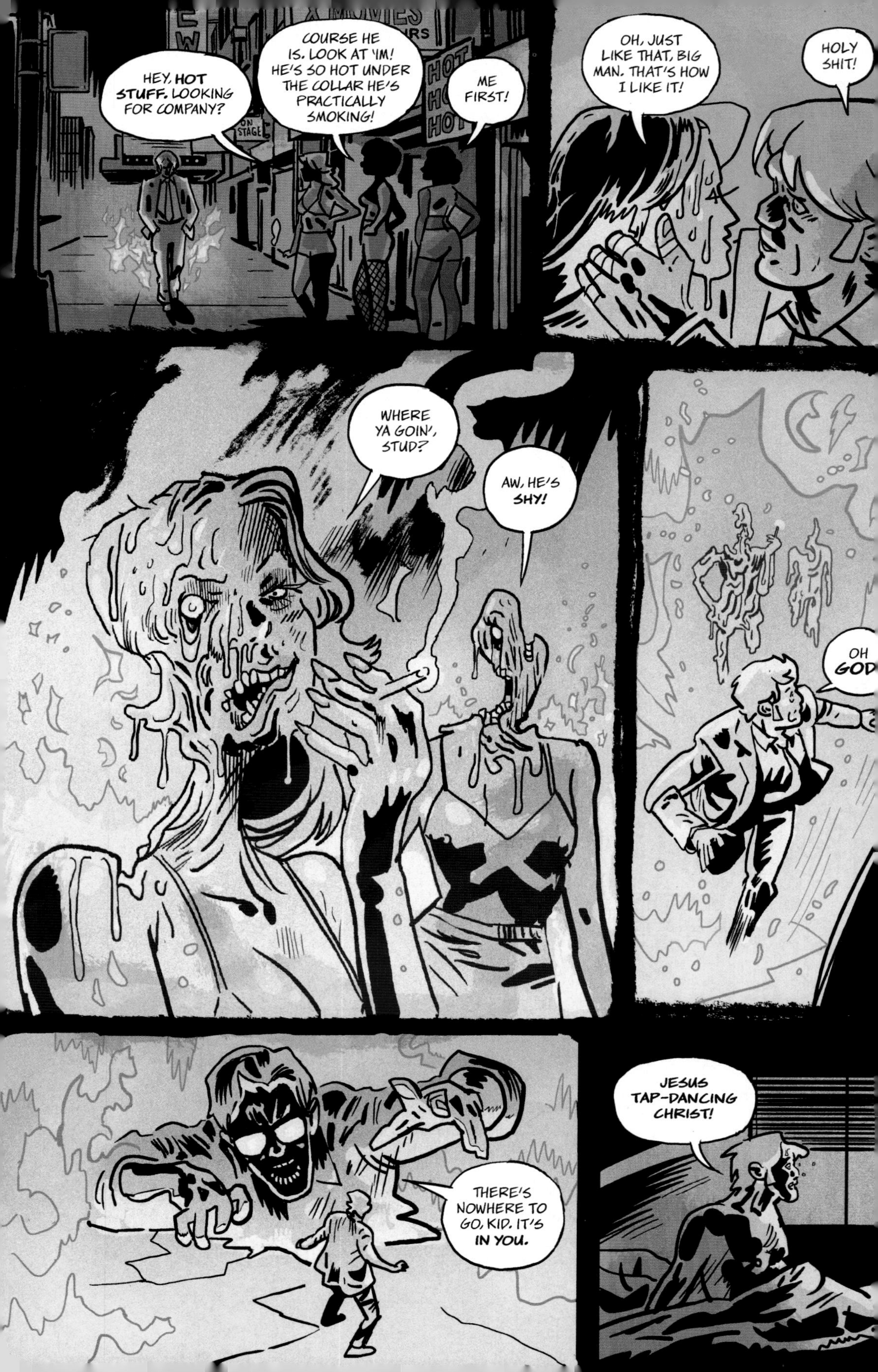
X MOVIES
HOT
ON STAGE
HEY, HOT STUFF. LOOKING FOR COMPANY?
COURSE HE IS. LOOK AT 'IM! HE'S SO HOT UNDER THE COLLAR HE'S PRACTICALLY SMOKING!
ME FIRST!
OH, JUST LIKE THAT, BIG MAN. THAT'S HOW I LIKE IT!
HOLY SHIT!
WHERE YA GOIN', STUD?
AW, HE'S SHY!
OH GOD
THERE'S NOWHERE TO GO, KID. IT'S IN YOU.
JESUS TAP-DANCING CHRIST!

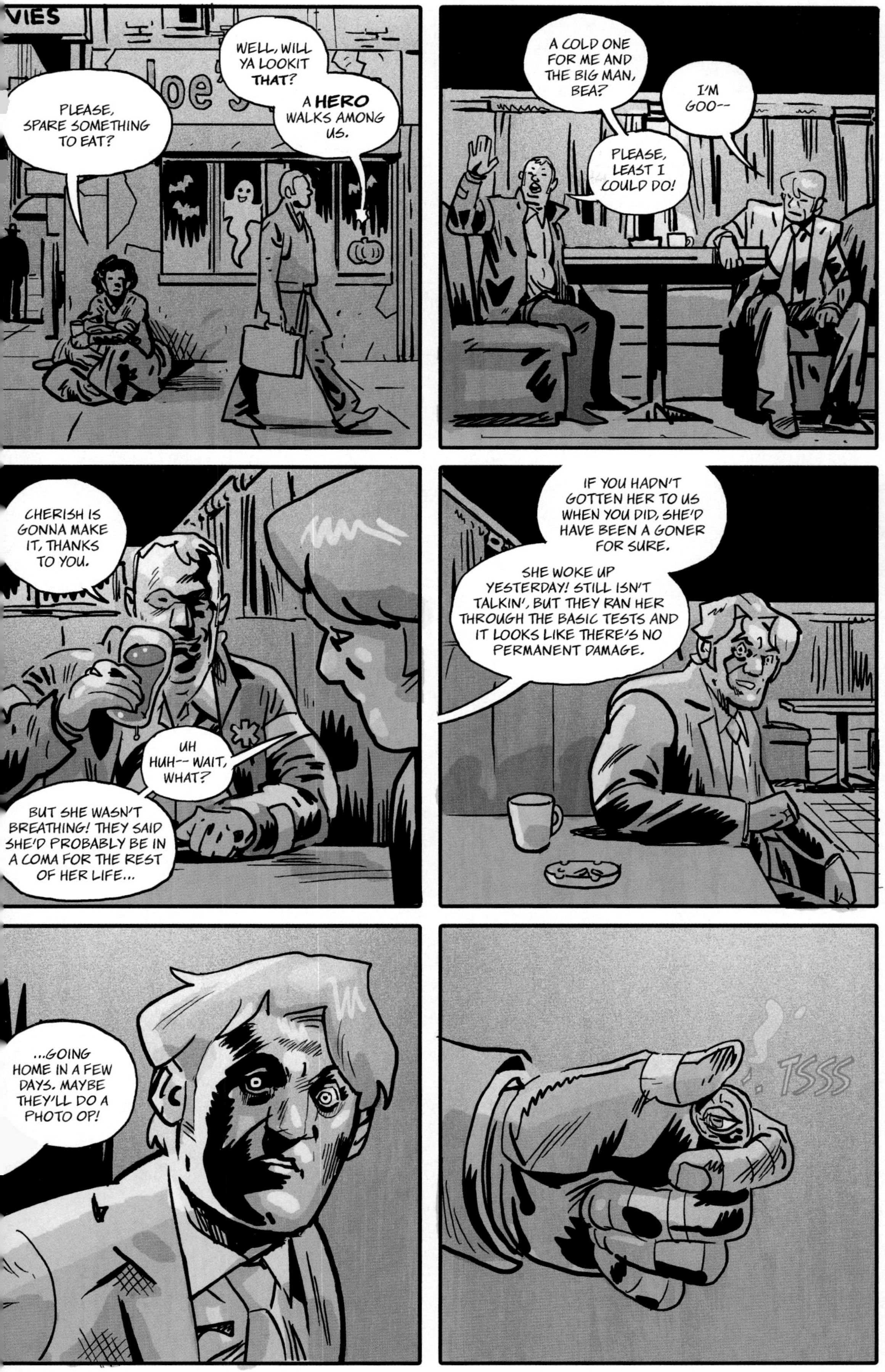
VIES
Joe's
PLEASE, SPARE SOMETHING TO EAT?
WELL, WILL YA LOOKIT THAT?
A HERO WALKS AMONG US.
A COLD ONE FOR ME AND THE BIG MAN, BEA?
I'M GOO--
PLEASE, LEAST I COULD DO!
CHERISH IS GONNA MAKE IT, THANKS TO YOU.
UH HUH-- WAIT, WHAT?
BUT SHE WASN'T BREATHING! THEY SAID SHE'D PROBABLY BE IN A COMA FOR THE REST OF HER LIFE...
IF YOU HADN'T GOTTEN HER TO US WHEN YOU DID, SHE'D HAVE BEEN A GONER FOR SURE.
SHE WOKE UP YESTERDAY! STILL ISN'T TALKIN', BUT THEY RAN HER THROUGH THE BASIC TESTS AND IT LOOKS LIKE THERE'S NO PERMANENT DAMAGE.
...GOING HOME IN A FEW DAYS. MAYBE THEY'LL DO A PHOTO OP!
TSSS

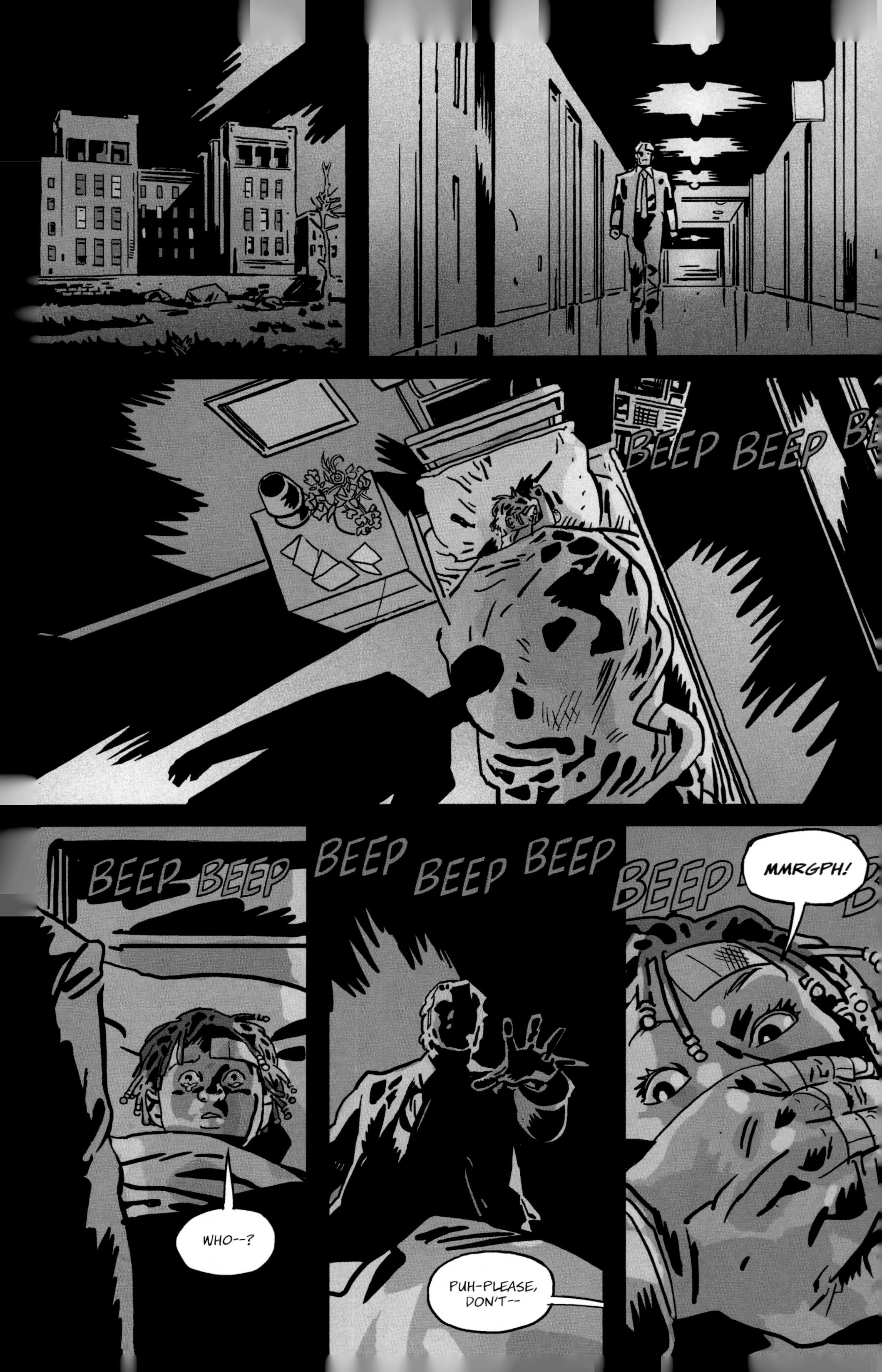
BEEP BEEP
BEEP BEEP
BEEP BEEP BEEP
WHO--?
PUH-PLEASE, DON'T--
BEEP
MMRGPH!

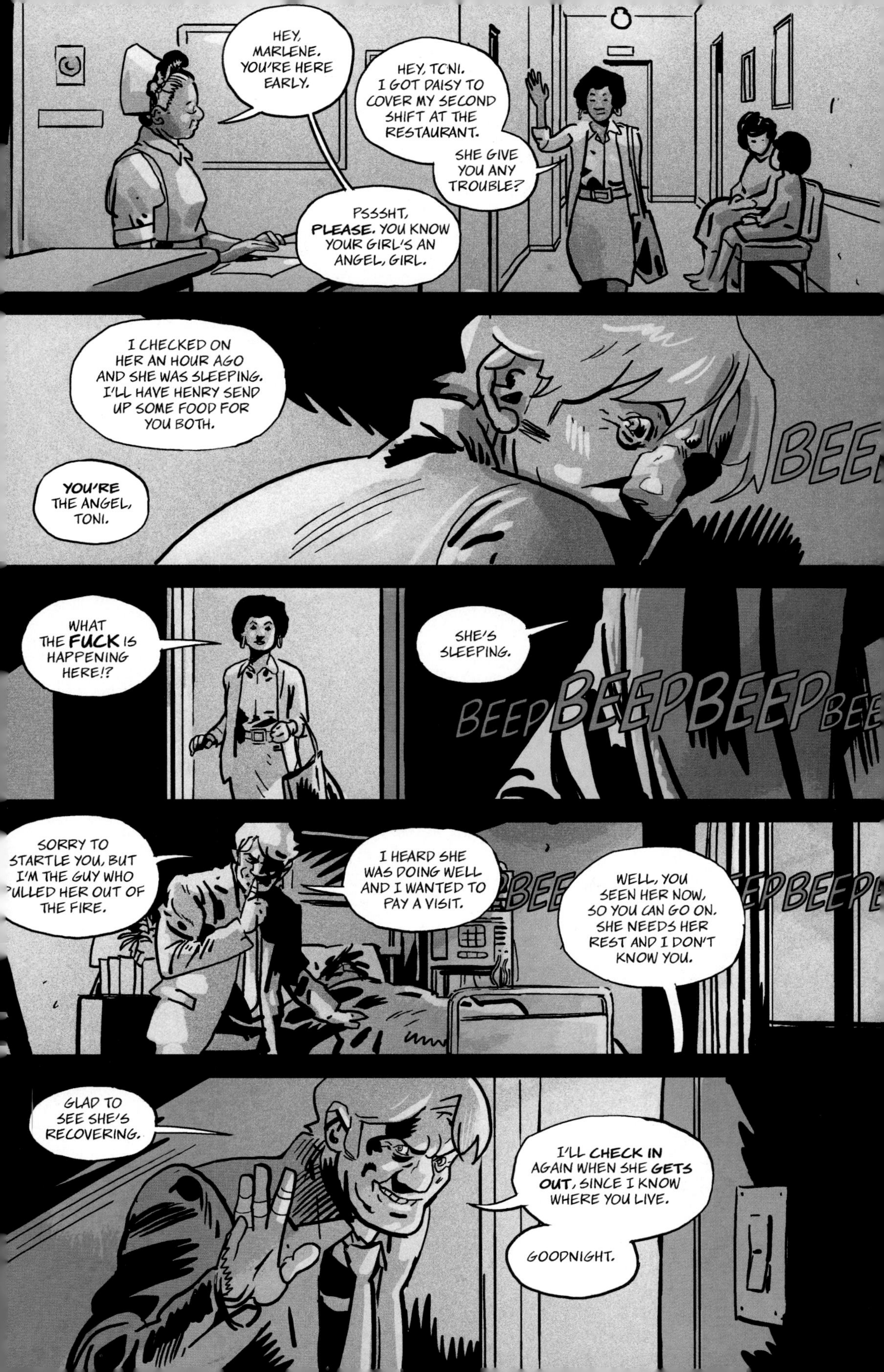
HEY, MARLENE. YOU'RE HERE EARLY.
HEY, TONI. I GOT DAISY TO COVER MY SECOND SHIFT AT THE RESTAURANT.
SHE GIVE YOU ANY TROUBLE?
PSSSHT, PLEASE. YOU KNOW YOUR GIRL'S AN ANGEL, GIRL.
I CHECKED ON HER AN HOUR AGO AND SHE WAS SLEEPING. I'LL HAVE HENRY SEND UP SOME FOOD FOR YOU BOTH.
YOU'RE THE ANGEL, TONI.
WHAT THE FUCK IS HAPPENING HERE!?
SHE'S SLEEPING.
BEEPBEEPBEEP
SORRY TO STARTLE YOU, BUT I'M THE GUY WHO PULLED HER OUT OF THE FIRE.
I HEARD SHE WAS DOING WELL AND I WANTED TO PAY A VISIT.
WELL, YOU SEEN HER NOW, SO YOU CAN GO ON. SHE NEEDS HER REST AND I DON'T KNOW YOU.
GLAD TO SEE SHE'S RECOVERING.
I'LL CHECK IN AGAIN WHEN SHE GETS OUT, SINCE I KNOW WHERE YOU LIVE.
GOODNIGHT.

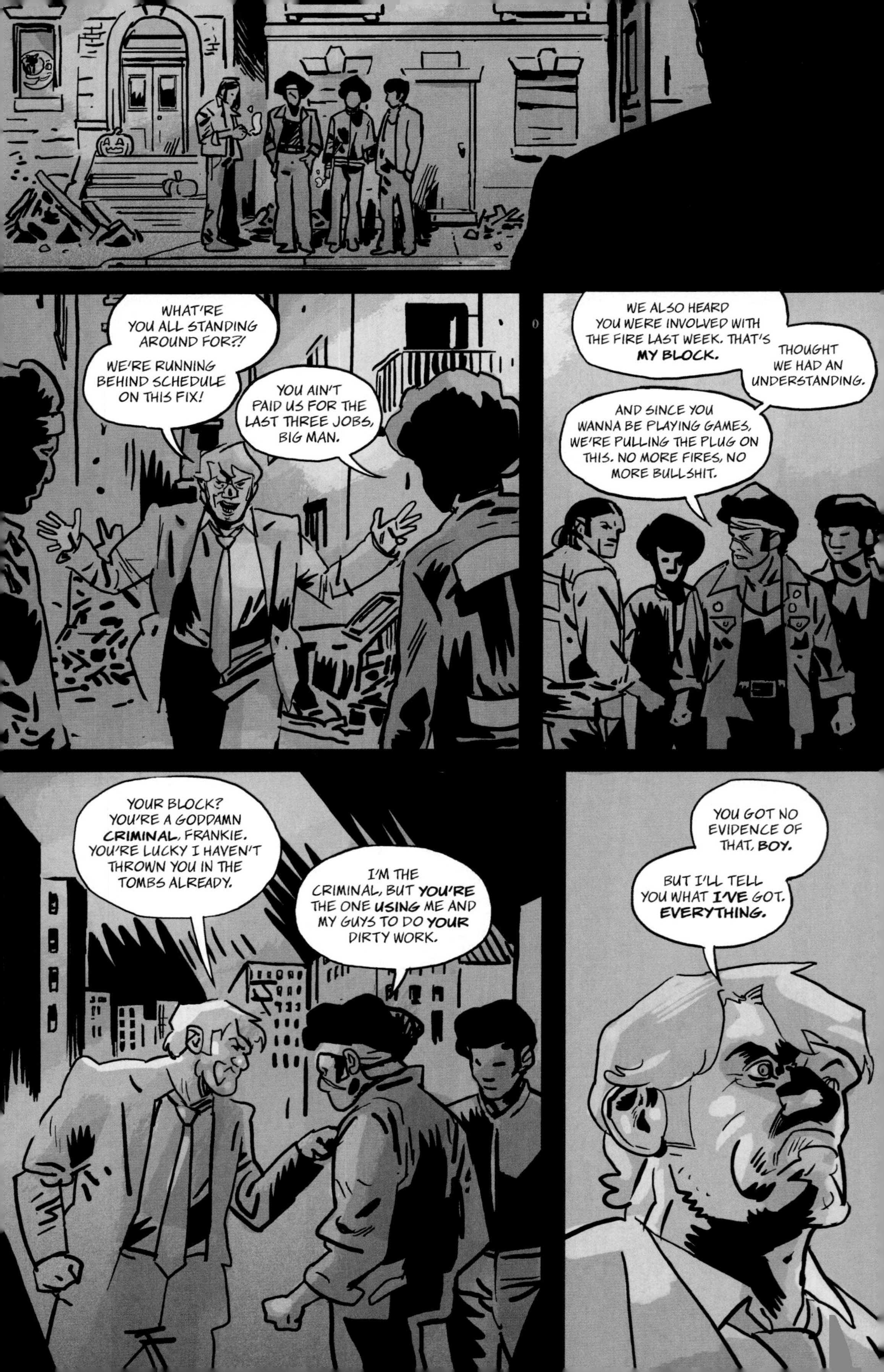
WHAT'RE YOU ALL STANDING AROUND FOR?!
WE'RE RUNNING BEHIND SCHEDULE ON THIS FIX!
YOU AIN'T PAID US FOR THE LAST THREE JOBS, BIG MAN.
WE ALSO HEARD YOU WERE INVOLVED WITH THE FIRE LAST WEEK. THAT'S **MY BLOCK.**
THOUGHT WE HAD AN UNDERSTANDING.
AND SINCE YOU WANNA BE PLAYING GAMES, WE'RE PULLING THE PLUG ON THIS. NO MORE FIRES, NO MORE BULLSHIT.
YOUR BLOCK? YOU'RE A GODDAMN **CRIMINAL**, FRANKIE. YOU'RE LUCKY I HAVEN'T THROWN YOU IN THE TOMBS ALREADY.
I'M THE CRIMINAL, BUT **YOU'RE** THE ONE **USING** ME AND MY GUYS TO DO **YOUR** DIRTY WORK.
YOU GOT NO EVIDENCE OF THAT, **BOY.**
BUT I'LL TELL YOU WHAT **I'VE** GOT. **EVERYTHING.**

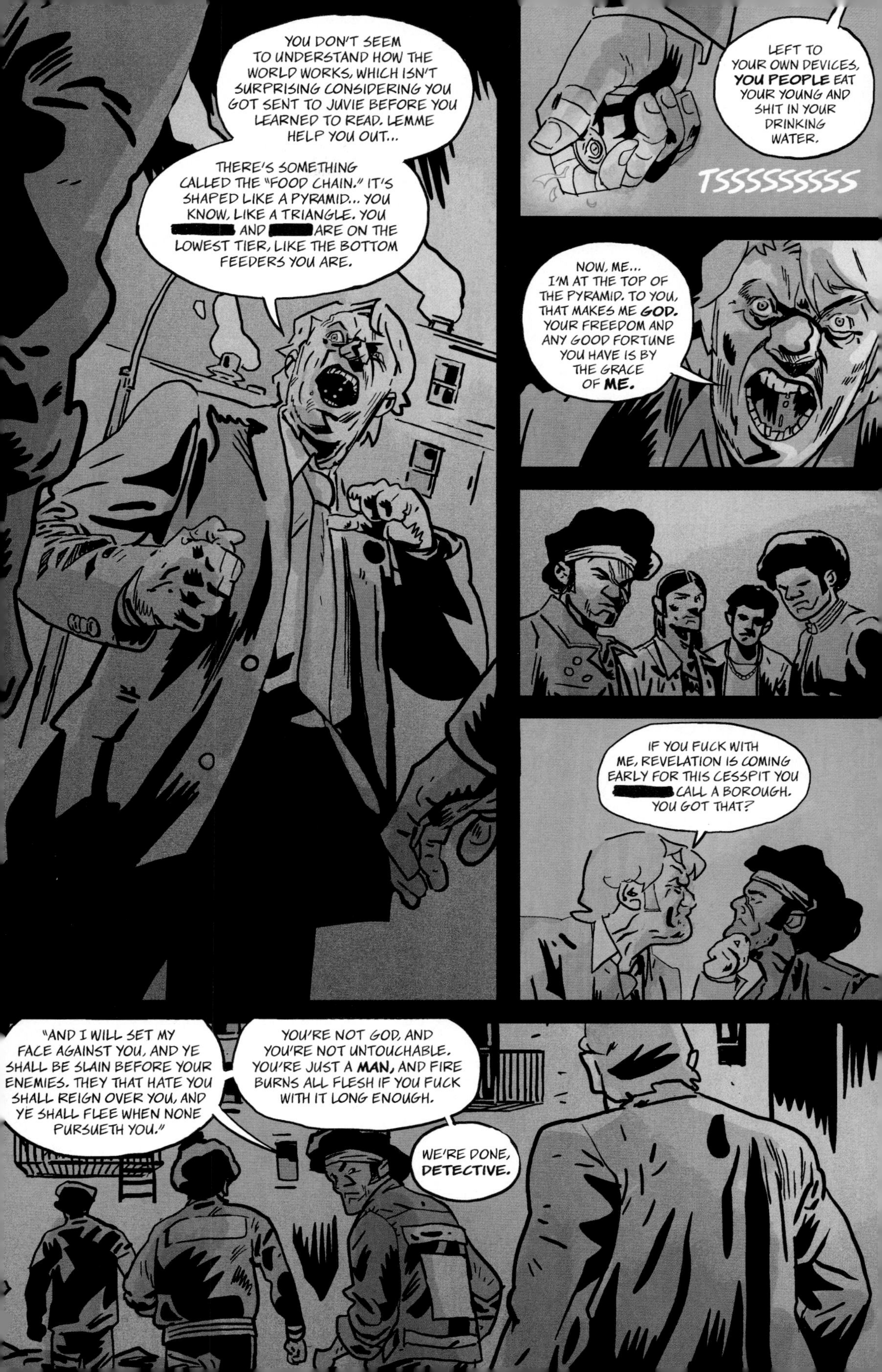

YOU DON'T SEEM TO UNDERSTAND HOW THE WORLD WORKS, WHICH ISN'T SURPRISING CONSIDERING YOU GOT SENT TO JUVIE BEFORE YOU LEARNED TO READ. LEMME HELP YOU OUT...
THERE'S SOMETHING CALLED THE "FOOD CHAIN." IT'S SHAPED LIKE A PYRAMID... YOU KNOW, LIKE A TRIANGLE. YOU [redacted] AND [redacted] ARE ON THE LOWEST TIER, LIKE THE BOTTOM FEEDERS YOU ARE.
LEFT TO YOUR OWN DEVICES, YOU PEOPLE EAT YOUR YOUNG AND SHIT IN YOUR DRINKING WATER.
TSSSSSSSSS
NOW, ME... I'M AT THE TOP OF THE PYRAMID. TO YOU, THAT MAKES ME GOD. YOUR FREEDOM AND ANY GOOD FORTUNE YOU HAVE IS BY THE GRACE OF ME.
IF YOU FUCK WITH ME, REVELATION IS COMING EARLY FOR THIS CESSPIT YOU [redacted] CALL A BOROUGH. YOU GOT THAT?
"AND I WILL SET MY FACE AGAINST YOU, AND YE SHALL BE SLAIN BEFORE YOUR ENEMIES. THEY THAT HATE YOU SHALL REIGN OVER YOU, AND YE SHALL FLEE WHEN NONE PURSUETH YOU."
YOU'RE NOT GOD, AND YOU'RE NOT UNTOUCHABLE. YOU'RE JUST A MAN, AND FIRE BURNS ALL FLESH IF YOU FUCK WITH IT LONG ENOUGH.
WE'RE DONE, DETECTIVE.

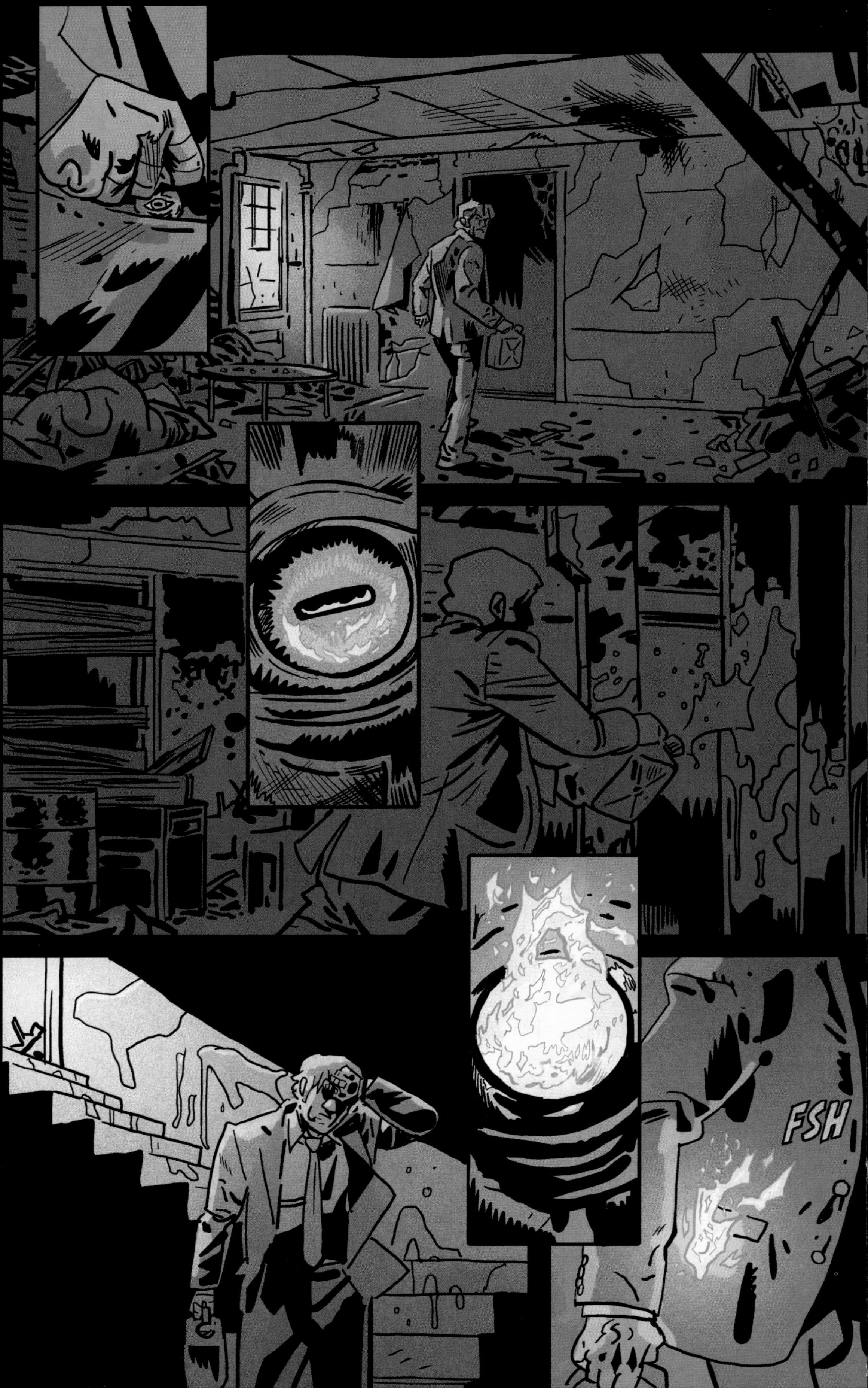
FSH

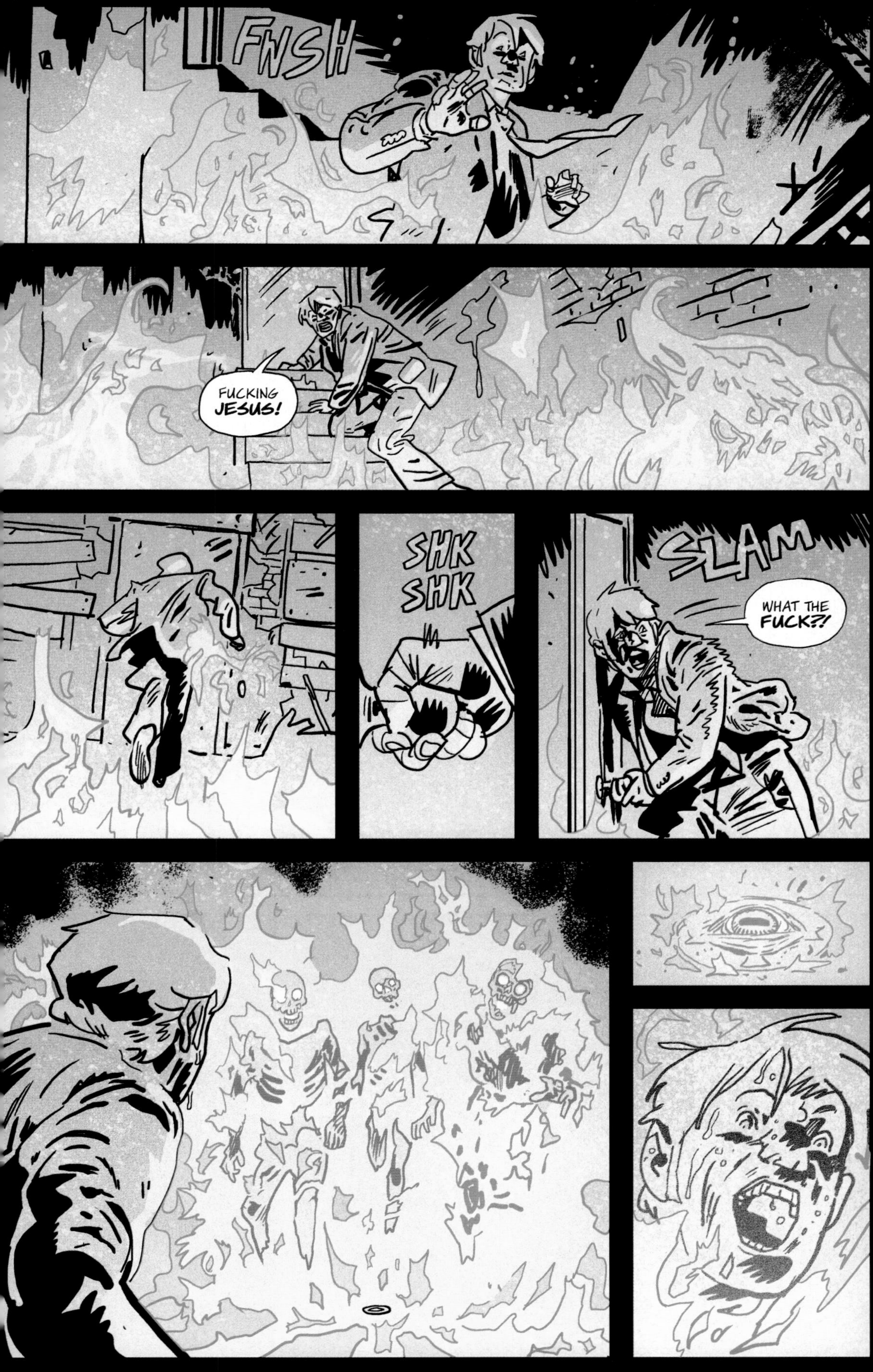
FWSH
FUCKING JESUS!
SHK SHK
SLAM
WHAT THE FUCK?!

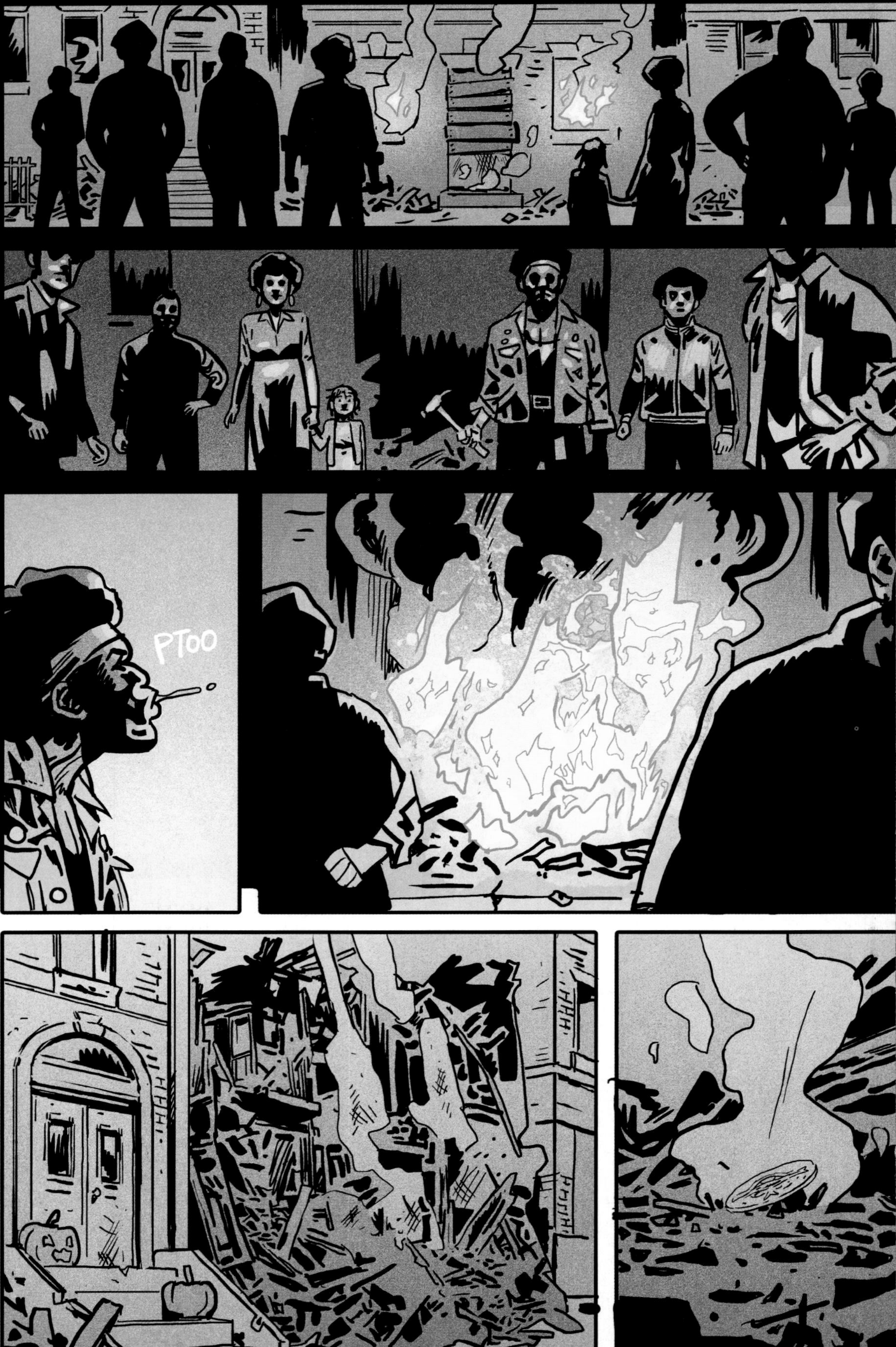
PTOO

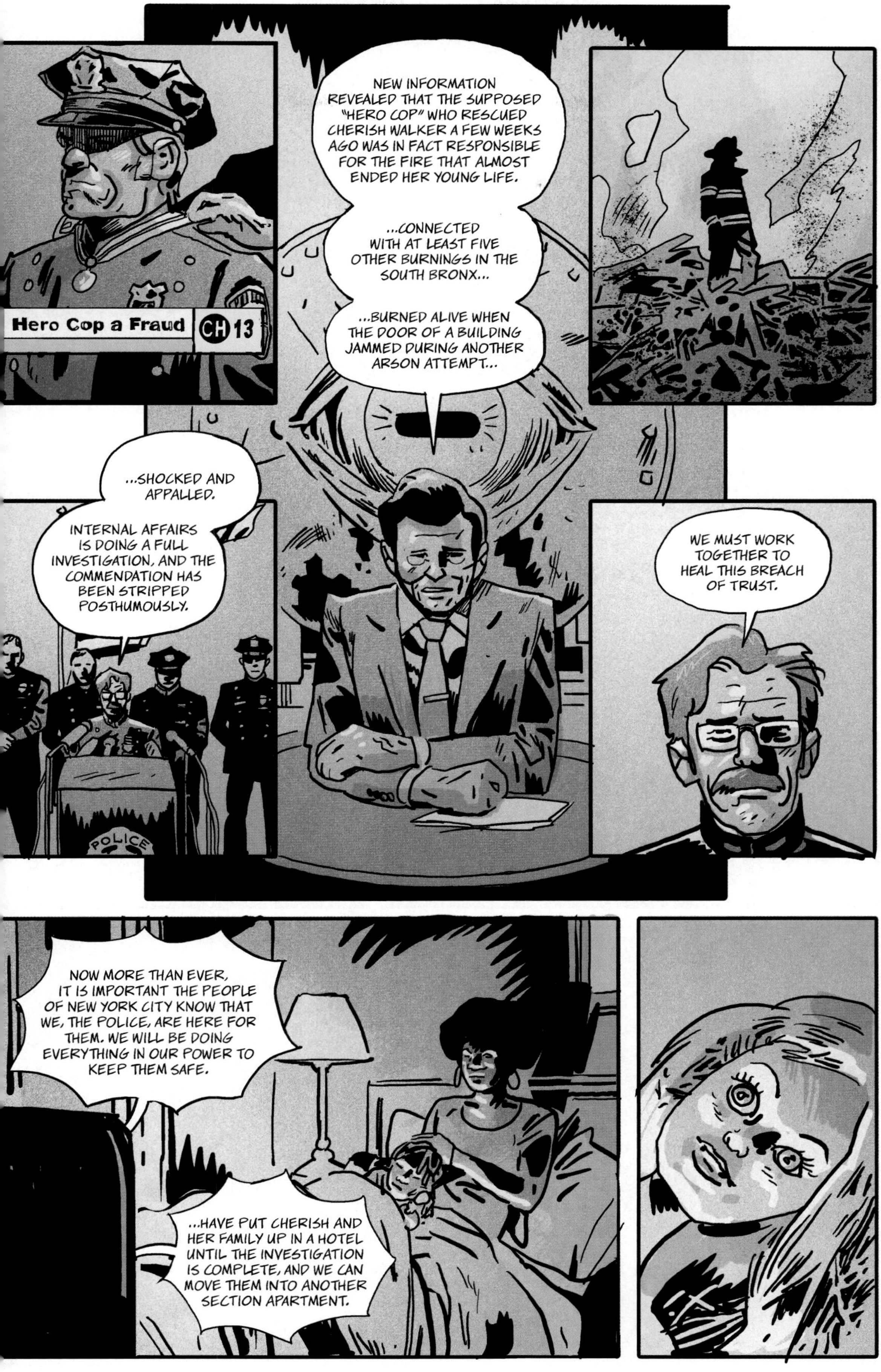

Hero Cop a Fraud
CH 13
NEW INFORMATION REVEALED THAT THE SUPPOSED "HERO COP" WHO RESCUED CHERISH WALKER A FEW WEEKS AGO WAS IN FACT RESPONSIBLE FOR THE FIRE THAT ALMOST ENDED HER YOUNG LIFE.
...CONNECTED WITH AT LEAST FIVE OTHER BURNINGS IN THE SOUTH BRONX...
...BURNED ALIVE WHEN THE DOOR OF A BUILDING JAMMED DURING ANOTHER ARSON ATTEMPT...
...SHOCKED AND APPALLED.
INTERNAL AFFAIRS IS DOING A FULL INVESTIGATION, AND THE COMMENDATION HAS BEEN STRIPPED POSTHUMOUSLY.
POLICE
WE MUST WORK TOGETHER TO HEAL THIS BREACH OF TRUST.
NOW MORE THAN EVER, IT IS IMPORTANT THE PEOPLE OF NEW YORK CITY KNOW THAT WE, THE POLICE, ARE HERE FOR THEM. WE WILL BE DOING EVERYTHING IN OUR POWER TO KEEP THEM SAFE.
...HAVE PUT CHERISH AND HER FAMILY UP IN A HOTEL UNTIL THE INVESTIGATION IS COMPLETE, AND WE CAN MOVE THEM INTO ANOTHER SECTION APARTMENT.

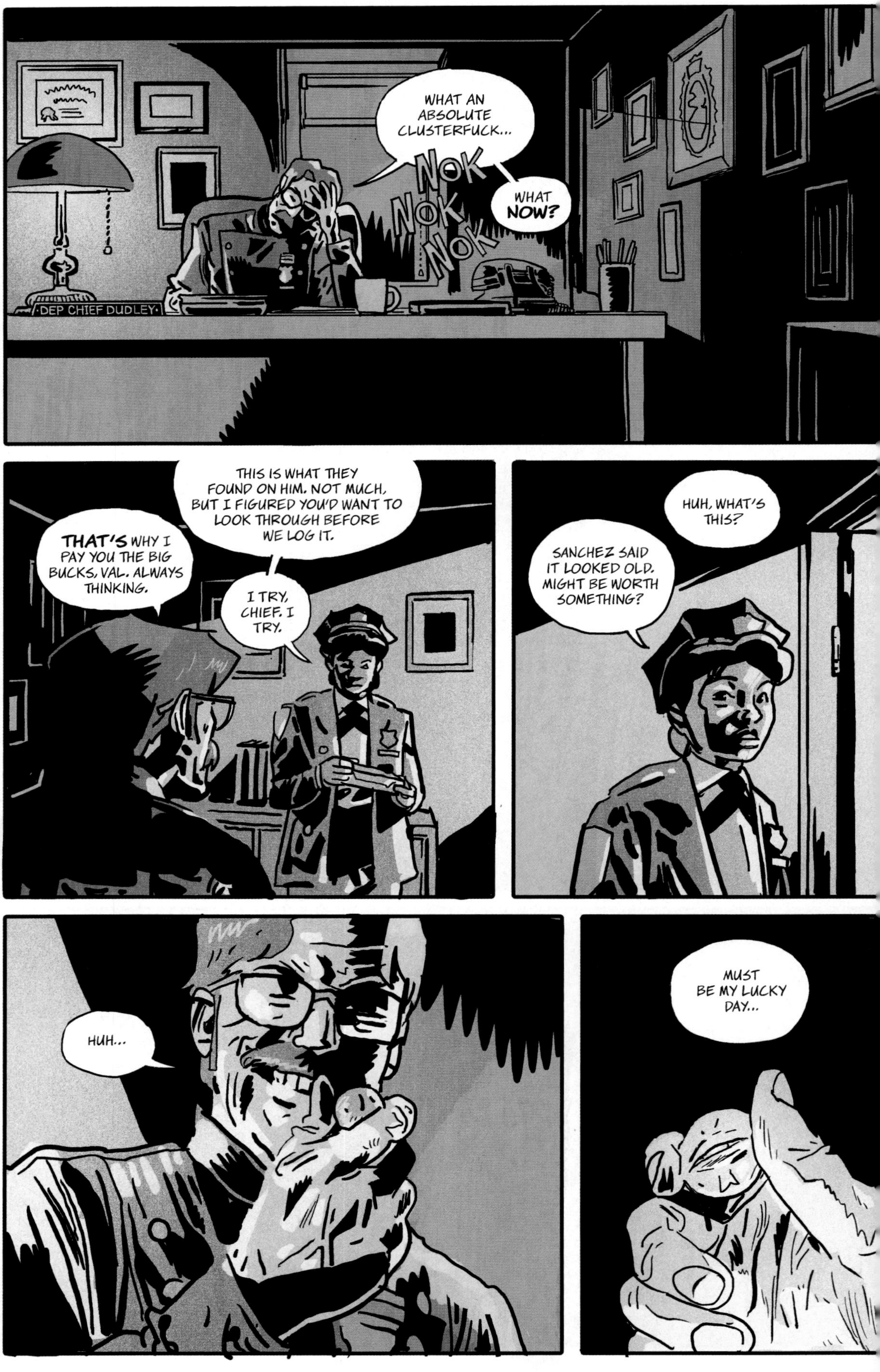
WHAT AN ABSOLUTE CLUSTERFUCK...
NOK NOK NOK
WHAT NOW?
DEP CHIEF DUDLEY
THIS IS WHAT THEY FOUND ON HIM. NOT MUCH, BUT I FIGURED YOU'D WANT TO LOOK THROUGH BEFORE WE LOG IT.
THAT'S WHY I PAY YOU THE BIG BUCKS, VAL. ALWAYS THINKING.
I TRY, CHIEF. I TRY.
HUH, WHAT'S THIS?
SANCHEZ SAID IT LOOKED OLD. MIGHT BE WORTH SOMETHING?
HUH...
MUST BE MY LUCKY DAY...

"THE BRONX IS BURNING."

Though the quote is apocryphal, it is an apt description of New York City in the 1970s.

A combination of plummeting property values (due partially to white flight and harmful government incentive practices) and extremely high unemployment rates, coupled with massive government spending cuts citywide, led to some of the worst urban decay New York had ever seen.

Absentee slumlords took advantage of the lack of resources for city inspection, often allowing their properties to fall into complete ruin.

Honest landlords were driven out, while those who waited to sell their properties found that most of the South Bronx had been redlined by the banks and lost big.

Unable to sell their properties, landlords began to burn their buildings in hopes of collecting the insurance money.

This would lead to the rise of "fixers" — white collar criminals who specialized in an insidious form of insurance fraud. They would buy up properties for pennies on the dollar, then use shell companies to sell and resell, artificially inflating the property value. They would then take out "no questions" fire insurance on the buildings (made possible because budget cuts on local government made it impossible to inspect all the buildings). Then, they'd burn the buildings and collect the cash.

Local street gangs were often conscripted by fixers to help strip buildings of anything of value that could be sold.

Many times, the properties were still inhabited by subsidized residents or squatters when they were "fixed."

Between 1970 and 1980, about 40 percent of the Bronx was abandoned or burned.

With little to no help, the population (mostly Black and Latin) was desperately disenfranchised, left to pick through the ashes in the aftermath.

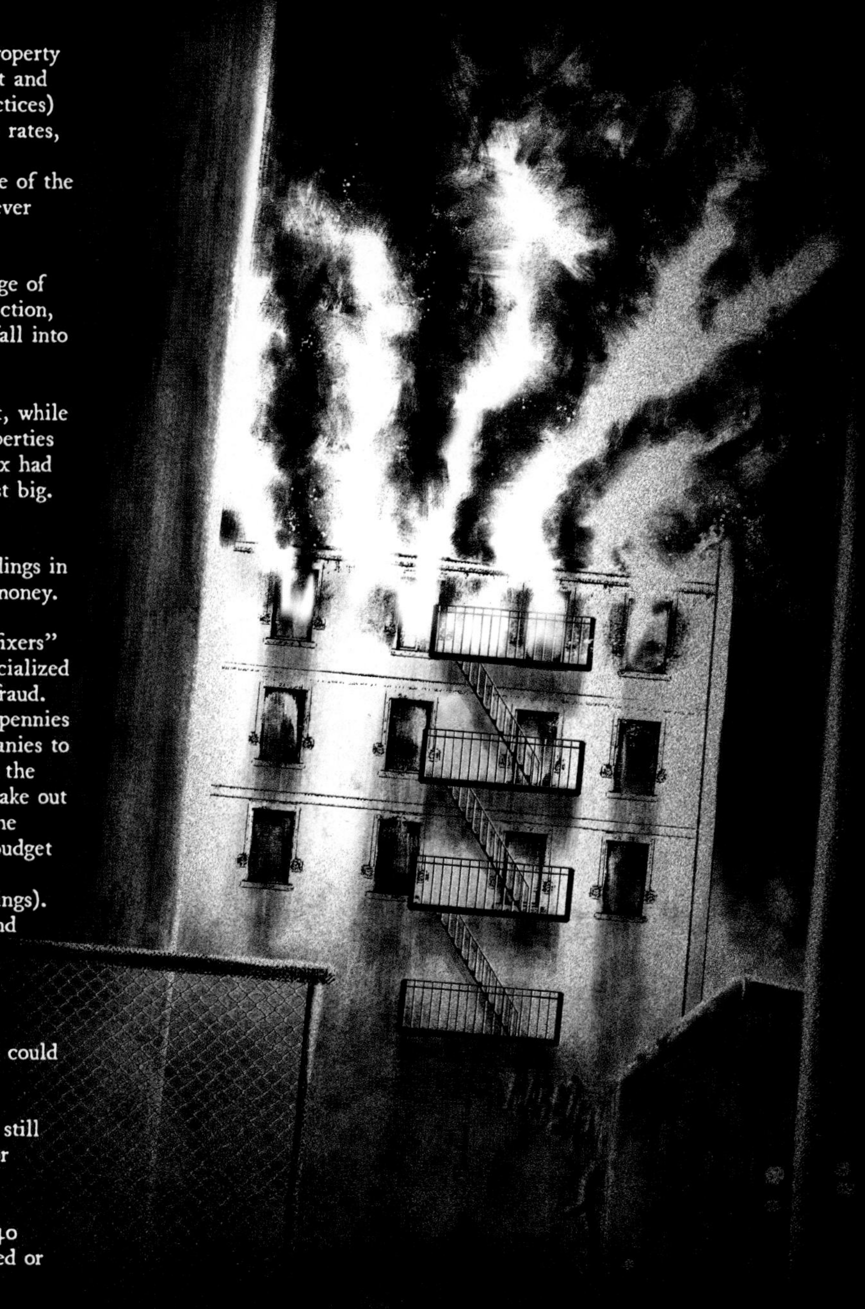

Covenant: Abomination

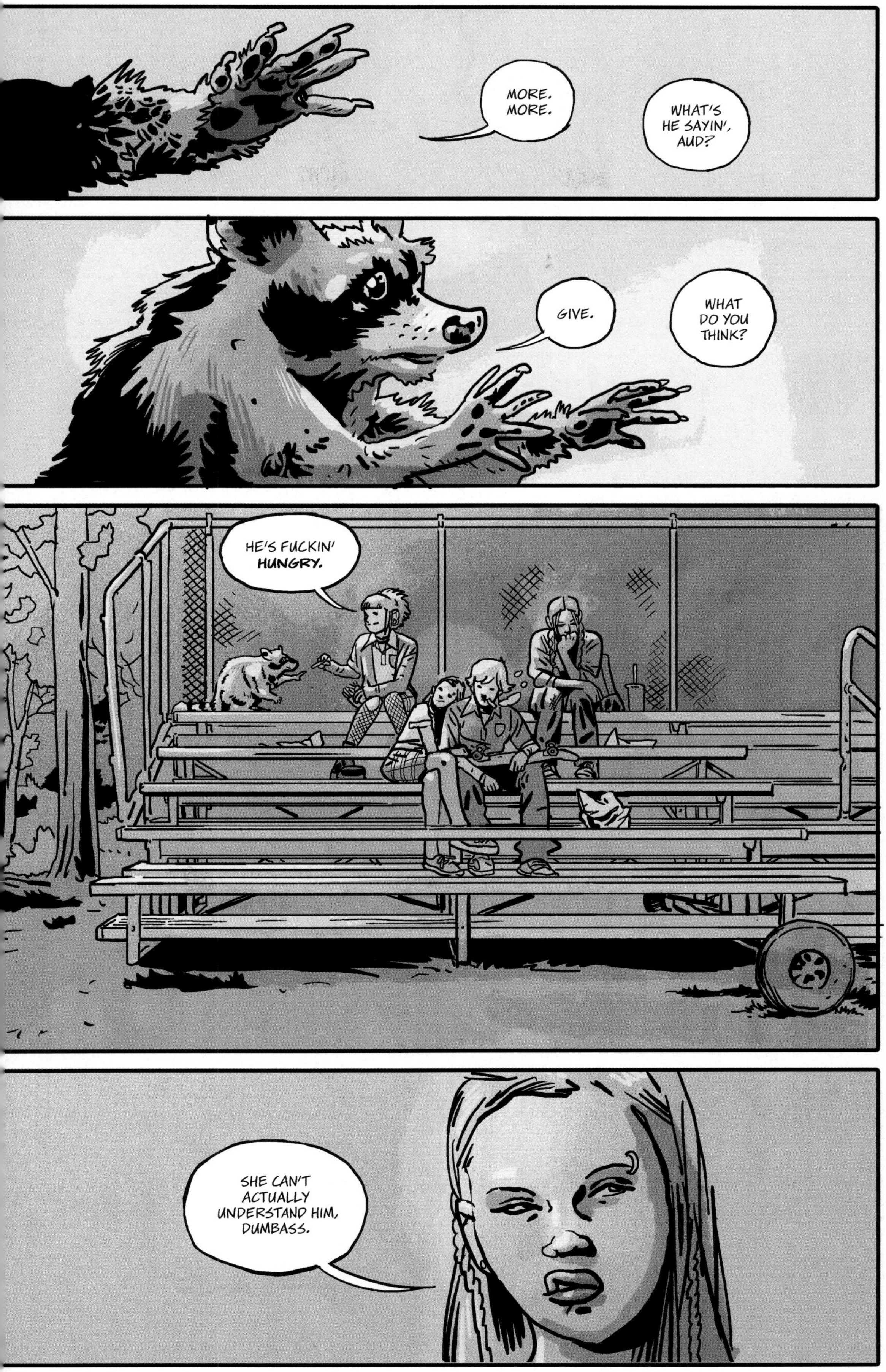
MORE. MORE.
WHAT'S HE SAYIN', AUD?
GIVE.
WHAT DO YOU THINK?
HE'S FUCKIN' **HUNGRY.**
SHE CAN'T ACTUALLY UNDERSTAND HIM, DUMBASS.

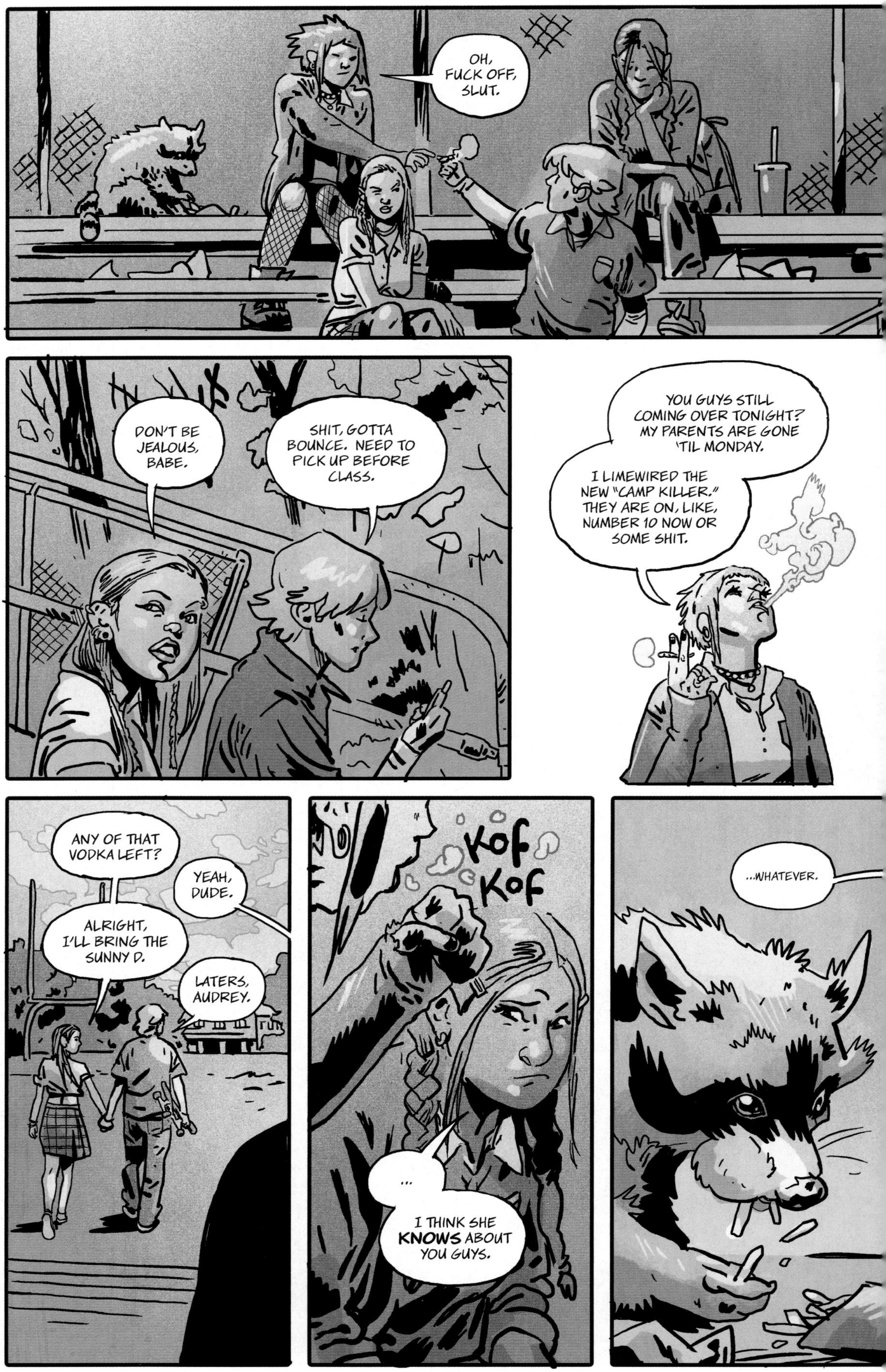
OH, FUCK OFF, SLUT.
DON'T BE JEALOUS, BABE.
SHIT, GOTTA BOUNCE. NEED TO PICK UP BEFORE CLASS.
YOU GUYS STILL COMING OVER TONIGHT? MY PARENTS ARE GONE 'TIL MONDAY.
I LIMEWIRED THE NEW "CAMP KILLER." THEY ARE ON, LIKE, NUMBER 10 NOW OR SOME SHIT.
ANY OF THAT VODKA LEFT?
YEAH, DUDE.
ALRIGHT, I'LL BRING THE SUNNY D.
LATERS, AUDREY.
KOF KOF
...
I THINK SHE **KNOWS** ABOUT YOU GUYS.
...WHATEVER.

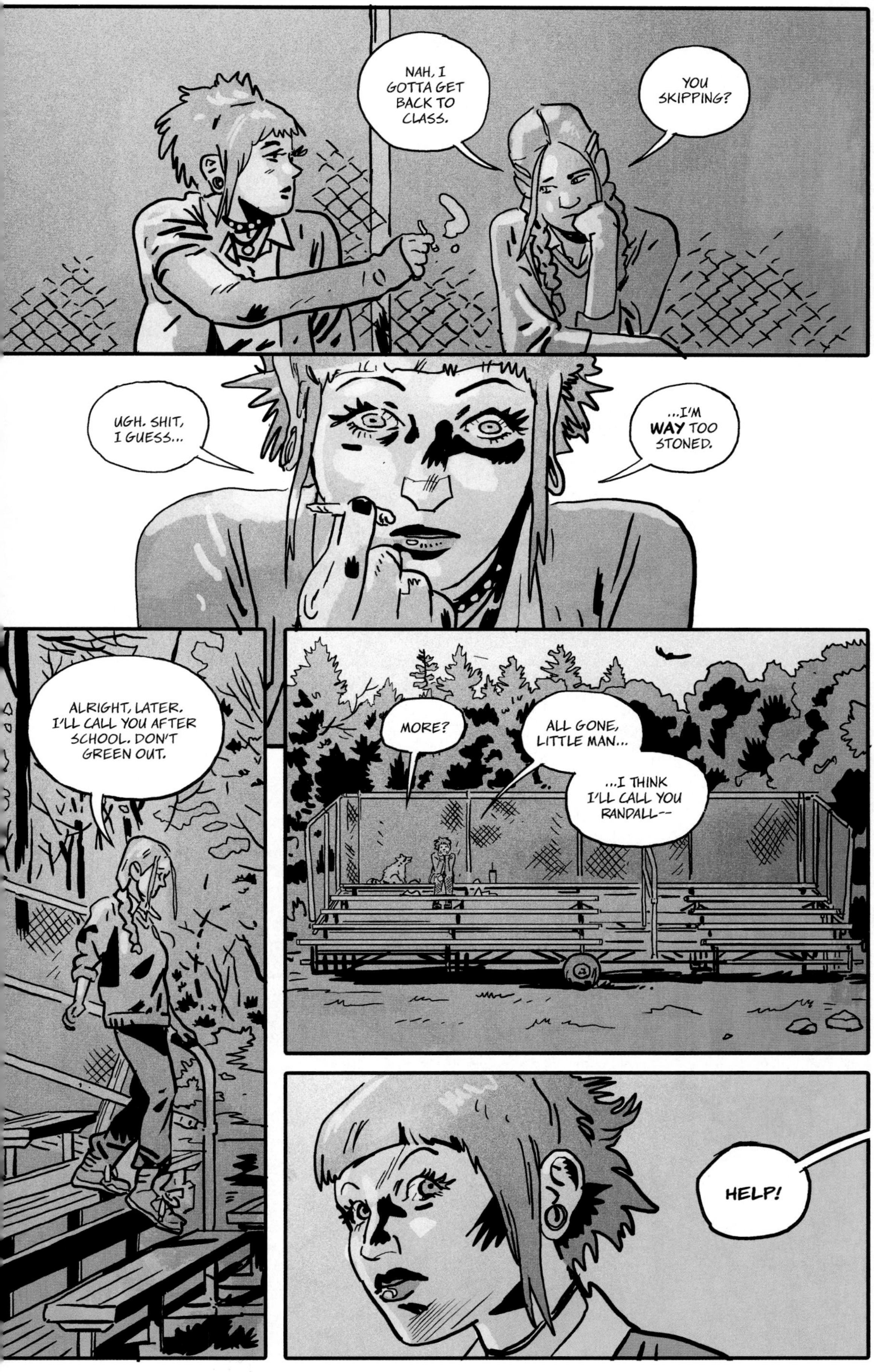
NAH, I GOTTA GET BACK TO CLASS.
YOU SKIPPING?
UGH. SHIT, I GUESS...
...I'M WAY TOO STONED.
ALRIGHT, LATER. I'LL CALL YOU AFTER SCHOOL. DON'T GREEN OUT.
MORE?
ALL GONE, LITTLE MAN...
...I THINK I'LL CALL YOU RANDALL--
HELP!

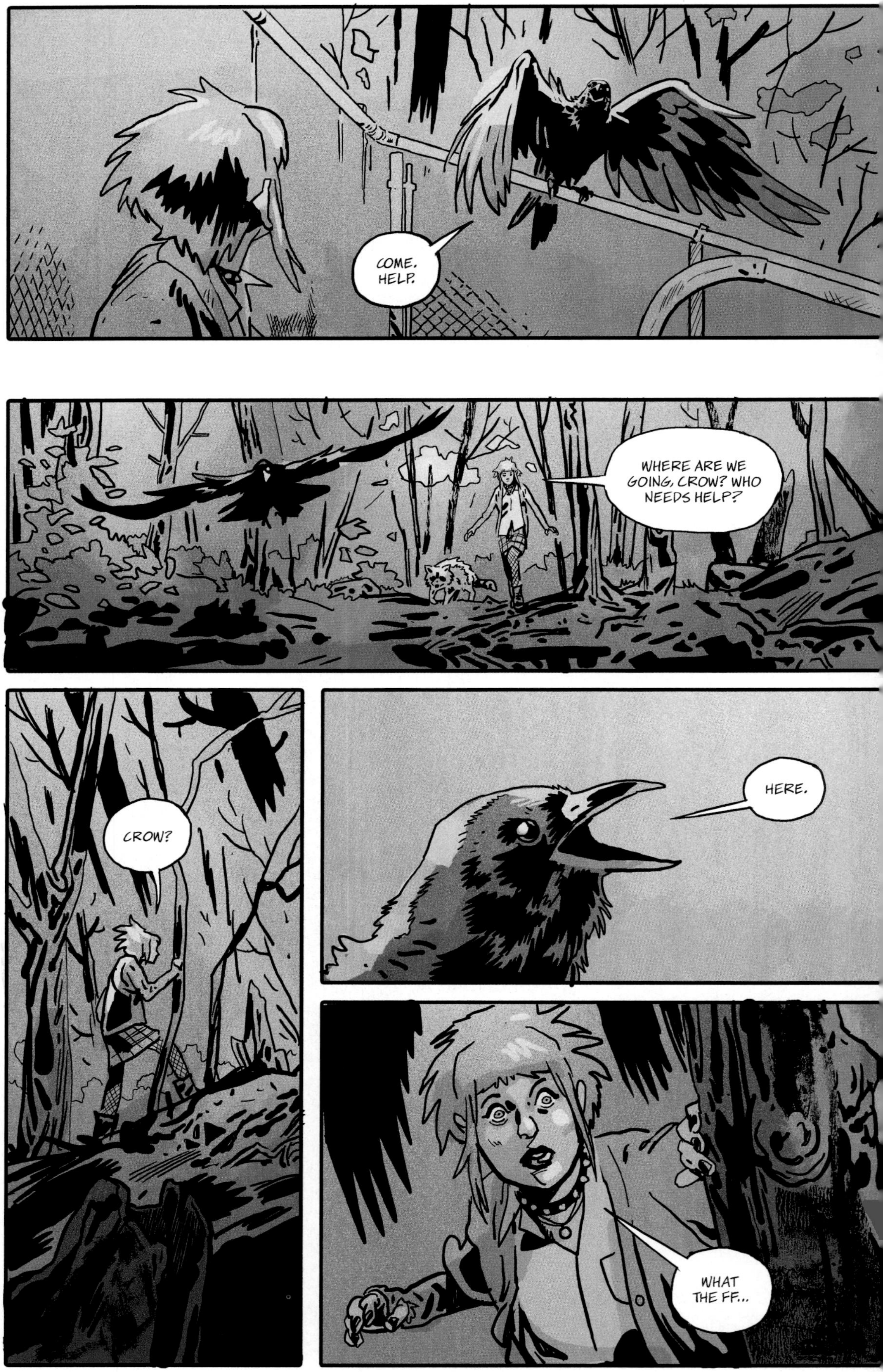
COME. HELP.
WHERE ARE WE GOING, CROW? WHO NEEDS HELP?
CROW?
HERE.
WHAT THE FF...

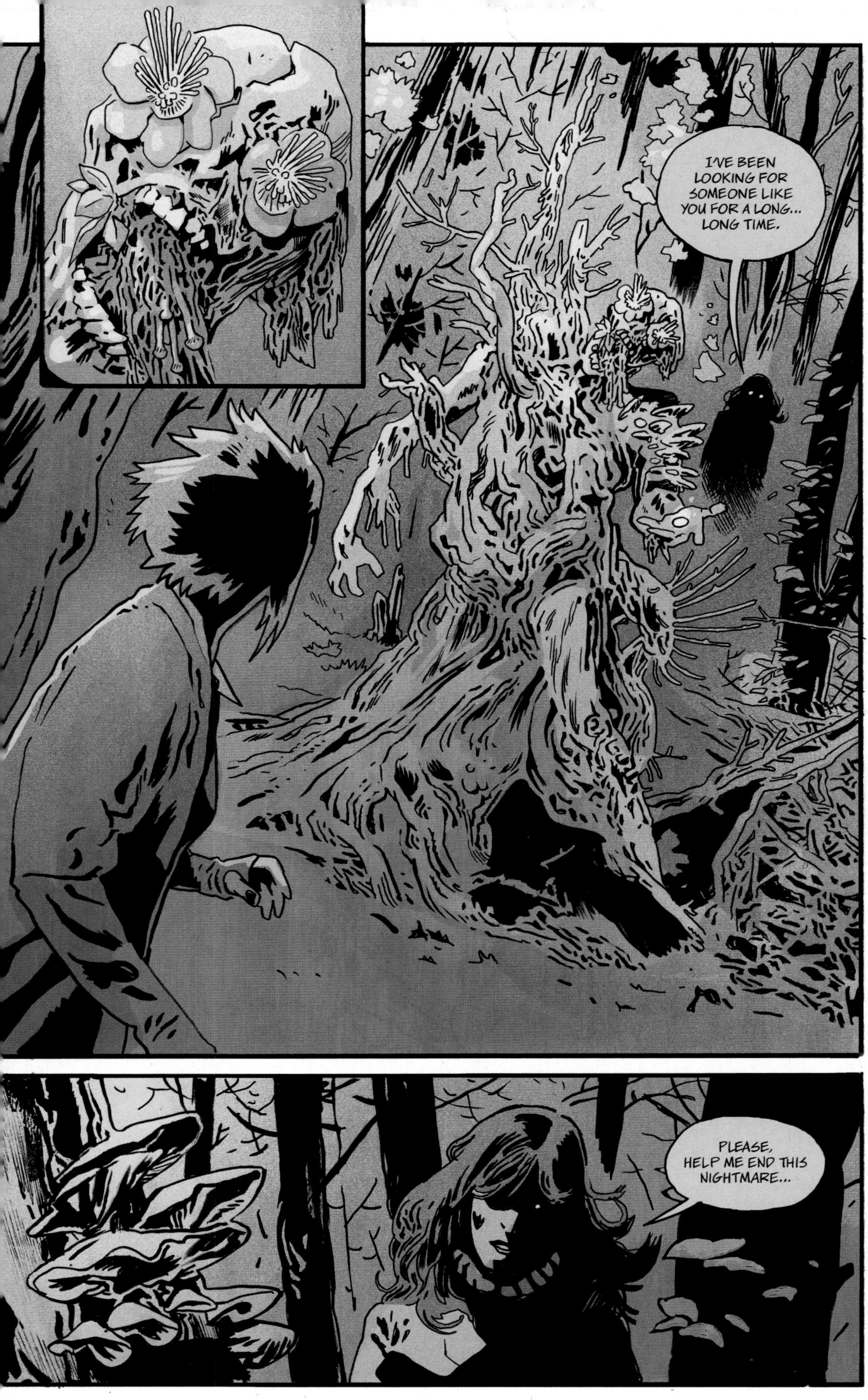
I'VE BEEN LOOKING FOR SOMEONE LIKE YOU FOR A LONG... LONG TIME.
PLEASE, HELP ME END THIS NIGHTMARE...

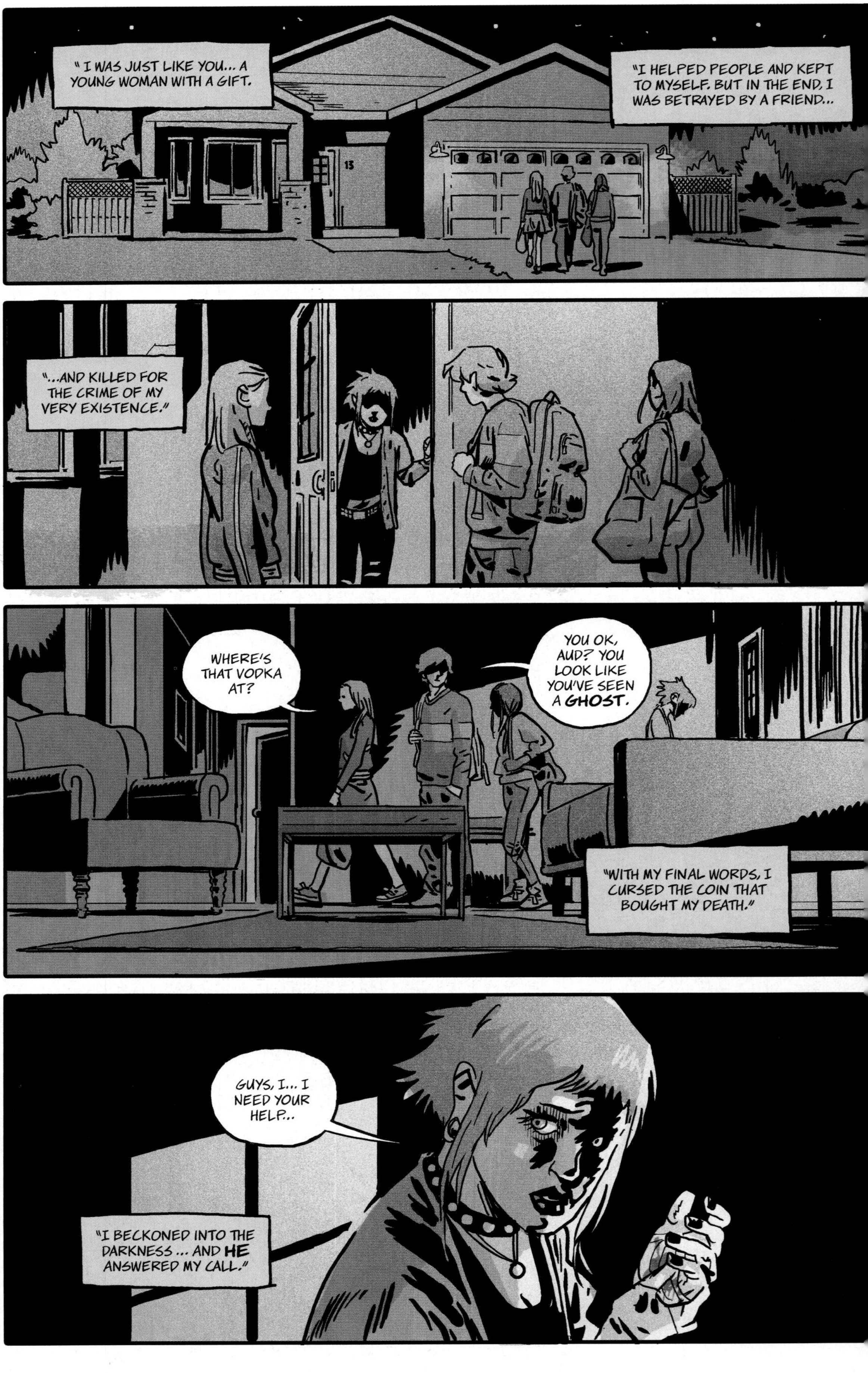
"I WAS JUST LIKE YOU... A YOUNG WOMAN WITH A GIFT.
"I HELPED PEOPLE AND KEPT TO MYSELF. BUT IN THE END, I WAS BETRAYED BY A FRIEND...
13
"...AND KILLED FOR THE CRIME OF MY VERY EXISTENCE."
WHERE'S THAT VODKA AT?
YOU OK, AUD? YOU LOOK LIKE YOU'VE SEEN A GHOST.
"WITH MY FINAL WORDS, I CURSED THE COIN THAT BOUGHT MY DEATH."
GUYS, I... I NEED YOUR HELP...
"I BECKONED INTO THE DARKNESS ... AND HE ANSWERED MY CALL."

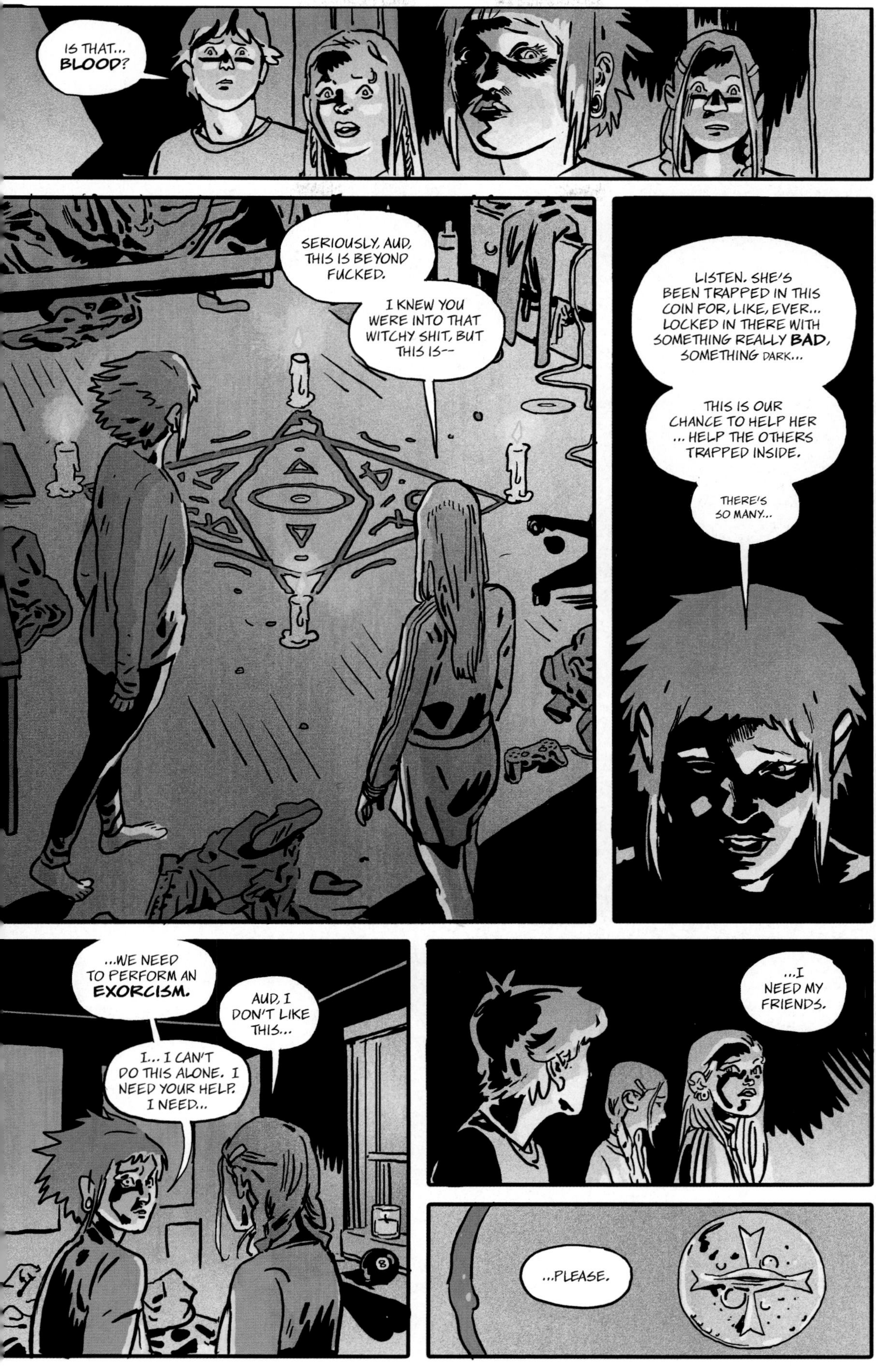
IS THAT... BLOOD?
SERIOUSLY, AUD, THIS IS BEYOND FUCKED.
I KNEW YOU WERE INTO THAT WITCHY SHIT, BUT THIS IS--
LISTEN. SHE'S BEEN TRAPPED IN THIS COIN FOR, LIKE, EVER... LOCKED IN THERE WITH SOMETHING REALLY BAD, SOMETHING DARK...
THIS IS OUR CHANCE TO HELP HER ... HELP THE OTHERS TRAPPED INSIDE.
THERE'S SO MANY...
...WE NEED TO PERFORM AN EXORCISM.
AUD, I DON'T LIKE THIS...
I... I CAN'T DO THIS ALONE. I NEED YOUR HELP. I NEED...
...I NEED MY FRIENDS.
...PLEASE.

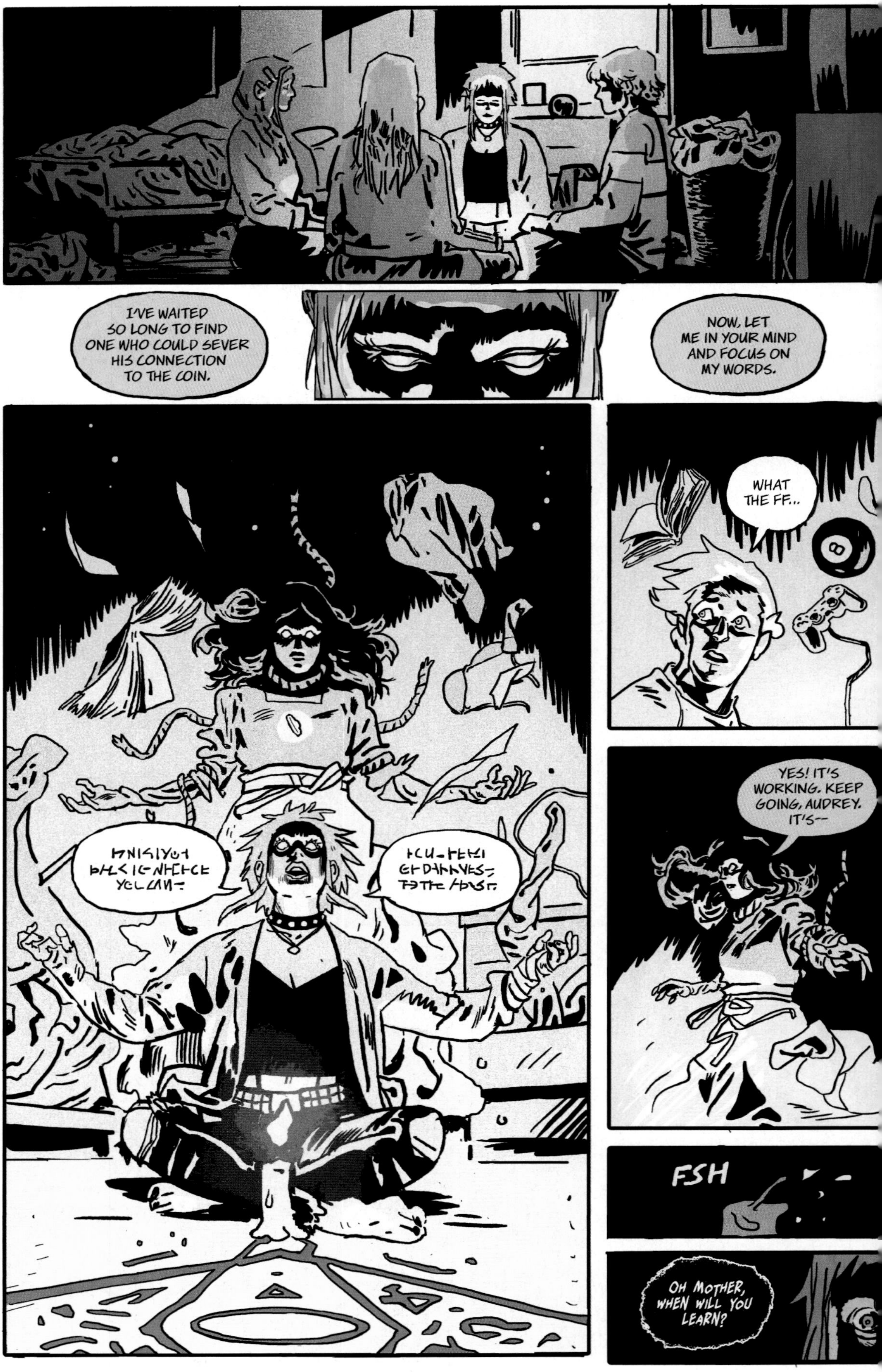
I'VE WAITED SO LONG TO FIND ONE WHO COULD SEVER HIS CONNECTION TO THE COIN.
NOW, LET ME IN YOUR MIND AND FOCUS ON MY WORDS.
WHAT THE FF...
YES! IT'S WORKING. KEEP GOING, AUDREY. IT'S--
FSH
OH MOTHER, WHEN WILL YOU LEARN?

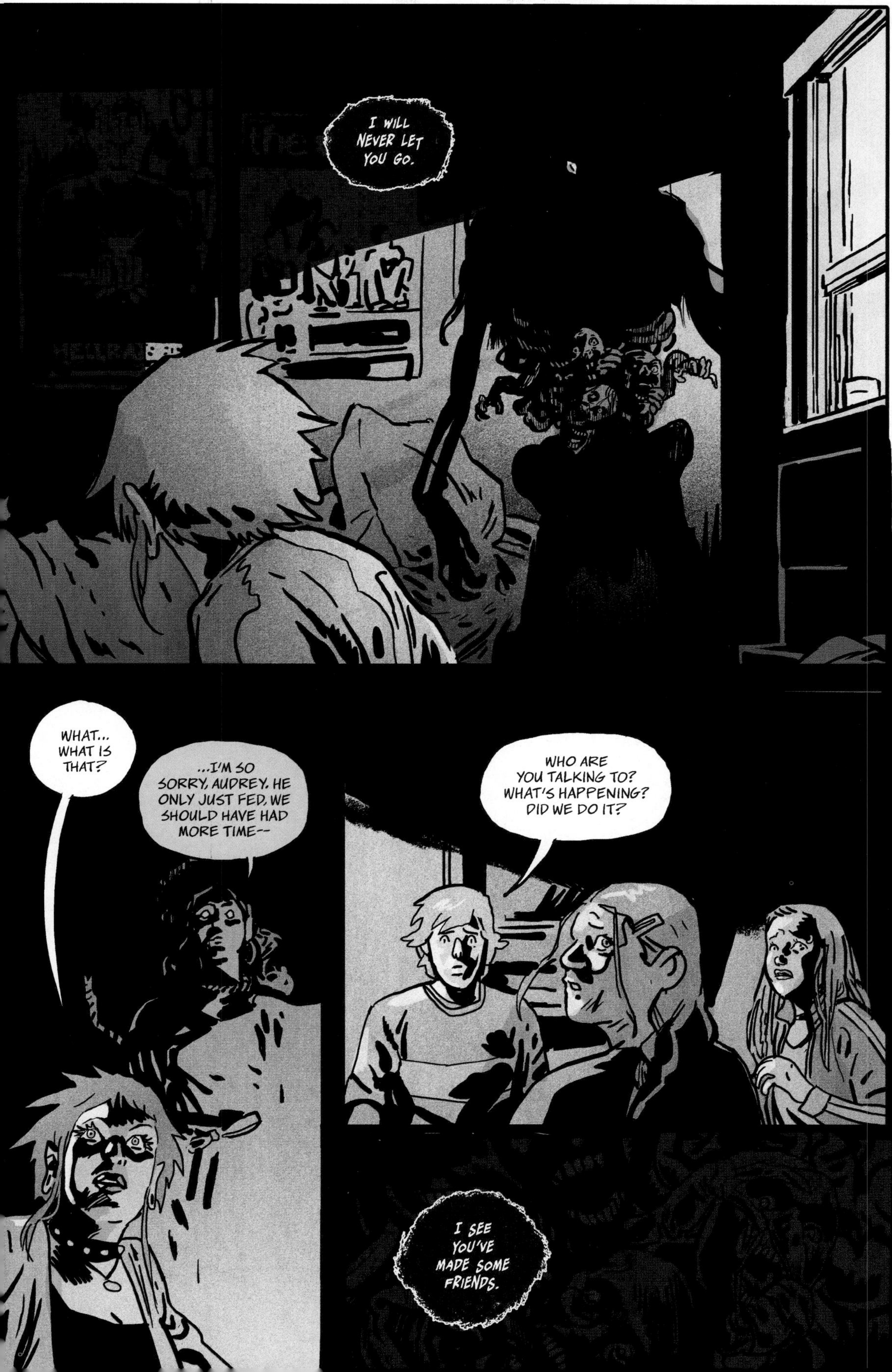
I WILL NEVER LET YOU GO.
WHAT... WHAT IS THAT?
...I'M SO SORRY, AUDREY. HE ONLY JUST FED, WE SHOULD HAVE HAD MORE TIME--
WHO ARE YOU TALKING TO? WHAT'S HAPPENING? DID WE DO IT?
I SEE YOU'VE MADE SOME FRIENDS.

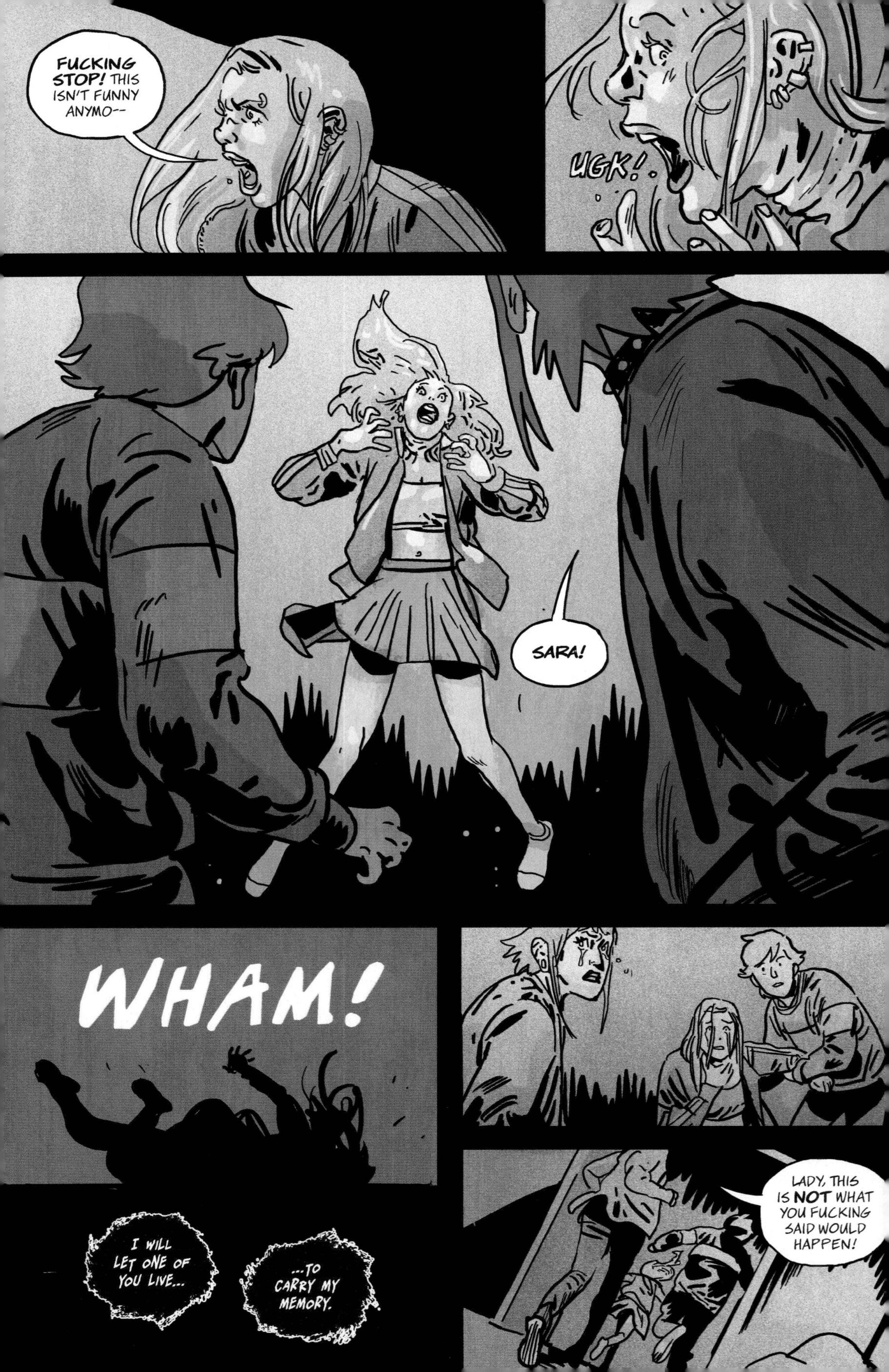

FUCKING STOP! THIS ISN'T FUNNY ANYMO--
UGK!
SARA!
WHAM!
I WILL LET ONE OF YOU LIVE...
...TO CARRY MY MEMORY.
LADY, THIS IS NOT WHAT YOU FUCKING SAID WOULD HAPPEN!

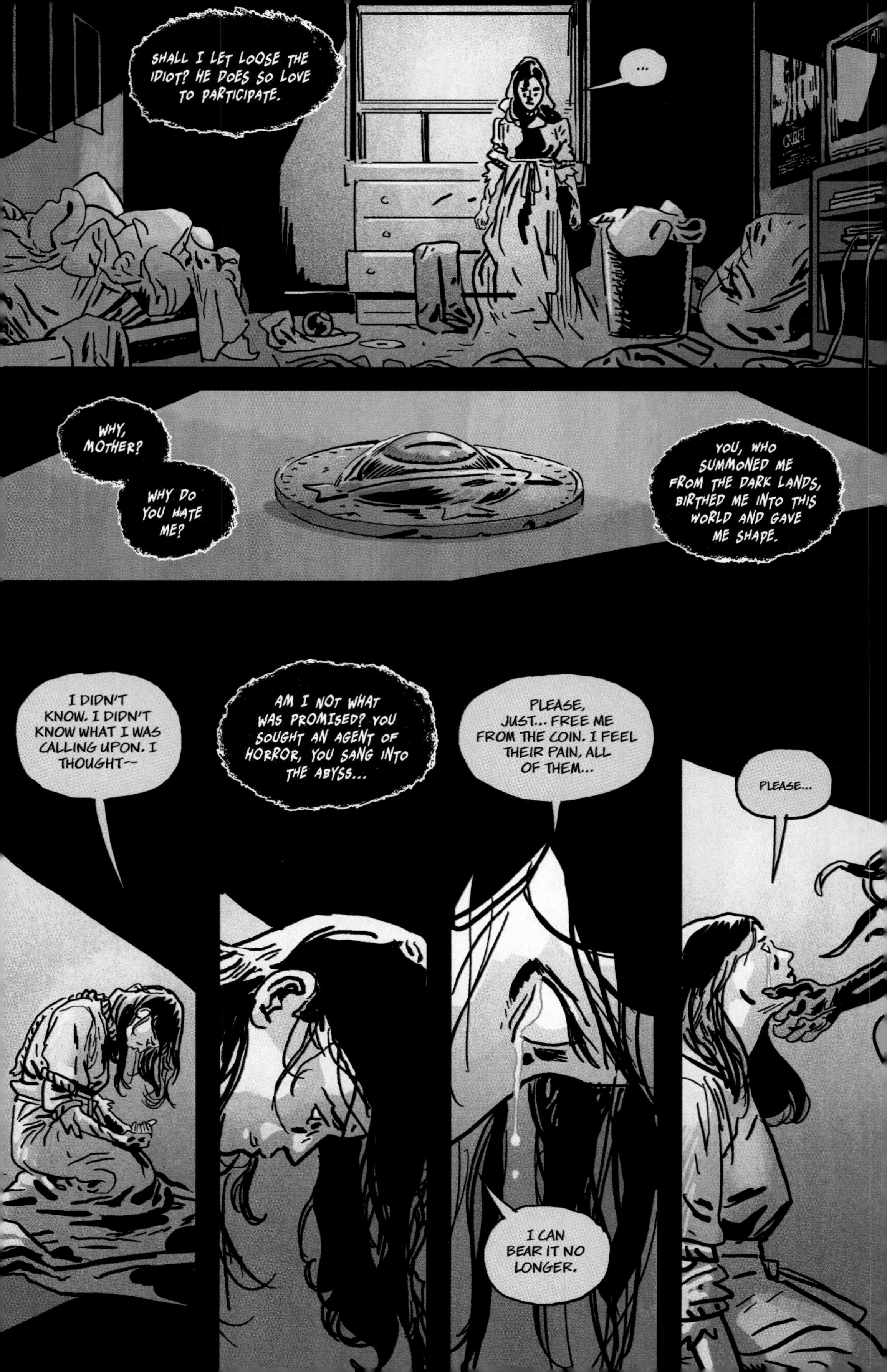

SHALL I LET LOOSE THE IDIOT? HE DOES SO LOVE TO PARTICIPATE.
...
WHY, MOTHER?
WHY DO YOU HATE ME?
YOU, WHO SUMMONED ME FROM THE DARK LANDS, BIRTHED ME INTO THIS WORLD AND GAVE ME SHAPE.
I DIDN'T KNOW. I DIDN'T KNOW WHAT I WAS CALLING UPON. I THOUGHT--
AM I NOT WHAT WAS PROMISED? YOU SOUGHT AN AGENT OF HORROR, YOU SANG INTO THE ABYSS...
PLEASE, JUST... FREE ME FROM THE COIN. I FEEL THEIR PAIN, ALL OF THEM...
I CAN BEAR IT NO LONGER.
PLEASE...

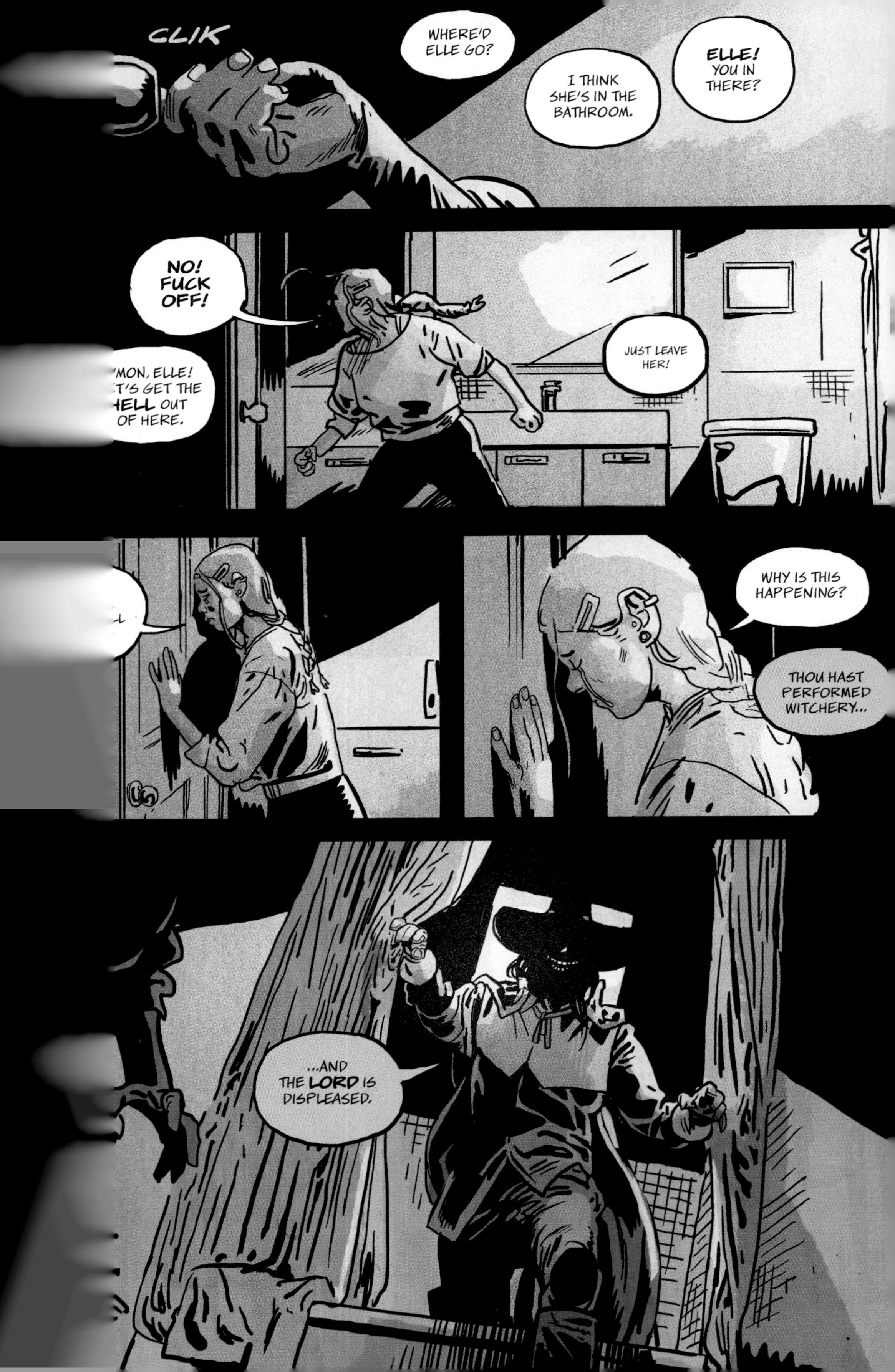
CLIK
WHERE'D ELLE GO?
I THINK SHE'S IN THE BATHROOM.
ELLE! YOU IN THERE?
NO! FUCK OFF!
'MON, ELLE! T'S GET THE HELL OUT OF HERE.
JUST LEAVE HER!
WHY IS THIS HAPPENING?
THOU HAST PERFORMED WITCHERY...
...AND THE LORD IS DISPLEASED.

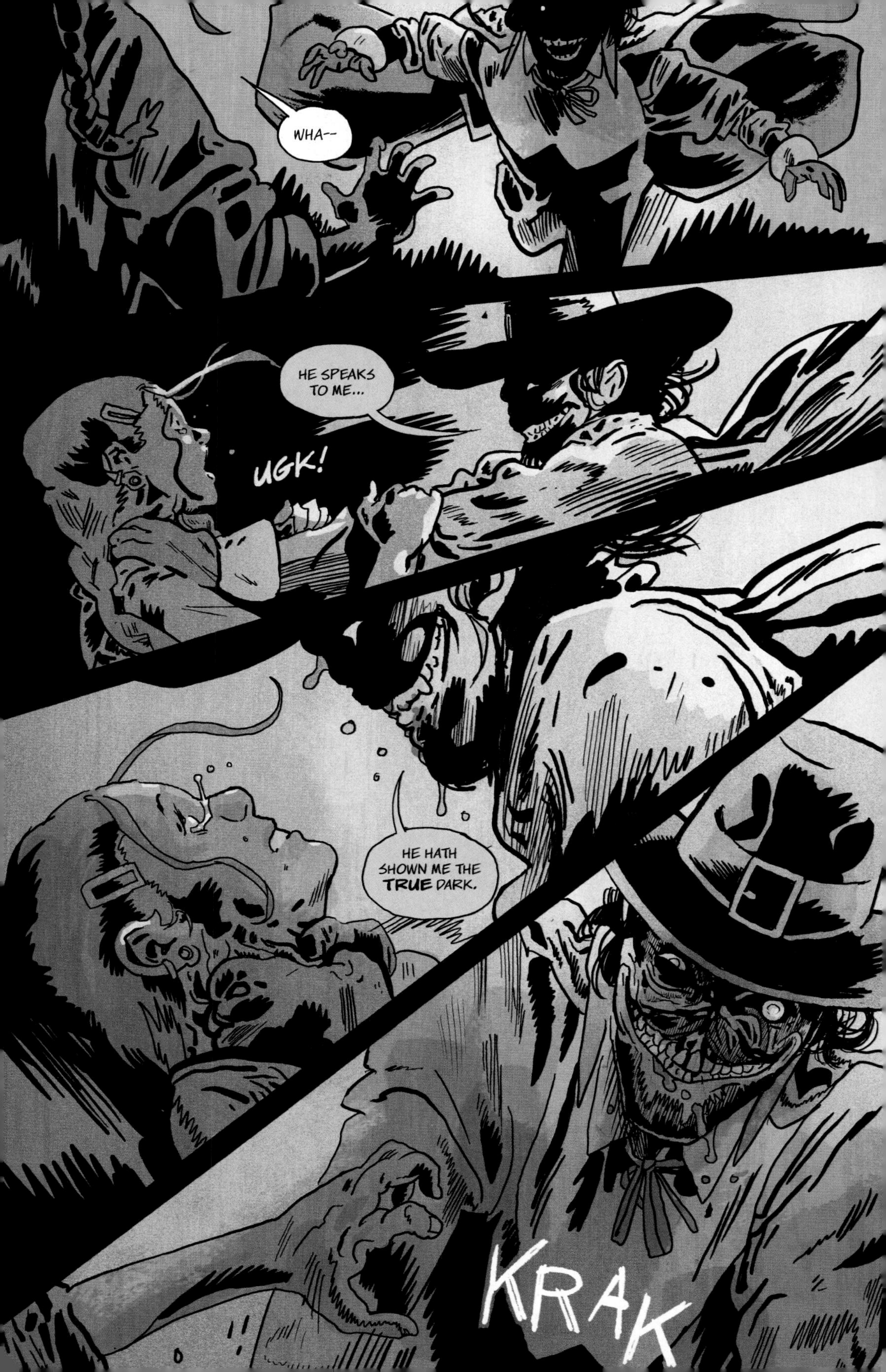
WHA--
HE SPEAKS TO ME...
UGK!
HE HATH SHOWN ME THE **TRUE** DARK.
KRAK

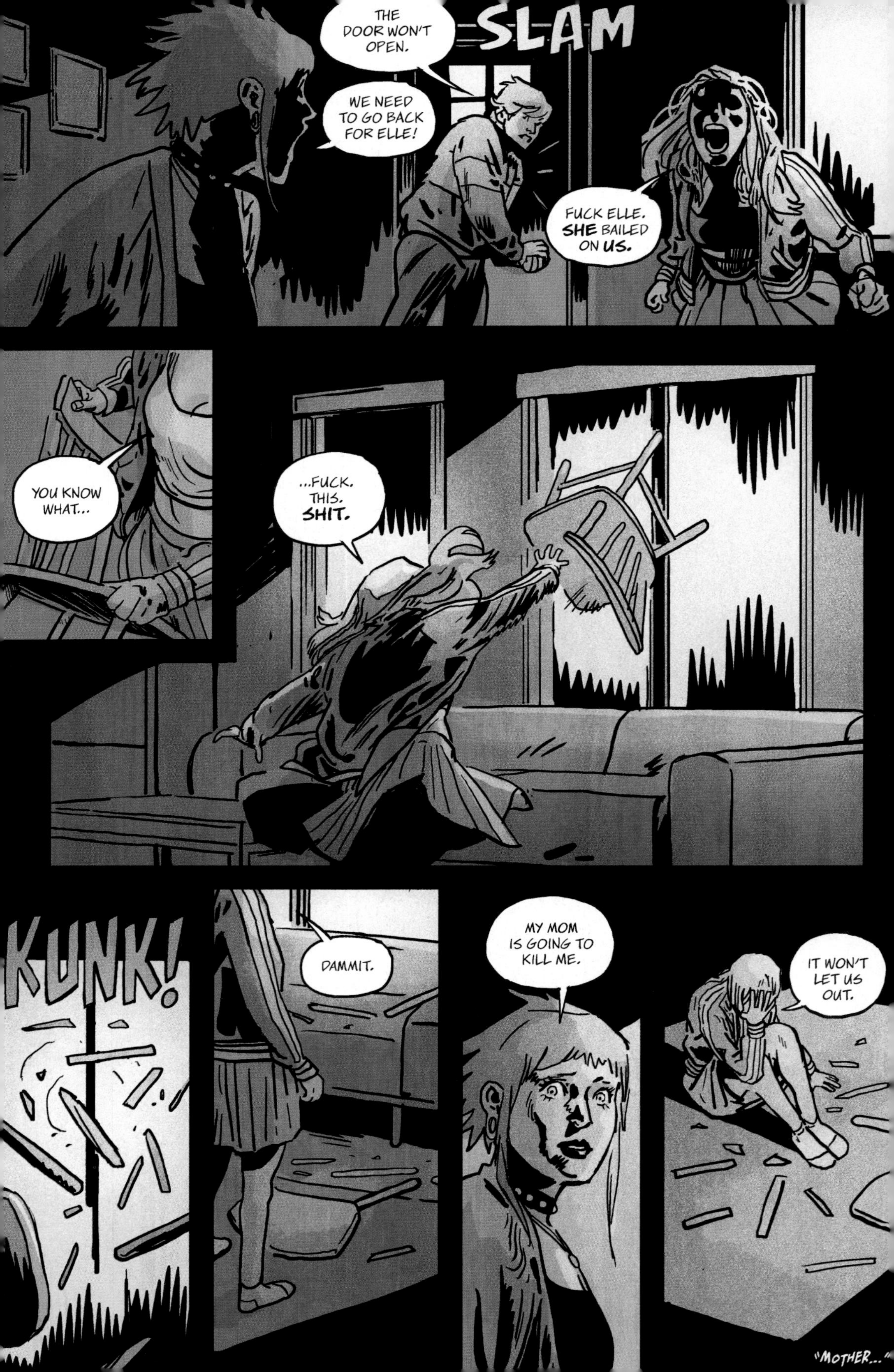
SLAM
THE DOOR WON'T OPEN.
WE NEED TO GO BACK FOR ELLE!
FUCK ELLE. SHE BAILED ON US.
YOU KNOW WHAT...
...FUCK. THIS. SHIT.
KUNK!
DAMMIT.
MY MOM IS GOING TO KILL ME.
IT WON'T LET US OUT.
"MOTHER..."

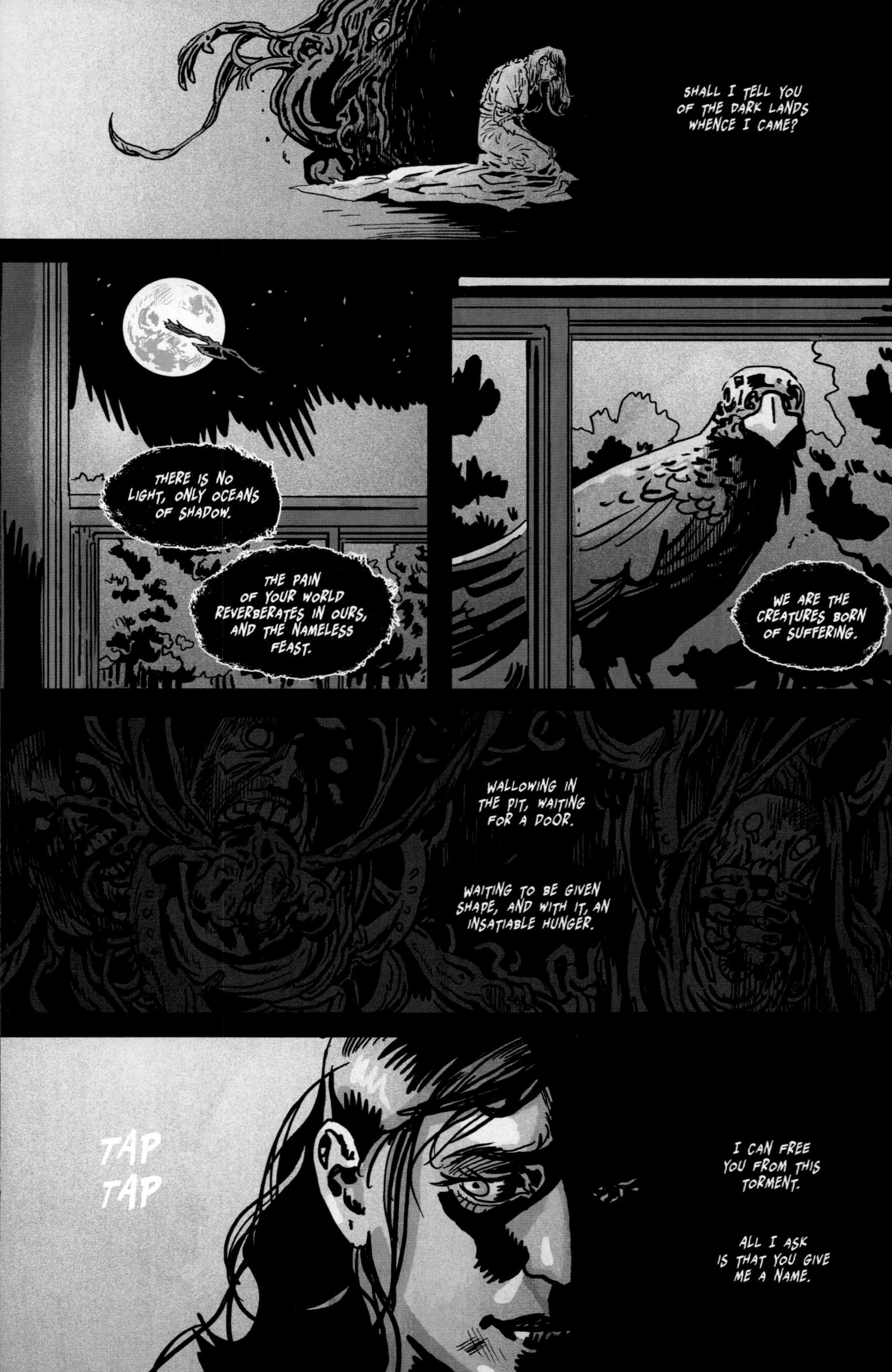
SHALL I TELL YOU OF THE DARK LANDS WHENCE I CAME?
THERE IS NO LIGHT, ONLY OCEANS OF SHADOW.
THE PAIN OF YOUR WORLD REVERBERATES IN OURS, AND THE NAMELESS FEAST.
WE ARE THE CREATURES BORN OF SUFFERING.
WALLOWING IN THE PIT, WAITING FOR A DOOR.
WAITING TO BE GIVEN SHAPE, AND WITH IT, AN INSATIABLE HUNGER.
TAP TAP
I CAN FREE YOU FROM THIS TORMENT.
ALL I ASK IS THAT YOU GIVE ME A NAME.

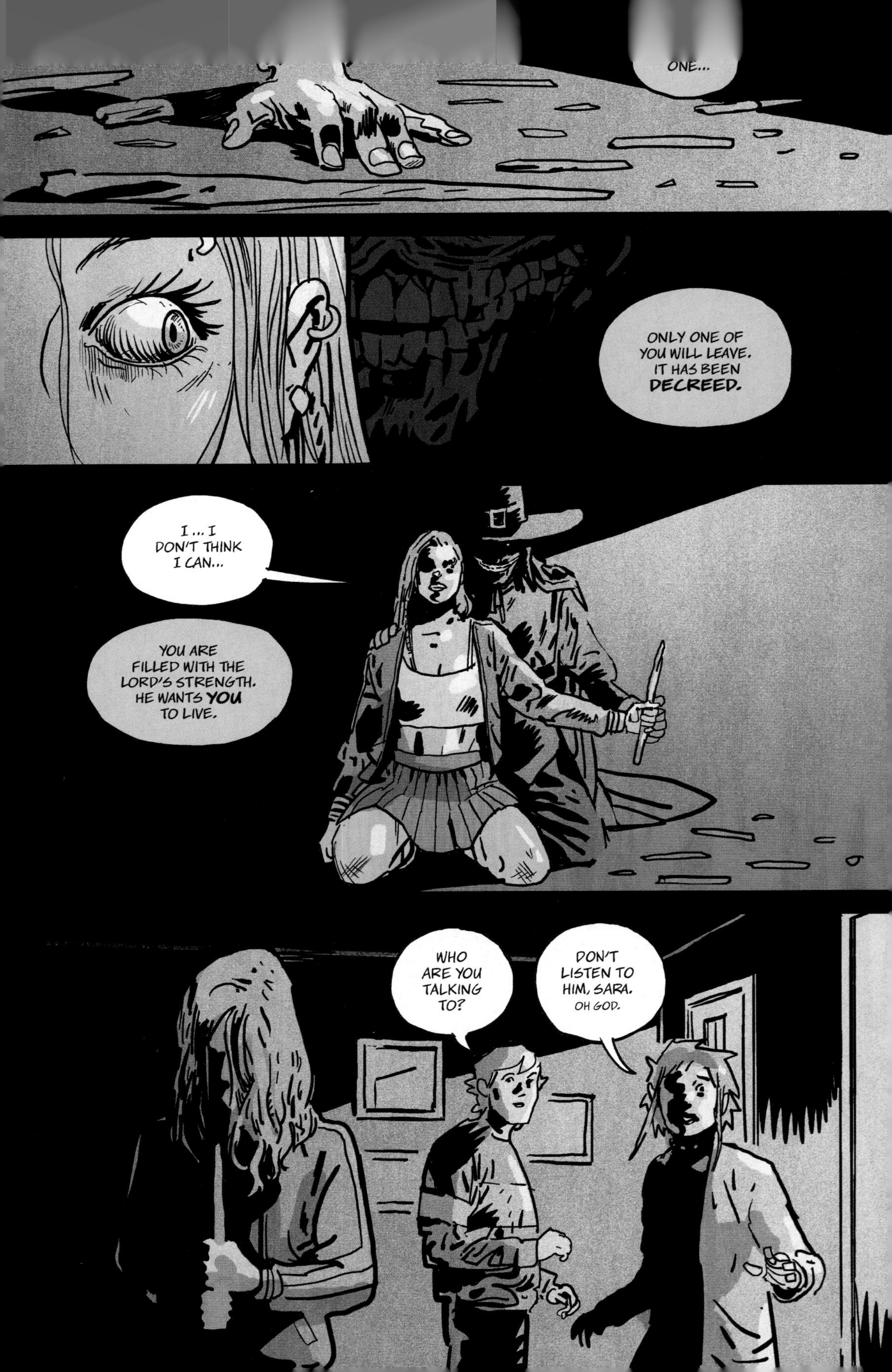
ONE...
ONLY ONE OF YOU WILL LEAVE. IT HAS BEEN DECREED.
I... I DON'T THINK I CAN...
YOU ARE FILLED WITH THE LORD'S STRENGTH. HE WANTS YOU TO LIVE.
WHO ARE YOU TALKING TO?
DON'T LISTEN TO HIM, SARA. OH GOD.

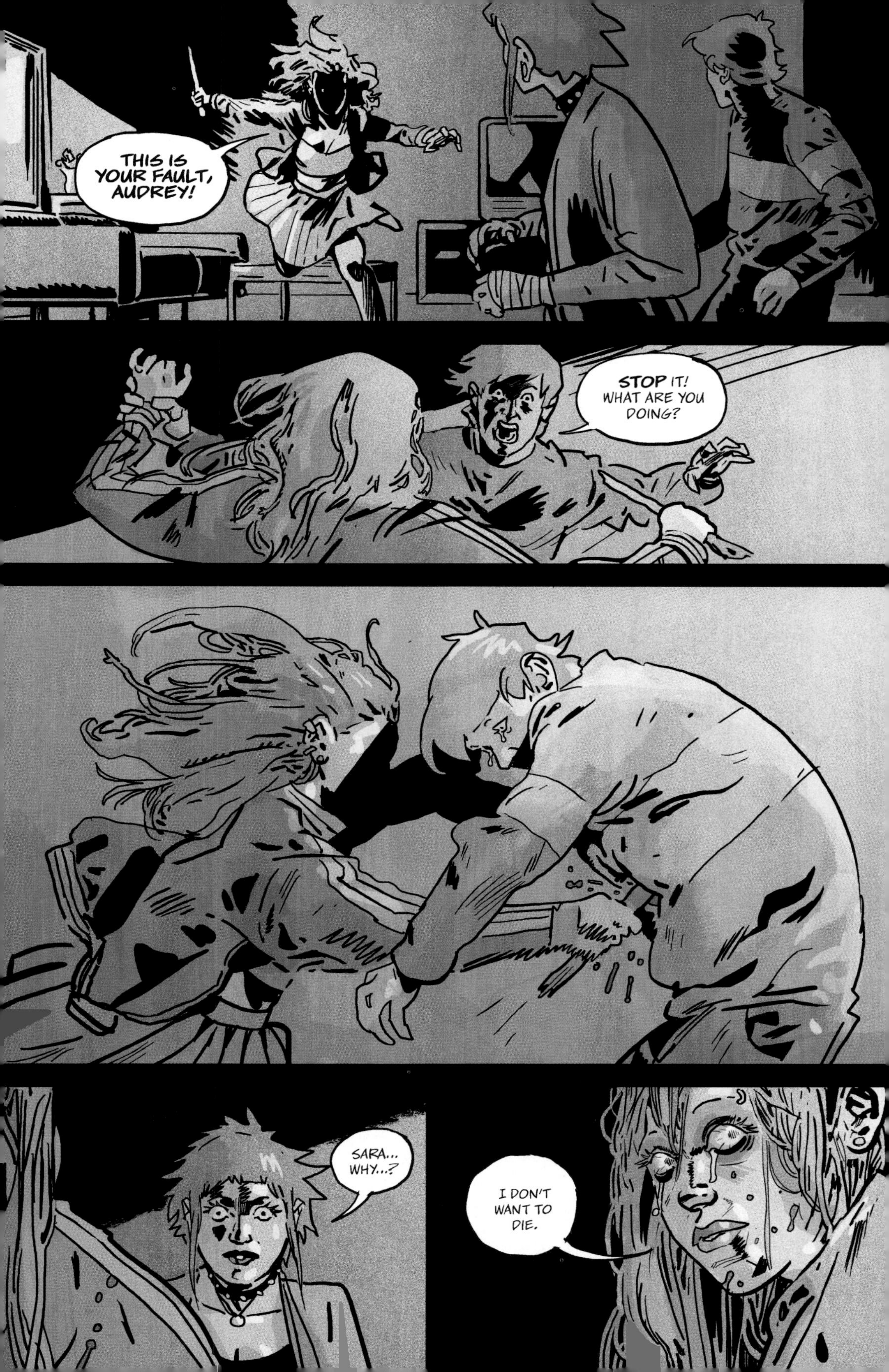
THIS IS YOUR FAULT, AUDREY!
STOP IT! WHAT ARE YOU DOING?
SARA... WHY...?
I DON'T WANT TO DIE.

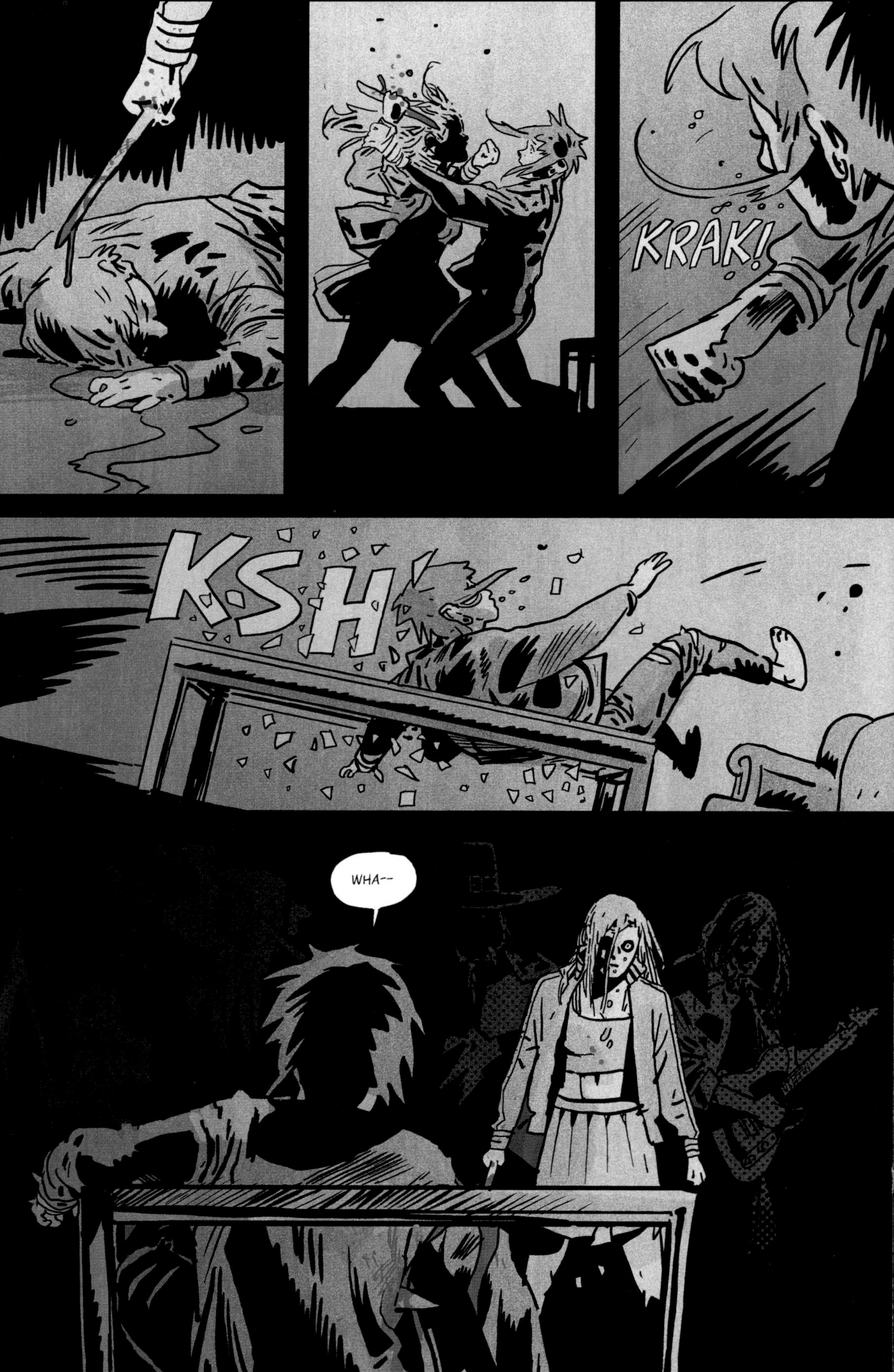
KRAK!
KSH
WHA--

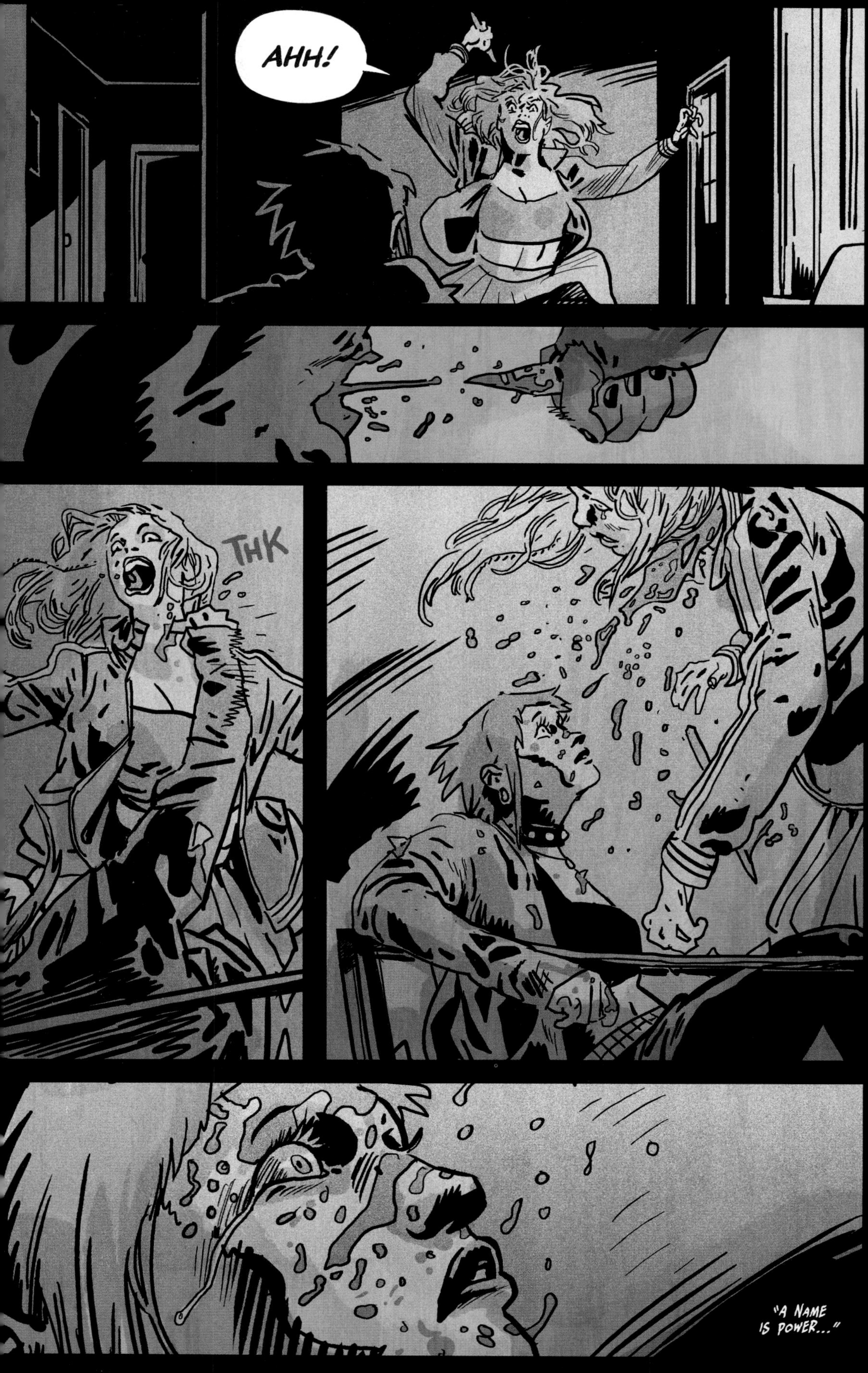
AHH!
THK
"A NAME IS POWER..."

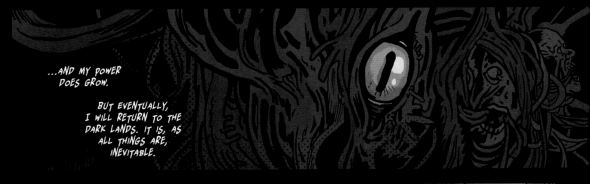

...AND MY POWER DOES GROW.

BUT EVENTUALLY, I WILL RETURN TO THE DARK LANDS. IT IS, AS ALL THINGS ARE, INEVITABLE.

WITH A NAME, LIKE BALHAMUT BEFORE ME, I WILL RETURN A KING.

SITTING UPON A THRONE OF SOULS, EVEN THE ABYSS WILL TREMBLE AT MY FEET.

NO!

DUNCAN. I CAN STAY NO LONGER, MY SOUL DECAYS.

WHEN I WAS YOUNG, I DREAMED THAT I COULD BE A **GOOD** WOMAN.

BUT NOW, I HAVE SEEN MY OWN SHADOW. THE FRUITS OF MY LABOR ARE **ROTTEN.**

YOUR NAME...

...ꞁꓵꓕ⅃ꓵꓭ...

MAY IT NEVER BE HEARD BY THE EARS OF MAN.

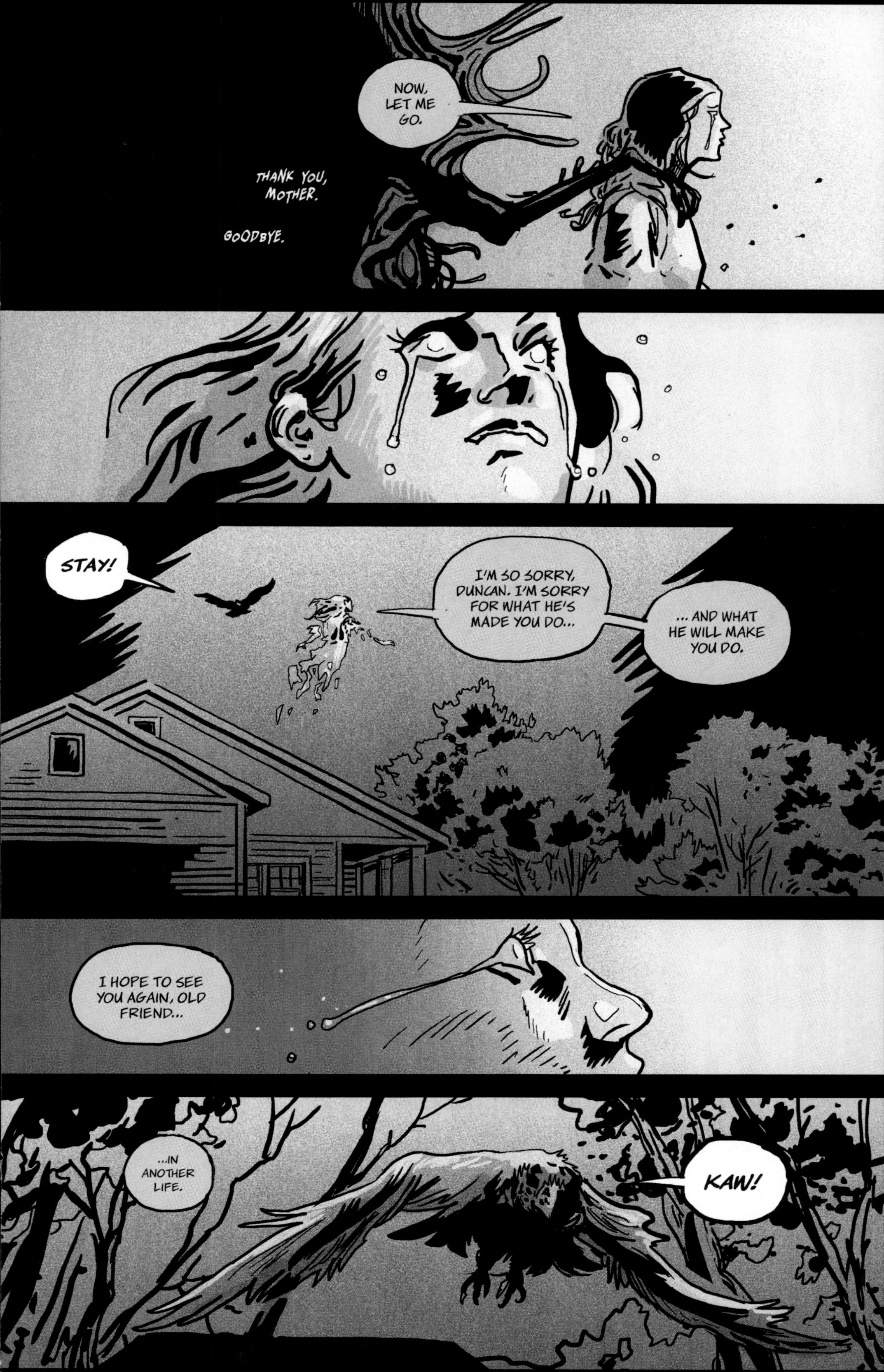
NOW, LET ME GO.
THANK YOU, MOTHER.
GOODBYE.
STAY!
I'M SO SORRY, DUNCAN. I'M SORRY FOR WHAT HE'S MADE YOU DO...
... AND WHAT HE WILL MAKE YOU DO.
I HOPE TO SEE YOU AGAIN, OLD FRIEND...
...IN ANOTHER LIFE.
KAW!

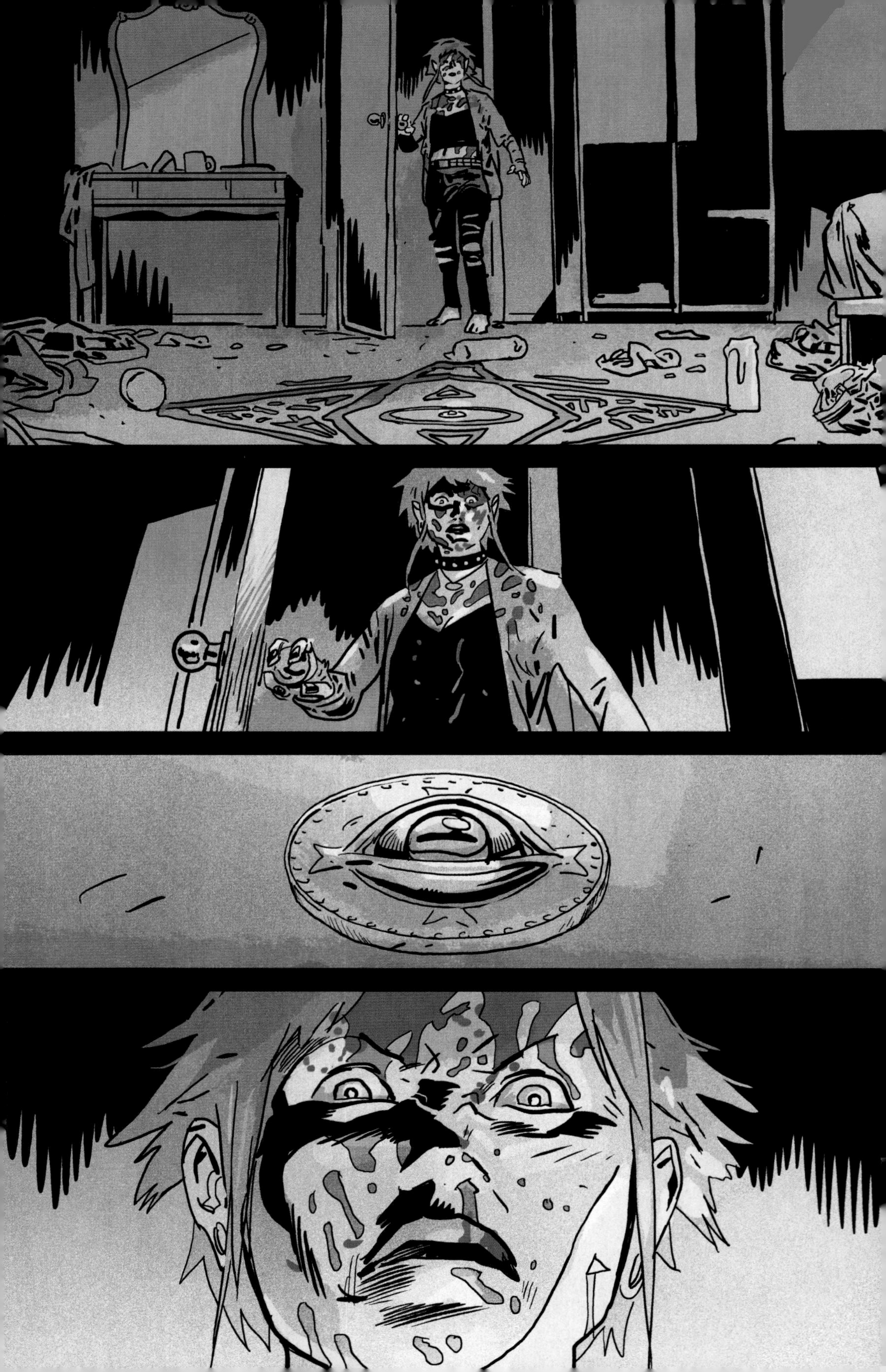

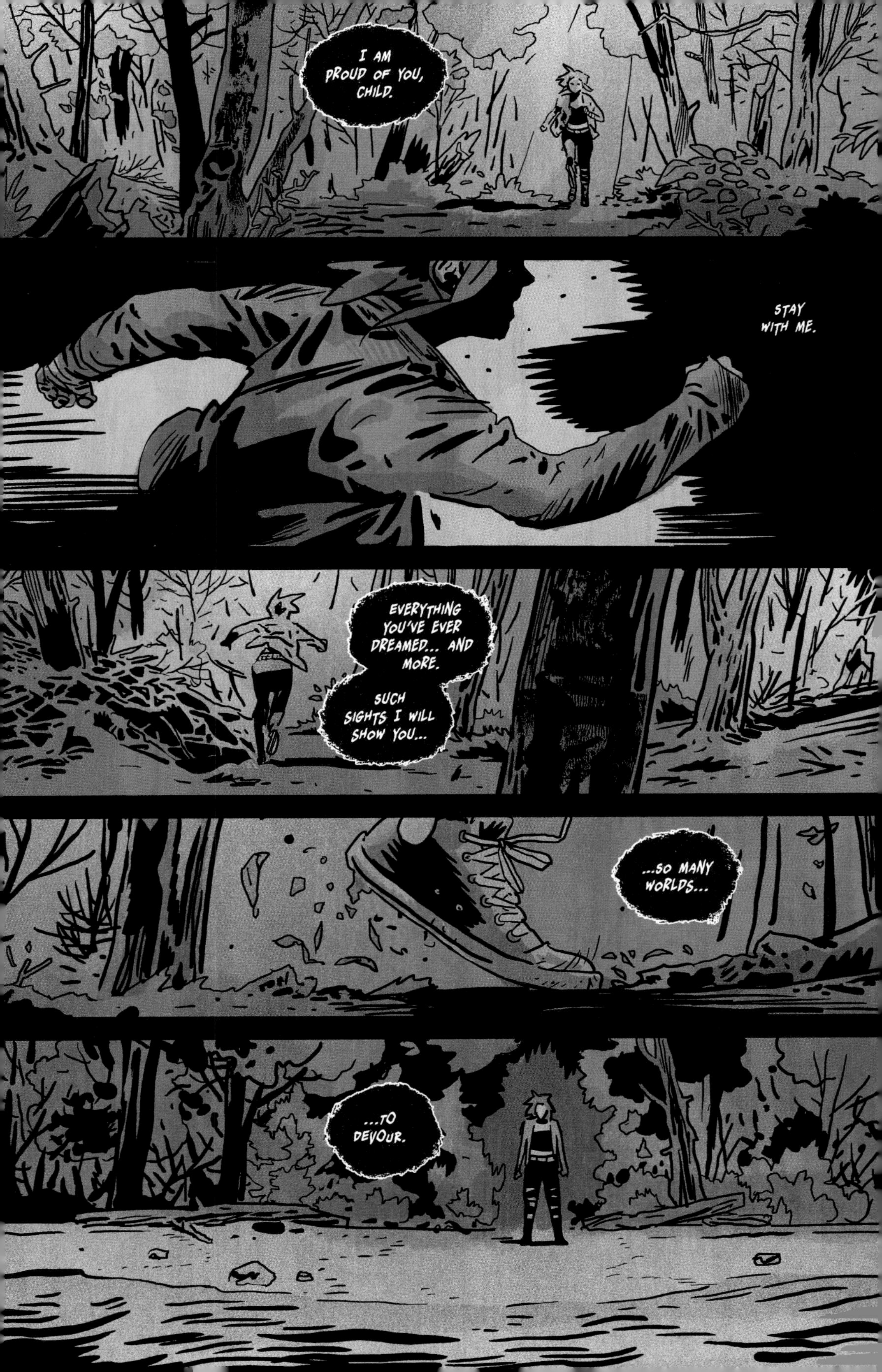
I AM PROUD OF YOU, CHILD.
STAY WITH ME.
EVERYTHING YOU'VE EVER DREAMED... AND MORE.
SUCH SIGHTS I WILL SHOW YOU...
...SO MANY WORLDS...
...TO DEVOUR.

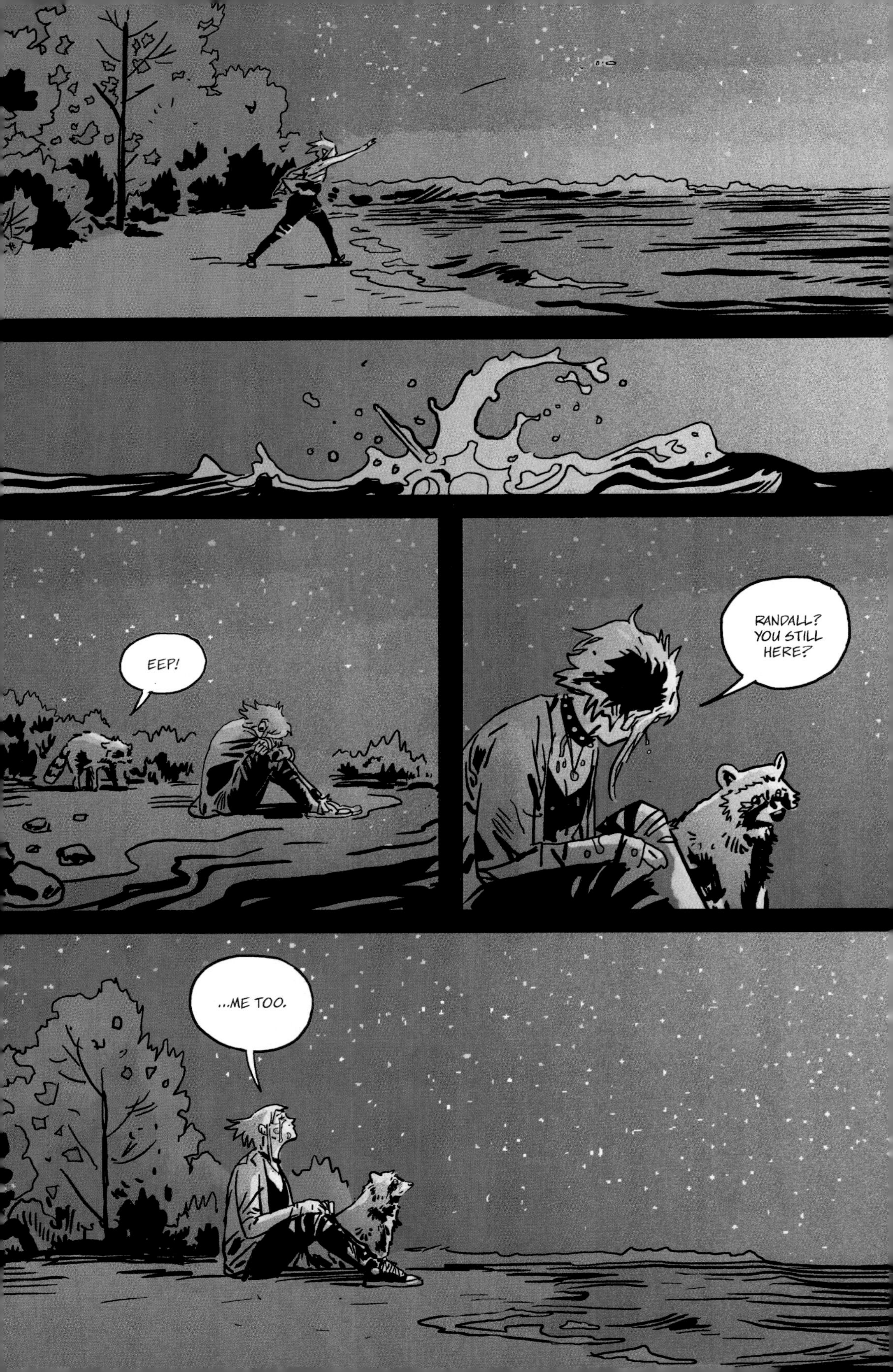
EEP!
RANDALL? YOU STILL HERE?
...ME TOO.

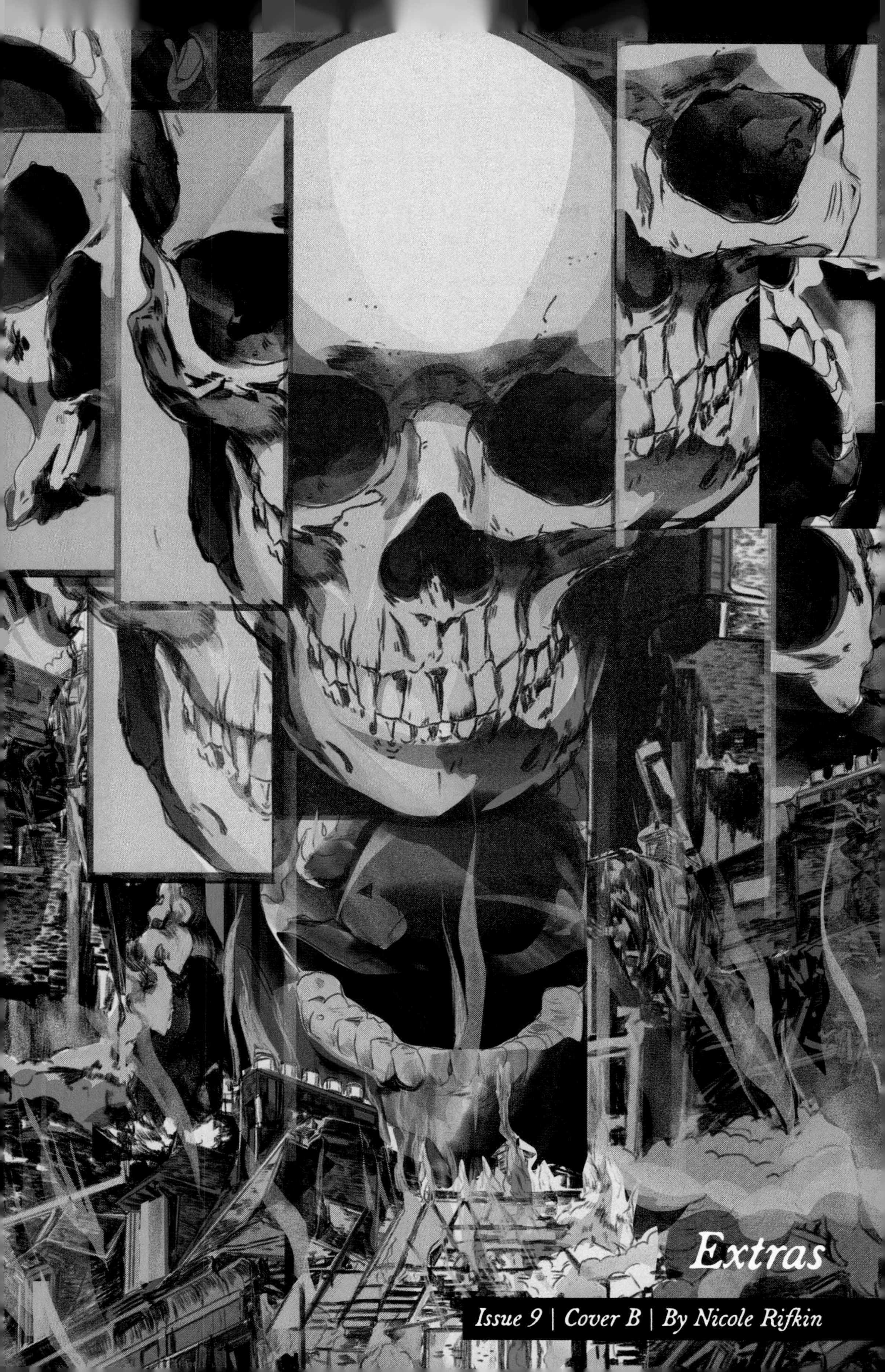

Extras

Issue 9 | Cover B | By Nicole Rifkin

Interview Transcript
Recorded 17th Sept. 2007
Subject: Sgt. Harry Bicks
Interviewer: Special Agent Severian
Eyes Only

S.A. Severian: Thanks for sticking around, Sergeant. I appreciate this might be a difficult conversation, but we thought it best to get the facts down as quickly as—

Sgt. Bicks: Yeah, no problem. It's my—well, it's the least I can do. *(Coughs.)*

Can we start as far back as possible? And, if you could, speak into the—

I know, I know. I've done a million of these. Yeah, so, this was—we were already investigating this Silver Coin business. A couple of local kids had gone missing, and it seemed like ... they were all frequenting these forums online—

You mean bulletin boards?

Whatever they're called, yeah. So there's a bunch of people discussing how there's this coin you find, and it—people have been tracking it for years. *Centuries*, they said. They had this whole fucking—sorry. They had this mythology worked out. The coin, it passes from owner to owner and ... it's been all over the world, and it does ... well, it does something for you, but you gotta ... *give* to it.

Could you be more specific?

They kept it kinda ... cryptic. Like, they all knew what they were discussing, so they didn't *need* to say it out loud. If you didn't know already, you didn't *deserve* to know. And they'd been busy. They had listings of where they thought the coin had been, maps to keep track, see if there was a pattern. People hunting it down like Sasquatch—

Or aliens?

(Laughs.) Yeah. Or aliens.

It's one coin?

Not always clear. At first, I figured it's just any silver coin. Like a silver bullet or whatever. But I think they believed it's a specific one. And it's been *around*. They had theories about where it'd come from. Puritan superstitions, some went further back—Rome, Aztecs, India, what have you. One guy thought it was a Native American revenge for their genocide. Or maybe it's one of Judas's thirty pieces of silver.

And you took this seriously?

Not at first. It was just something we'd found in common for all these kids—all boys, by the way. Nerds. They were into comics, sci-fi and all that nonsense. Glasses, acne. Suddenly, they go missing, and they've all been obsessed with this thing, something called the Silver Coin, right before they disappeared. A couple of them had told their friends to join these forums. But even then, we were looking at other things—high schools, sports teams, hell, maybe they played together as kids. But Merman's brother ... he didn't fit any of those.

Yes. Detective Merman.

He was lead on the whole thing. He talked to these kid[s'] friends, found out about the forums. He even set up the what's it called? The operation.

You mean the stings?

Yeah, dummy posters who'd pretend they're in on th[e] whole thing and who could see if any of these people we[re] actually involved in any dangerous sh—stuff.

You can swear, Sergeant.

That's alright. I'd prefer not to. *(Coughs.)* So yeah—*(coughs.)* sorry, I got a frog in my throat. Could I get some water?

Of course.

(Recording pauses, then resumes.)

So, Merman's brother ... Dan, his name was. He's n[ot] a nerd. I don't think he's even seen a computer. Good k[id,] plays football, lives with his parents. And Merman's talki[ng] to him one day and—oh god, I just realized. *(Heavy breat[h]ing.)* I didn't—I'm sorry. It's just sinking in.

Breathe, Sergeant. Just tell us what you knew.

(15 seconds silence.) So Merman's talking to his paren[ts] one day, and they mention that his brother's just g[ot] interested in coin collecting. Merman asks them to put hi[m] on, and he knows immediately what the kid's talki[ng] about. And the kid says there's this bunch of people, th[ey] have this coin. Like, it's their *god*. There's a priest a[nd] everything. And they have these ceremonies. And the k[id] he's excited about it, and wants to join this ... church. T[he] idea is that you worship this coin, and it gives you ever[y]thing you desire. And a friend of Dan's is going to bring hi[m] in. What Merman realizes is that his brother's about to g[o] missing if he doesn't do something. That *Dan* is what th[is] guy is going to *give* to the coin, you get me? And [he] realizes his brother isn't thinking straight. Classic cult stu[ff.] So he says that before going to this church meeting wi[th] his friend, Dan should come and meet him somepla[ce] safe. Tell him about it, y'know?

What happened next?

Merman goes to this place with the idea that he's gon[na] talk Dan out of this stuff, or, if it comes to it, he's going [to] bring him in, for his protection, so the cops can get it o[ut] of him.

And did Detective Merman tell anyone about this at th[e] time?

Obviously not. Because next thing we know, Merma[n's] barging into the station, hollering that his little brothe[r's] gone missing. Merman waited, but the kid never showe[d,] and he's not at his parents'. Merman was gonna try and g[et] the location of the church out of him, so now, nobo[dy] knows where the kid's gone.

Did the boy have a cell phone?

Left it at home. Look, we did all the investigation on th[at,] that's not what we're—

I apologize. Please continue.

Merman's distraught. We mount a search for the kid. Bu[t] of course, we never find him. Merman's placed on comp[...]

ory leave, but he's just raring to come back after a week, and throughout his leave, he insists on helping with the ...ting operation. Now, the coin is the focus. We're trying to get any real details on people: addresses, phone numbers, IPs.

...nd nothing?

...ot a thing. There's a whole protocol here we're not ...eeing. It's like they can tell exactly who's the real deal and ...ho's just a dabbler or a cop. And Merman's sitting at ...ome, *obsessing* over this to see if he can still save his ...rother.

...ow long did it take?

...was three months later. Merman's running five of the ...ummy accounts himself.

...nd you thought that was a good idea?

...0 seconds silence.) (Whispered.) That part's my fault, ...n't it?

...ould you speak louder, please? Into the machine.

...orry. I really thought it would help. He was so ... driven. ...ke he couldn't think of anything else. I don't think he even ...et his parents after the funeral. I just don't ... do you think ...'s all my fault? *(20 seconds silence.)* I didn't want to ... *...rying.)*

(...ecording pauses, then resumes.)

... your tea. I'm sorry about that. Please continue.

...erman, he ... So Merman gets a PM on one of his ...ccounts. Private message. It says that they've noticed his ...ctivity on the forum, and he seems like a true believer. ...hey send over instructions to wipe his account, set up ... new one using this dark web thing that lets you hide ...verything. They even give him a new username to ...egister with, so they know it's him. It's how they've been ...ole to keep a backchannel going and how they know ...ho's already in, and who's just playing.

...nd this works?

...eah. It's a whole 'nother experience of the same site. It's ...ke augmented reality or something. He's getting access ...o all the weird codewords they're using, and we start ...aking all these connections. We figure this is a whole ...eligion—it's worldwide, and it's all underground. And ...ey've got churches all over the place. Including here. ...takes a while, but finally, they invite him. He's gotta bring ... friend and he can join the church. But he has to get this ...end to believe, *really* believe. So that takes some time ... ...o convince them we're actually doing that stuff. Then, ...ur days ago, we get an address.

...hat easy?

...asy? Have you been *listening*? I don't—what the hell, man? *...eavy breathing.)*

...meant nothing by it. Ignore me, Sergeant. Just ... in your ...wn time.

...0 seconds silence.) So we put together a SWAT team. It's ...e, Merman, and the SWAT. We get to the address, and it's ...st some kind of converted warehouse. Merman takes the ...ad. I know what you're gonna say. Shit idea. *I know.* ...nyway, he *insists* on taking the lead, and like an idiot, I let ...m. Then, it's him and the SWAT. I'm waiting outside, and ...e got Merman on the walkie-talkie.

...o you didn't go in with him?

No, but one of the SWAT guys had a helmet cam, and it was playing on a laptop.

You saw the whole thing from there?

No, I ran inside when I heard the shots, but I—they played it back for me before you folks showed up. So I could be sure what I thought happened ... had happened.

Tell me. In your words.

We're seeing this grainy footage of them walking through dark corridors, with these maze-like turns, so you're not quite sure where to go—unless you know, of course. And the SWAT guy loses Merman. Then they—and I—we hear this loud yelling from somewhere. And the SWAT guy runs in that direction. Next thing I know, there are shots. So I ran inside, and I just ... I followed the noise, and there was this red room, and at first, I thought it was just the light, but, oh my god, it was the floor. The fucking *floor* was red. It was blood, and—and their robes were soaked in it. They were all—they were all lying on the floor, and Merman— Merman, he was sitting on top of one of them, his face all spattered, and he was holding the kid up by the neck and shouting—fuck—he was shouting, *"LIARS! All of you liars! It's mine! It'll ALWAYS BE MINE!"* And in his other hand, he had this coin he was holding up. Oh fuck, I can't ... *(Crying.)* Oh, fuck, oh my god.

So the cultists?

They were just ... kids. They were nerds. Cosplayers, they called themselves. *(Heavy breathing.)* Two of them were still alive, and they said it was this game. They knew about this coin thing, and they'd just made up this goofy shit around it. None of it was real. He killed them for a *game.*

And the missing kids?

Oh my god, I'm gonna throw up. It was—*(heaving sounds)*— I'm so sorry. *(Heaving sounds.)*

It's no problem. We'll have it cleaned up.

No, just ... *(Sounds of drinking.)*

Do you need a minute to—

It was Merman, wasn't it? He killed them all. He killed his brother. I don't know where he heard about this coin nonsense, but he was clearly fucking—

And the coin, Sergeant?

—clearly crazy. I'm sorry what? The coin?

The one Detective Merman was holding? It wasn't on him in custody.

It ... it was just a coin, man. Just a coin.

Was it silver?

I don't fucking know. Didn't you see it in Evidence?

We can't find the coin, Sergeant. It's not *in* Evidence.

I don't ... Merman was *crazy*, man. What does the *coin* matter? It was just a coin.

We'd still like to find the coin. To see if it is indeed this Silver—

IT WAS JUST. A FUCKING. COIN.

I'm sorry. Of course. That was insensitive of me. We can talk about this later. Get some rest, Sergeant. There'll be more questions for you. *(Chair scraping.)* Cleanup in here, pl—

(Recording ends.)

Shiny Thing

written by Chris Hampton • art by Gavin Fullerton

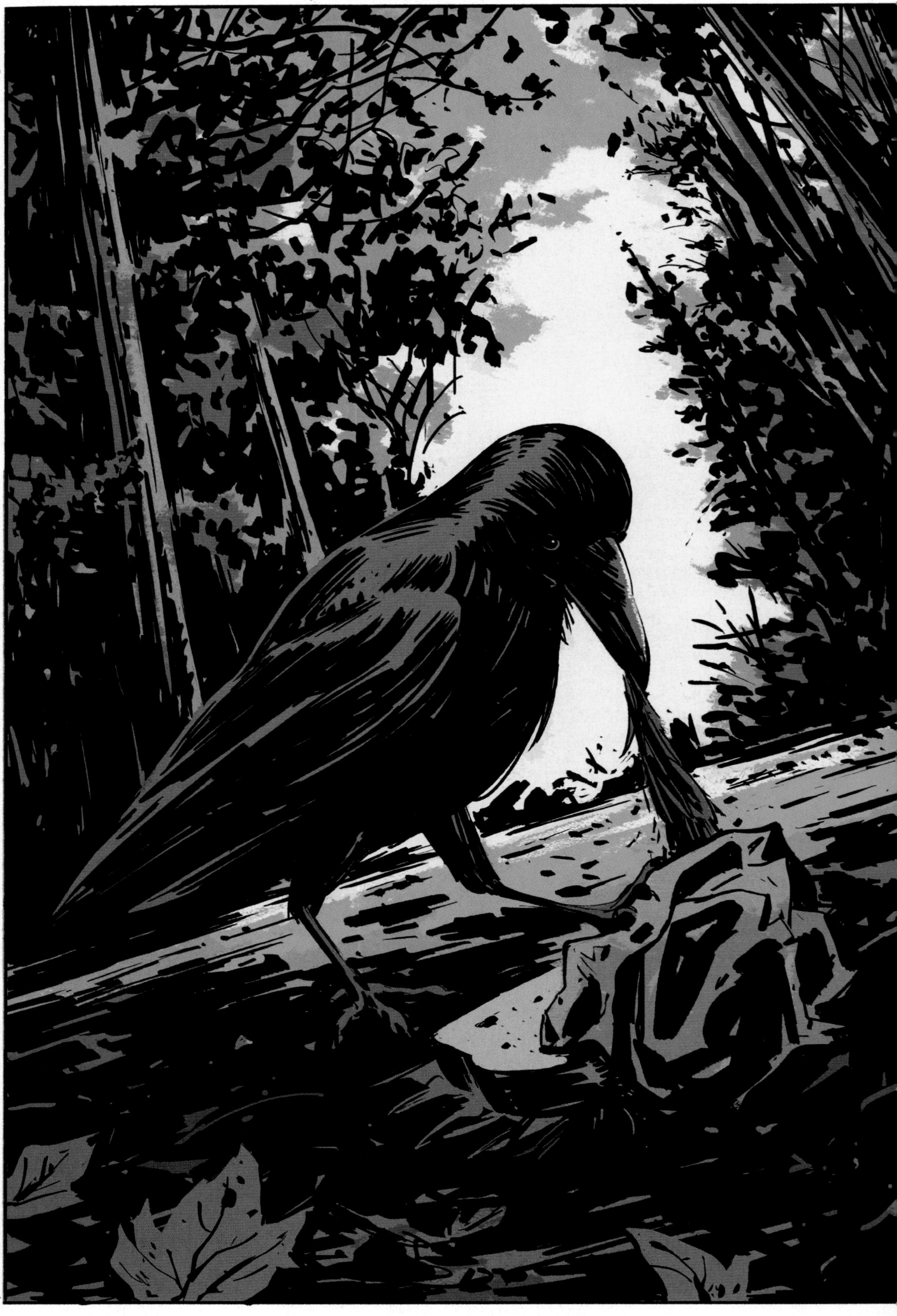

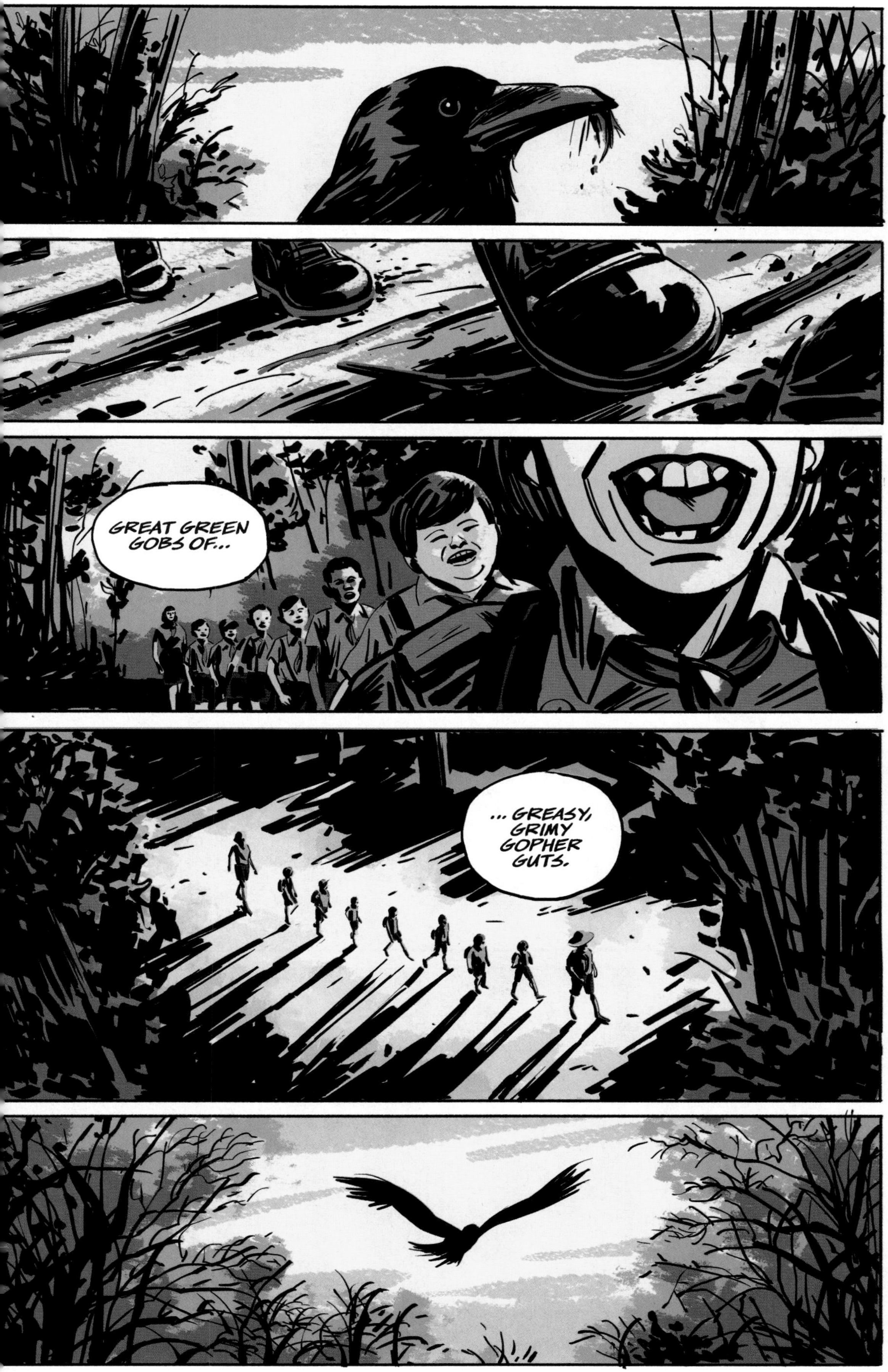
GREAT GREEN GOBS OF...
... GREASY, GRIMY GOPHER GUTS.

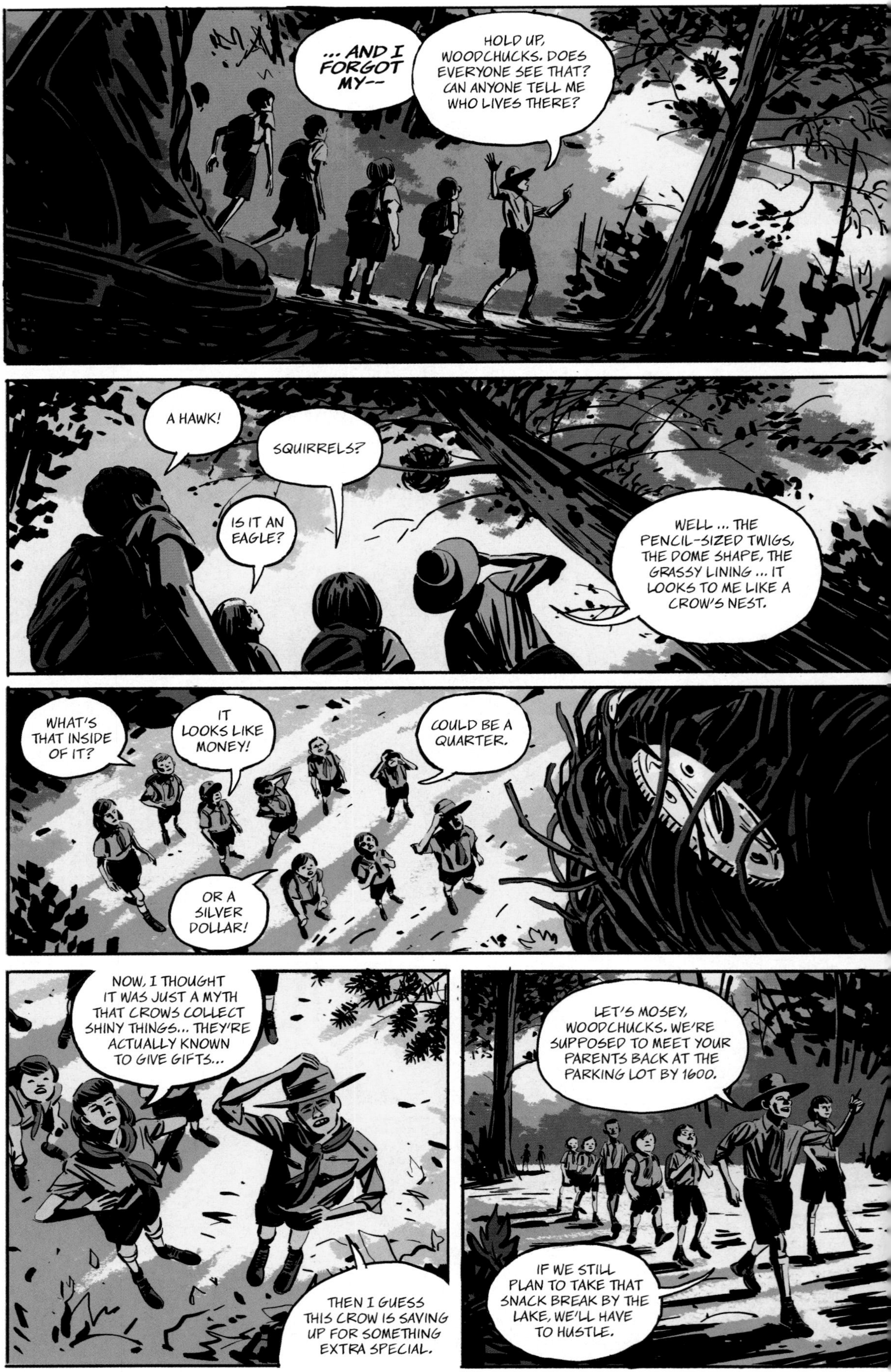
... AND I FORGOT MY--
HOLD UP, WOODCHUCKS. DOES EVERYONE SEE THAT? CAN ANYONE TELL ME WHO LIVES THERE?
A HAWK!
SQUIRRELS?
IS IT AN EAGLE?
WELL ... THE PENCIL-SIZED TWIGS, THE DOME SHAPE, THE GRASSY LINING ... IT LOOKS TO ME LIKE A CROW'S NEST.
WHAT'S THAT INSIDE OF IT?
IT LOOKS LIKE MONEY!
COULD BE A QUARTER.
OR A SILVER DOLLAR!
NOW, I THOUGHT IT WAS JUST A MYTH THAT CROWS COLLECT SHINY THINGS... THEY'RE ACTUALLY KNOWN TO GIVE GIFTS...
THEN I GUESS THIS CROW IS SAVING UP FOR SOMETHING EXTRA SPECIAL.
LET'S MOSEY, WOODCHUCKS. WE'RE SUPPOSED TO MEET YOUR PARENTS BACK AT THE PARKING LOT BY 1600.
IF WE STILL PLAN TO TAKE THAT SNACK BREAK BY THE LAKE, WE'LL HAVE TO HUSTLE.

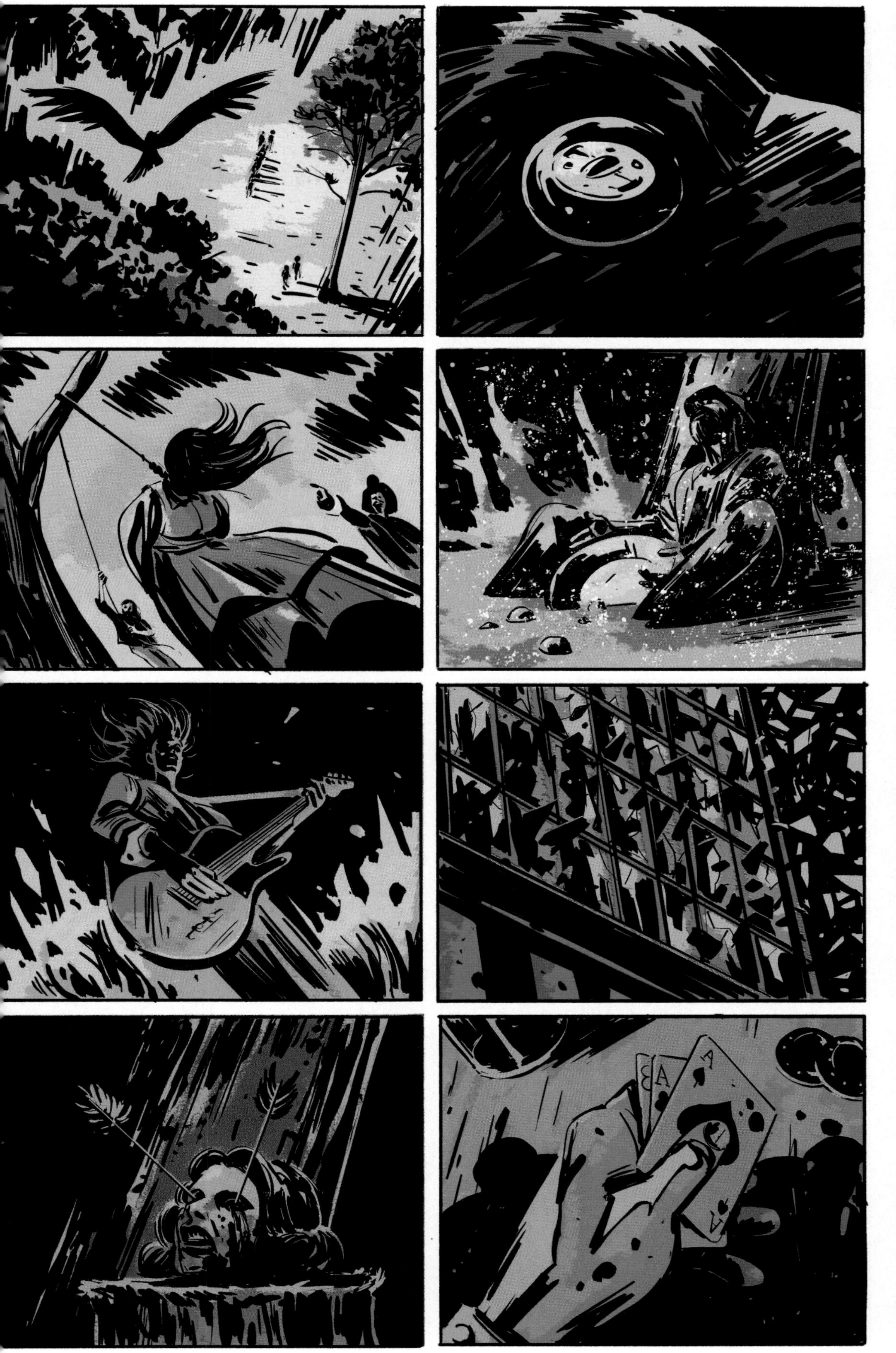

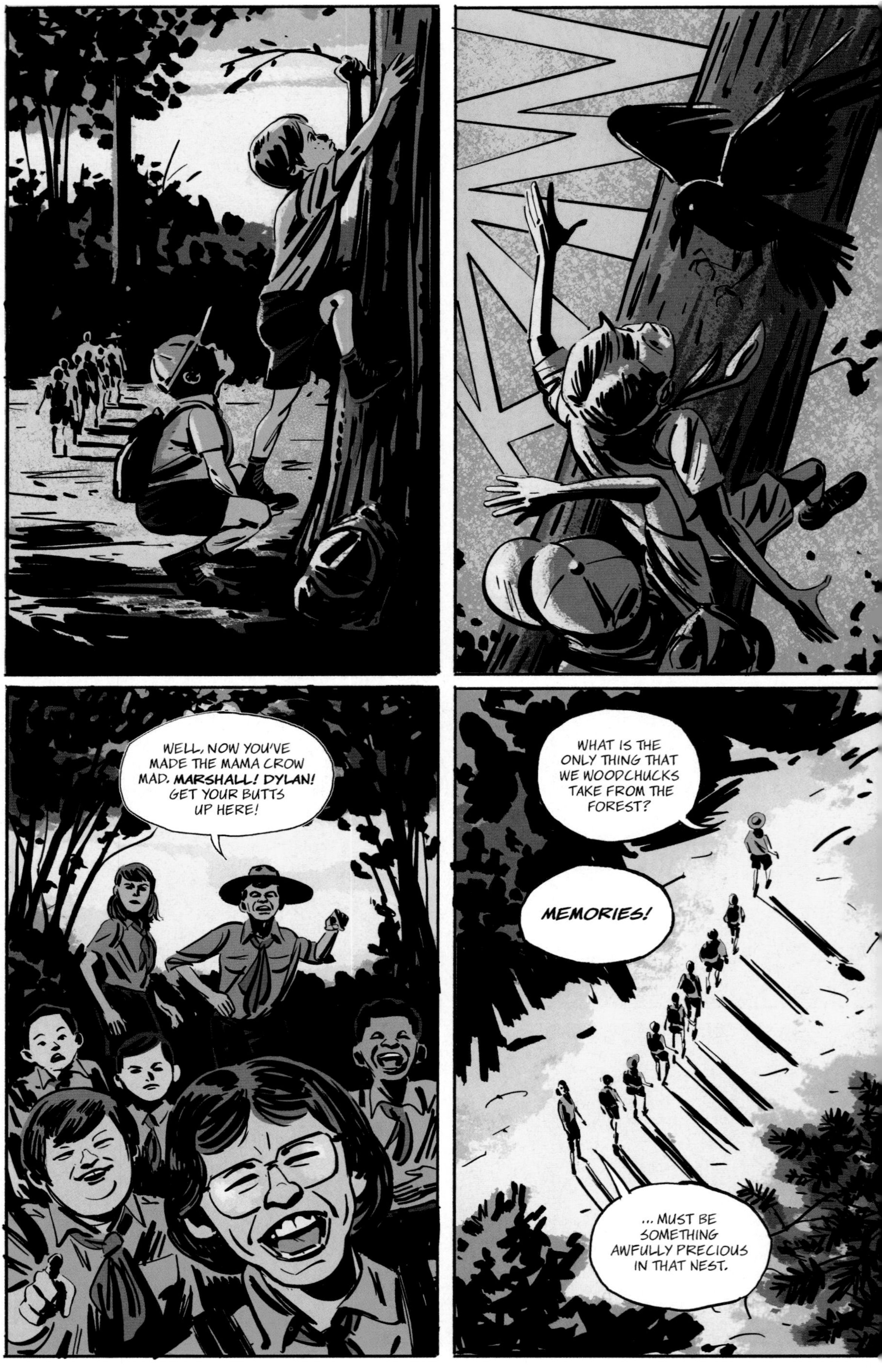
WELL, NOW YOU'VE MADE THE MAMA CROW MAD. **MARSHALL! DYLAN!** GET YOUR BUTTS UP HERE!
WHAT IS THE ONLY THING THAT WE WOODCHUCKS TAKE FROM THE FOREST?
MEMORIES!
... MUST BE SOMETHING AWFULLY PRECIOUS IN THAT NEST.

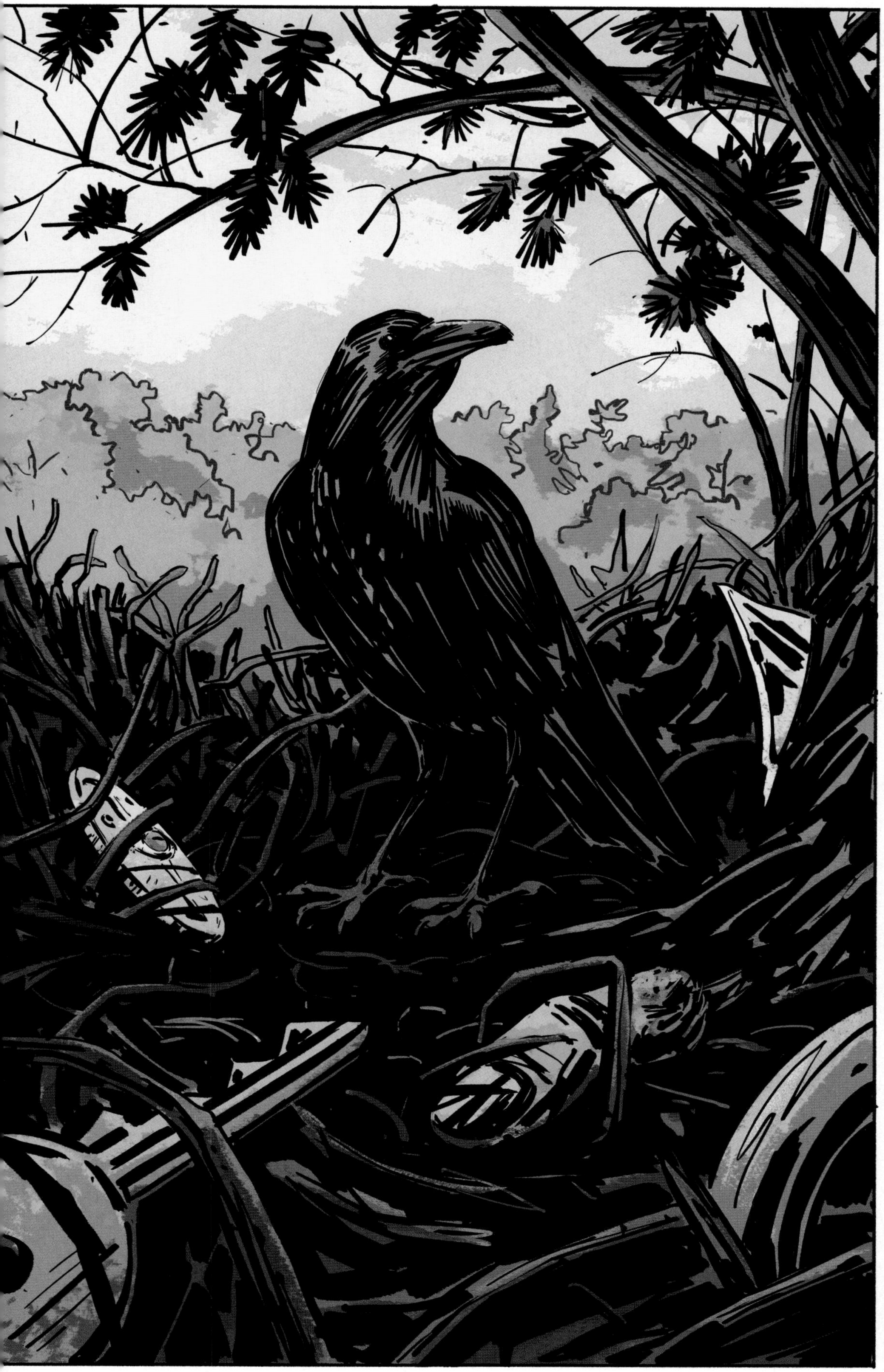

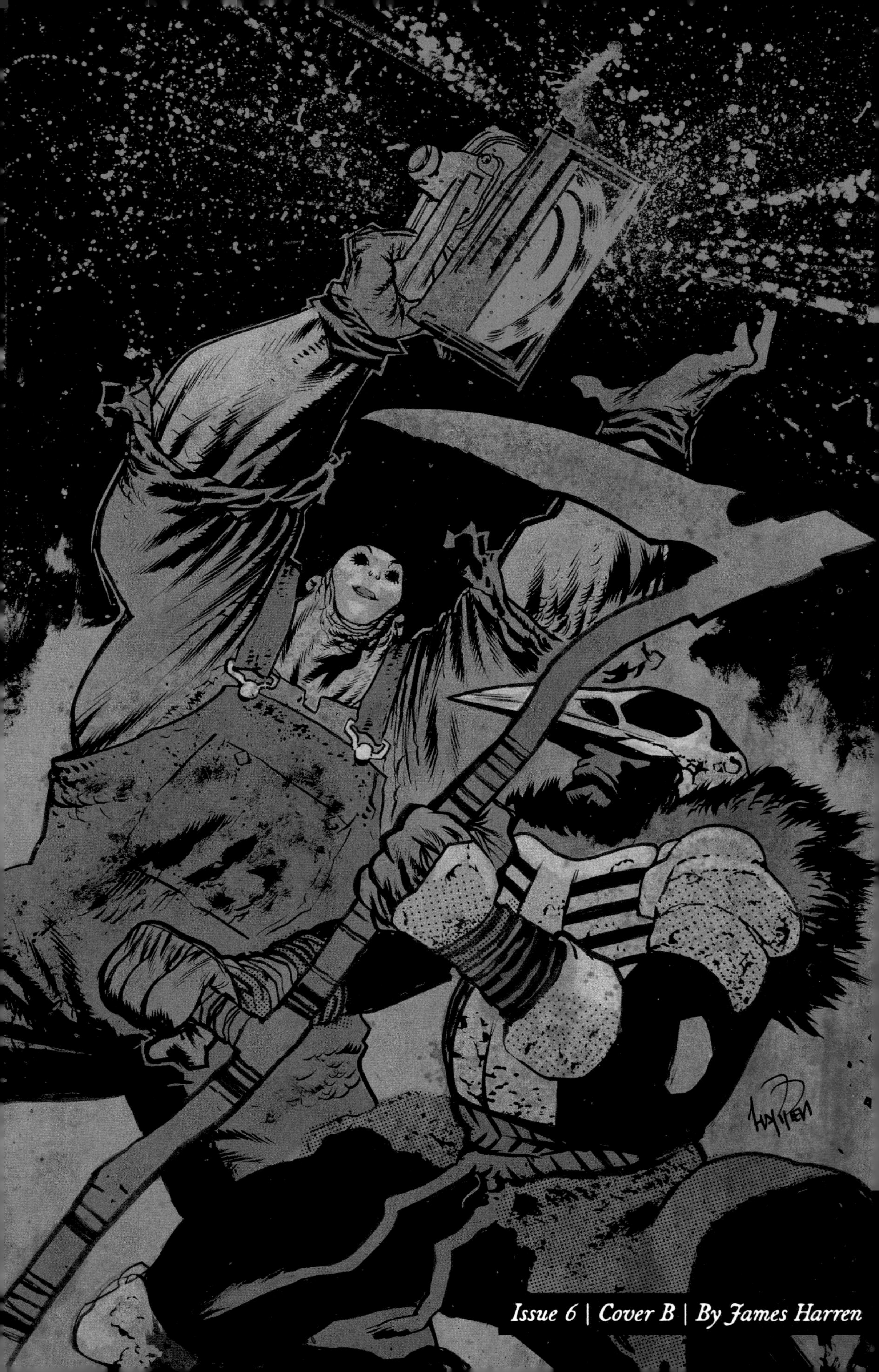
HARREN

Issue 6 | Cover B | By James Harren